Build
It BIG

101 Insider Secrets from Top Direct Selling Experts

Direct Selling Women's Alliance

Dearborn™
Trade Publishing
A **Kaplan Professional** Company

This publication is designed to provide accurate and authoritative information in regard to the subject matter covered. It is sold with the understanding that the publisher is not engaged in rendering legal, accounting, or other professional service. If legal advice or other expert assistance is required, the services of a competent professional person should be sought.

Vice President and Publisher: Cynthia A. Zigmund
Acquisitions Editor: Michael Cunningham
Senior Managing Editor: Jack Kiburz
Interior Design: Lucy Jenkins
Cover Design: Scott Rattray, Rattray Design
Typesetting: Elizabeth Pitts

The Direct Selling Women's Alliance, Principle-Centered Coaching, and my dswa.org are trademarks of the Direct Selling Women's Alliance. America's Dream Coach is a trademark of Dream Coach, Inc. Get Fired Up Without Burning Out is a registered trademark of Anderson Programs, Inc. The Lemon Aid Lady is a trademark of Lemon Aid Learning Adventures. Natural Selling is a registered trademark of Natural Selling Inc. ServiceQuest is a registered trademark of ServiceQuest MLM LLC. The Technology Tamer is a trademark of TechTamers. Other product, service, and company names mentioned herein may be the properties of their respective owners.

Published by Dearborn Trade Publishing
A Kaplan Professional Company

Printed in the United States of America

11 12 13 14 10 9 8

Library of Congress Cataloging-in-Publication Data

Build it big : 101 insider secrets from top direct selling experts / Direct Selling Women's Alliance.
    p. cm.
Includes index.
ISBN 0-7931-9277-3 (pbk.)
1. Direct selling. I. Direct Selling Women's Alliance.
HF5438.25.B85 2005
658.8′72—dc22

                                         2004018058

■ Acknowledgments

To the women and men who put their heart and soul into their direct-selling business every day.

It has been said that writing a book that reveals the wisdom of 89 individuals is like herding butterflies. How true it is. This book wouldn't exist if not for our remarkable editing team who stood ready—butterfly nets in hand—to capture the brilliance of our contributors. What a pleasure it was to work with such gifted, positive people who truly appreciate our profession. We are grateful for the opportunity to cocreate with you in such a significant project. Our heartfelt thanks go to Susan Raab, who came to the project with a delightful, can-do attitude and a clarity of vision that inspired us to hold ourselves to a higher standard than we ever thought possible. To Nolan Hale: we are grateful for your steady, calming manner and willingness to do whatever it took. You brought a keen eye and valuable perspective to every insight you touched. To Garvin DeShazer, our knight in shining armor: thank you for lending your talents to draw out your contributors' unique brilliance and capturing it so ably. Every life you touch shifts in a positive direction. To Kathie Nelson, who came through with flying colors: you were there when we needed you with your industry experience and love for the profession. To Michael Cunningham at Dearborn Trade Publishing, who saw the potential of this industry and asked for this book: you gave us the idea, trust, support, and space we needed to create a book worthy of the Direct Selling community. We are truly grateful!

We want to acknowledge the distributors, speakers, trainers, and industry experts featured in these pages, for they are the true leaders of our profession, working daily to teach, inspire, and uplift direct sellers around the world. Your willingness to share your knowledge and experience is making a significant difference in the lives of others. Thank you for holding a greater vision for our profession.

We are eternally grateful to the DSWA team, Advisory Board, and Council members. Your contributions go far beyond the scope of this book. You have been there for us since the very beginning, investing your time and talents toward our shared vision of greater success for all direct sellers. And to the countless supporters who work behind the scenes to make the DSWA what we know it can be—we thank you!

Words cannot express the love and appreciation we have for our families, who have supported us since the journey began. To our husbands, Saf, Maui, and Mario: you are each the rock we cling to when things get tough. Thank you for bringing such peace and joy into our lives. To our children, Isea, Kahea, Kaala, Alex, Paola, and Dane: big smoochies for being the light of our lives!

To God we give thanks for the hand you have had in this project and in everything we do. We do not take lightly this responsibility you've given us, and we strive to be good stewards of the blessings that you send our way.

Nicki Keohohou
Jane Deuber
Grace Keohohou Lee

■ Contents

■ Foreword

Celebrate the Greatness within You
By Richard Neihart
Inspirational voice of the Direct Selling profession

They burst like blazing comets from the cosmos of Hollywood headlines: superstars whose acting exploits astonish and excite us. Larger than life, they surge across the silver screen—and although we're mesmerized and enthralled, we're also reminded of all that we're not. Not bright enough. Not built enough. Not brave enough.

I guess that's why I'd like to open this wonderful book by taking a moment to celebrate you—the real heroes in life—to respectfully remind you that the greatest exploits in this world are not in movies. And the greatest heroes in life are not featured on film.

Real heroes are people just like you. With courage and character, you step into the role life hands you. With dignity and discipline, you play that role to the best of your ability—without the right lighting and background music. No props. No pyrotechnics. You simply walk out and give life your best performance. No stunt doubles. No stand-ins.

> **I**'d like to open this wonderful book by taking a moment to celebrate you—the real heroes in life.

Real life is not a 120-minute screenplay. It's a day-by-day drama, lived out hour by hour, moment by moment. No rehearsals. No retakes.

As a keynote speaker and seminar leader in the Direct Selling profession, I've come to know a lot of you pretty well. Aside from the honor of speaking, what I like most about your conferences is the awards event. I sit there amazed, so proud of you I could just holler—and sometimes I do! So extraordinarily ordinary, you're often as amazed as anyone to be standing there in the spotlight.

> **I** *know that at some point you made a cold, calculated commitment to create your future; to write and perform your own script; to become the star of your own production.*

I may not know the particulars of your life, but I do know you're on that stage for a reason. I know that at some point you made a cold, calculated commitment to create your future; to write and perform your own script; to become the star of your own production. While others wished, you worked. While others made excuses, you made changes. The very reason why others quit their direct-selling business was the reason you were unstoppable.

So in the moments when you're not feeling all that "great," remember this: Your tireless prospecting; your ceaseless bookings; your endless caring; and the coaching of your leaders will pay off in rewards that promise to surpass any efforts you are now investing.

In the meantime, I just want to remind you of your greatness. You're smart enough and you're strong enough to achieve your dreams in this wonderful business called direct selling. Go ahead . . . look within yourself and see just how special you are!

> *You're more than your age*
> *or an hourly wage,*
> *You're more than your e-mail address.*
> *You're not just some size*
> *or the shape of your thighs*
> *or the make of the car you possess.*
>
> *You're more than your PIN*
> *or the shade of your skin*
> *or the place you were born or the date.*
> *You're not your IQ*
> *or the width of your shoe,*
> *your zip code, your height, or your weight.*

You can't be defined
by your Zodiac sign
or the lines in the palm of your hand.
It's not who you know
or the money you owe,
your blood type or cereal brand.

You're much too complex
for just race, creed, or sex,
you're wonderfully multidimensional.
You're one-of-a-kind
with a fabulous mind
and a spirit that's quite unconventional.

That makes you a treasure
which cannot be measured
with numbers and checks on a chart.
You're truly tremendous,
amazing, stupendous!
Believe it with all of your heart!

■ Preface

What Is Direct Selling?

Today, more than ever before, people are considering the possibility of starting their own business. The promise of time freedom, prestige, independence, and fulfilling work pulls seductively at our heartstrings as an alternative to being unfulfilled and underpaid. But the truth is, starting a traditional small business is backbreaking work, requiring long days that stretch late into the night, never-ending amounts of capital, and strong mental stamina to juggle the many roles and responsibilities of today's entrepreneur. Is this any way to live? We don't think so.

Enter the direct-selling business—small, lean, and incredibly efficient. As a direct-selling professional, you can choose from hundreds of fine companies that sell every product or service imaginable— from women's apparel to state-of-the-art nutritional products. In exchange for a minimal investment (most under $100), the company agrees to research, design, test, manufacture, store, ship, and, in many cases, service its product—all at its expense. You, in turn, agree to become the company's "marketing department," acting independently to share the products and find new customers, who then become your clients. For every sale that you make, you are paid a commission ranging from 20 to 50 percent. As a direct-selling professional, you have the opportunity to work part-time or full-time and can expand your business enterprise by engaging and training other people, who also love the products, share their enthusiasm for the business, and gain new customers. For this you are paid additional bonuses.

But it doesn't stop there. Your company has a stake in your success and goes to great lengths to inspire you with incentives that range from free products to all-expense-paid trips to exotic destinations. Companies understand that their success depends on your success and provide ongoing support in the form of training material and live events to inspire you to continually grow and learn. Unlike traditional entrepreneurs who usually fly solo, you are never alone in your direct-selling business. You always have someone to support you along the way. And last but not least, you'll form lifelong friendships with some of the most incredible people you've ever met.

So if you are one of the hundreds of thousands of individuals who is thinking about starting a small business, be sure to look before you leap into the life of a traditional entrepreneur. You might be surprised to learn that the trappings of a conventional business limit your freedom instead of enhancing it. So why not consider starting a direct-selling business of your own? Perhaps like thousands of others before you, you'll discover more rewards than you ever thought possible.

■ Introduction

If you own a home-based business or have thought about starting one—a direct-selling business or otherwise—this book is written for you. Its pages reveal 101 innovative insights on how to succeed in business, shared by the women and men who don't just talk about success—they live it. Although this book was written specifically for the more than 44 million people worldwide who are independent distributors with direct-selling companies, the information applies equally to anyone who owns a small business or is looking to begin one. Through these insights, we speak to the essence of your success and provide an enlightened perspective of every facet of growing your business, from getting started to becoming a leader and coaching your team.

The idea and design for the book came, not from the boardroom of the DSWA, but from the members. During a conference call, which we hold monthly with our Leaders Task Force, we posed the question: "If you could design the ideal book on success in direct selling that you would want to recommend to everyone on your team, what would it look like?" From their answers we crafted the vision for this book—a book that is easy to read, comprehensive in subject matter, innovative in content, inspirational in nature, and valuable beyond measure. We believe the book you are holding in your hands fulfills that vision.

The individuals who contributed to this book were selected not just because they have attained considerable success in direct selling but also because they have done so with a spirit and sense of integrity that exemplifies the best of our profession. These leaders oversee a collective organization of nearly 1 million distributors, with teams ranging in size from 400 to 400,000 distributors. They've walked in your shoes, experienced your joys, and triumphed over the same challenges you face every day. These leaders want you to learn from their mistakes and graciously offer their tried-and-true secrets to success. The experts included here are the most sought-after keynote speakers and trainers in our industry. Their energy, enthusiasm, and ability to teach and inspire nearly jump off the pages, as they impart some of their most treasured insights on how to grow your direct-selling business while living a more fulfilling life.

What can you expect in exchange for the time you invest in reading this book? At the heart level, we believe you will gain a new sense of pride—a feeling of excitement that you are a part of this great profession. Your dreams and deepest desires will become crystal clear and your determination strengthened. And last, we believe the experience of discovering these insider secrets will inspire greater confidence in both you and your business, making it easier to share what you do with others.

But we won't leave you there, full of hopes and dreams and nowhere to turn. We go on to give you the answers you seek to some of your most pressing challenges: where to find more customers, how to juggle family and business, what to do when your top leader wants to throw in the towel, and how to find your next superstar. These are just a few of the gems these pages offer.

However, finding the answers to your challenges is merely the first step. The purpose of this book is to inspire you into action—to offer concrete steps you can take to begin to experience greater results in your business. To that end, we have provided clear, concise action steps at the close of every insight. These simple, yet significant, steps can be completed within 48 hours and are designed to help you grow personally and professionally.

Our wish is that you internalize the wisdom shared by the authors. Recognize that you have the privilege of building a business and, at the same time, the honor of making a positive impact on so many people's lives. The truth about your success in direct selling is that it is ultimately up to you. Allow us the honor of extending a hand so that we can make the journey just a little smoother, more profitable, and above all, more fulfilling. Come with us and feel the exhilaration of becoming the person you know you can be—to see yourself as a more confident, professional, and purposeful you!

■ How to Use This Book

How can you make the most of the material presented here? First and foremost—finish the book. Don't allow yourself to be among the majority of book buyers who never make it past the first ten pages. You're not like them. You're not a quitter, or you wouldn't be in this profession to begin with. Our second bit of advice is to pace yourself. Some of you have such an insatiable thirst for more information on how to succeed in direct selling that you will be tempted to blaze through the first six insights, never bothering to stop and write down the action steps you are committed to take. Still others will approach this book nonchalantly, allowing it to gather dust on their bedside until they have a really rotten day and come searching for answers. Our challenge to you is to not fall into either of these groups but to find a comfortable middle ground that keeps you consistently moving through the book, implementing the ideas and bringing forth the results you know you deserve.

There are many ways to use the book to your advantage. You can partner with another direct seller and commit to reading one insight per day. Then meet for breakfast or lunch every two weeks to discuss how the actions you are taking are impacting your success. If you are a leader, select a particular insight and use it as the educational focus for your meeting. Ask team members to read it and implement the action steps prior to the meeting and then share their experiences. You can join one of the many Build It Big Circles, popping up throughout the country. These groups of direct sellers often start in local DSWA Chapters, which meet regularly to share and support one another and implement the ideas presented in this book.

Finally, designate one special journal as your Build It Big Journal. In it, record ideas and tips that you want to capture. Your BIB Journal is also where you will record your commitments and action steps that grow out of each insight. Use this journal to record your thoughts, your experiences, and your growth. Before you know it, you too will *build it big!*

Starting Your Direct-Selling Business

World-class sprinters spend lots of time perfecting their start. They know that no matter how fast they run in the race, a slow or faltered start can cost them a victory. Even though a career in direct selling is a little more forgiving, it is just as important to focus your energy and attention on getting your direct-selling business off to a great start. But what exactly is a good start? For most, it looks something like this:

- You develop a love of your product and company.

- You cultivate a good working rapport with your upline.

- You can see the beginnings of your team develop.

- You seize numerous opportunities to share the product and business opportunity.

- You begin to make money.

- You see yourself growing, learning, and gaining confidence.

- You enjoy the journey!

The insights that follow are aimed at helping you meet these objectives. Take them to heart, infuse them into your business, and make your first three months the best months you have to give. If you have been in business for years, treat today as if it *is* your first day in business, because every day brings another opportunity to begin anew.

■ Treat Every Day Like Your First Day in Business!

By Les Brown
The Master Motivator

KEEPING FRESH

Every day has 1,440 minutes, meaning we have 1,440 daily opportunities to make a positive impact. Unfortunately, many a direct seller allows those opportunities to slip away unnoticed. Why? Because of burnout, reaching a plateau, or finding herself stuck in a rut. Before she knows it, minutes have turned into years of lost chances. I call it "The Curse of the Comfort Zone." This is not the title of a horror movie but a real-life epidemic barring many people's rise to greatness. Fortunately, there are *solutions that will help you crown every day with that first-day freshness, enthusiasm, and determination.*

Think back to some of the finest first days you've had in life—a new job, a new school, a budding relationship. You felt that adrenaline rush as you surveyed new opportunities and savored every magical moment. Your passion was to be the best and brightest, and you worked hard at it. You looked for opportunities to shine and innovate. As time passed, you may have lost some of your enthusiasm. Boredom replaced energy; clutter replaced fresh ideas; routines replaced creativity. You went from having pep in your step to not wanting to get out of bed.

FINDING THE MAGIC

How do you rekindle and keep that first-day enthusiasm? Consider these solutions.

Remember Every Day Is a Gift to You

The best gifts are cherished *and used.* Each day is a gift filled with opportunities to rise above fear, self-doubt, and mediocrity. Make each day count by setting specific goals to succeed, then making every effort to exceed your own expectations.

Use the Power You Already Have

We were all born with internal power. One key to success is discovering this innate power and using it to deal with our challenges. Don't wait for others to open your doors. People in the direst circumstances have made ways to open doors to freedom, education, and business success *by finding their power.* Make a conscious effort to find your power source, use it to fuel your passion, and release the greatness within you.

Stay Alert

When you ignore new opportunities, you open doors to boredom, resulting in complacency and lack of growth. Open your eyes and see yourself as a go-getter with the power to turn a No into a Yes. Be determined to blaze new trails to success.

Determination Finds Many Ways to Succeed

Many people become discouraged when facing resistance in reaching their goals. Most successful people overcome obstacles to reach success. Their golden achievements came after doors closed, dreams were derailed, and hecklers berated them. However, the difference between those who won and those who gave up in defeat was often just their level of persistence. In tough times, the winners found in themselves that incredible resolve every human being possesses and stood firm against the odds. If you encounter a roadblock, think of a dozen ways to get around it and take action. Remember, there's more than one road to success.

Constantly Improve Yourself

As the global marketplace changes, stay abreast of what's going on and constantly improve your knowledge and skills. Make a daily commitment to be better, more knowledgeable, and more in touch than you were yesterday. Enroll in classes or access self-help toolkits that will help you improve yourself.

Actions for Today and Tomorrow

Going forward, here are three things to do in the next 48 hours that will help you treat each day like your first day in business:

1. Start a journal of your accomplishments and the things you need to improve. Pat yourself on the back for your good points and make immediate plans to improve any weaknesses you note. This will help you to stay focused on your goals and what you need to do to reach them.

2. As you begin each workday, see yourself as a true champion. Visualize yourself speaking positively and confidently; walking or sitting with good posture; remembering names and details; receiving praise and rewards for your efforts.

3. Keep a highly visible plaque, picture, or inspiring quote in your workplace to remind you of your purpose and why your work is important. It should be a visual so powerful that it inspires you each time you see it. This reminder will help you to maintain that fresh, first-day focus as you press toward your goals. ■

■ Connect with Your "Why"

By Caterina Rando, MA
Helping you achieve success with ease

SEEING BEYOND DEFEAT

A fanatic is sometimes defined as one who, having lost sight of her goal, redoubles her pace. *Losing sight of your goal, or your Why, could not only result in fanaticism but could alternatively result in discouragement and a hopeless loss of direction.*

When speaking to a group of women in direct selling one day, I asked Serina, "Why are you in this business?" She responded, "To make life better for myself and my family." When I asked how it was going, she paused, sighed deeply, and said, "Okay, I guess." Her listless lack of enthusiasm signaled that even though she had a general idea of why she was in business, she had not yet created a compelling vision to drive her success. She had not yet clearly defined her *Why*—the central, significant reason for devoting herself and her time, talents, and energy to her business. Here are some ideas to help you find your Why.

CREATING YOUR COMPELLING VISION

You probably have at least a general idea of why you opted to work in the Direct Selling industry. Take that general idea, whatever it is, and make it concrete and tangible. For example, ask yourself, "What will happen when you do well in your direct-selling business?" You should be able to come up with a series of specific life changes that will happen when you reach an appropriate level of success.

Now, on a piece of paper list all these tangible and specific ways your life will be different when you achieve the direct-selling success you desire. Don't just hold these thoughts in your mind—write them down and revisit the list every day.

Once you have your reasons why you opted to work as a direct seller, create a picture so alluring and appealing that you will do *whatever* it takes to make it real. The picture can be cut out of a magazine, or you can create your own picture.

Here is why creating this picture is so important. We have three brains:

1. The *reptilian brain* is the oldest and unconsciously takes care of our physiological functions like breathing and heartbeat.

2. The youngest brain is the *neocortex* brain. It understands language and does our conscious thinking.

3. The middle part of our brain is the *mammalian* brain. It does not understand language—only pictures. This brain is also where

our unconscious thoughts and our emotions live. Creating a picture of what your goal achievement looks like speaks the language of this brain, and you will *feel* it in your body. Engaging your mammalian brain gives you the drive to move forward despite the odds.

When I asked Serina what her picture would be—a snapshot of *why* she wants success in her business—she said, "I see myself dropping my kids off at grammar school. They are wearing their private school uniforms and laughing as they get out of my car. As I watch them enter the building, I wave and drive off feeling so proud and happy that I am giving them and me a better life."

What is your compelling vision? What represents the achievement of your Why? Once you have it, write out your vision in detail and find a picture to make it real to your mammalian brain. Every day, spend time with it, read it, look at the picture, carry it around with you in your mind, and *feel it in your body.* When you do this every day, it will create momentum for you and motivate you to keep going, no matter what comes your way.

Congratulations, you now can find your Why! Now use the vision of your Why to hold steady to your goal and fuel your success.

Actions for Creating Your Vision Today

- If you haven't done it already, sit down and formally define *why* you are building this business. Be specific.

- Find or create a picture that invokes the feelings of your Why every time you see it. Post this picture someplace where you can easily see it daily and refer to it often. ■

■ Start Your Business Off Right

By Rachel Kerr Schneider
Lighting the way for others

STARTING QUICKLY

Now that you've made the decision to begin your own home-based business, it is important that you get started *immediately* and experience early success. **Setting and attaining goals within your first 90 days of business will keep you motivated and start making money for you.** Some companies refer to this time as a "Quick Start." Whatever you choose to call it, just do it—*fast!*

GETTING OFF THE STARTING LINE

Take control of your calendar. It's critical to form this habit early so that you manage your business rather than letting your business manage *you*. Meet with your family, spouse, and any others who have a claim on your time and decide when you are and are not available to work on your business. This simple act of marking off time on the calendar for family and other commitments establishes boundaries that will give you clarity in making appointments, scheduling phone time, doing presentations, and attending trainings. You and your family will find it much easier to operate when everyone knows the schedule. Family scheduling should become a *weekly, scheduled* meeting.

Host a Business Kickoff event at your home. Personally invite guests to come and see what you are doing, sample your product, and give their opinion. Everyone has an opinion—and is usually willing to share it when asked.

Don't spend a lot of time organizing an office. A phone, calendar, and your enthusiasm are your most critical components of success. Forget fancy handouts and blasting e-mails. Your personal connection is the key that will unlock the door to your success.

Talk to as many people as possible. Direct selling is just a numbers game. The more people you talk to, the more appointments you will book and the more people you can share the business with.

Be consistent. The business of direct selling is not difficult but demands consistency in sales and sponsoring. If you are consistent, you can generate a steady and growing income while keeping your life manageable. When others see you incorporating your new venture into your life without turning your life upside down, they will be more inclined to support you and eventually join you.

Make "FRANK" a friend in your business development. This is a well-known acronym for *F*riends, *R*elatives, *A*cquaintances, *N*eighbors, and *K*ids, and is a memory jogger to help you build a list of individuals to introduce to your product or business. This list, with phone numbers, needs to be with you at all times so that you can make that call when you have a moment and add names as they come to you. This document is a most important piece of your business development, as it focuses you to stay on top of your prospects at all times.

Order business cards and give them out at every opportunity. When people ask for your name, phone number, or other contact information, hand them a card. Surveys show that people hang on to business cards—for a long time. It's an easy way to publicize your business without being intrusive.

Use the resources available to you and attend trainings regularly. Your sponsor and leaders are available to mentor and model successful business practices for you. Listen in on their calls, go with them to appointments, and watch them make presentations. Schedule this on-the-job training time just as you would any other business activity.

Embrace and incorporate these activities into your first 90 days of business. Teach others the same principles and watch your income multiply.

Actions for Today and Tomorrow

- Set a date and time for your family scheduling meeting. Emphasize how important it is to you that *everyone* makes a point to be there *every week.*

- Set a date for your Business Kickoff event and set goals for the number of guests, total sales, number of bookings, and potential team members you would like to gain from the show.

- Begin your FRANK list and commit to add at least three names every day. ■

■ Treat Your Business Like a Business

By Shan Eisler
Business Builder Extraordinaire

WIFE, MOTHER, CEO

One of the truly remarkable benefits of direct selling is that it can bind your family together. For that to happen, *the first sale you must make is to your family members.* They are part of your business, too, and can be a tremendous help if you let them. Key to making that sale is your commitment to making the business work for you. I found I had to be very creative to balance and fulfill all my commitments.

My kids were five and six when I started. I made a large Smiley Face sign and a Stop sign to post on my office door. When I could be interrupted, I put up the Smiley Face. When I was making calls, I put up the Stop sign. The kids understood and supported me, even though they were small.

My kids had two sets of toys. The premium, really fun stuff came out when I had the Stop sign on my door. These special toys were put away when the Smiley Face went up. A favorite was an easel and art tools. We were careful to prominently display their art in the kitchen, so they got recognition for helping to build Mommy's business.

I paid a neighborhood teenager to come in and play with my kids during times the Stop sign was up. This way, I was accessible to them but could focus on work until they needed me.

I enlisted the help of my husband early on. This wonderful man has taken on much of the work required in running our home. To help that happen, we agreed on specific tasks that he could do to allow me the time to grow my business.

MANAGING YOUR TIME AND RESOURCES

- Open your business every day. In direct selling, *you* get to decide whether you are employed or unemployed every day. You are only employed if you are open for business—doing the things required to conduct business.

- I found out early on that I needed to have a fairly detailed schedule for integrating family activities with work. A clear idea of what needed to happen allowed us to make sure the family was fully cared for, even when I was deeply involved in business.

- You have to figure out whether you are a morning person or a night person. The best hours for your business doors to be open are from 9 AM to 9 PM. These are the hours when you can work with people. If you are a morning person, do your paperwork in the morning, before 9 AM; if a night person, do your paperwork after 9 PM.

- I also did the math and found that if I were earning $35 per hour, it didn't make sense for me to do my own cleaning when I could pay someone else $10 an hour to do it for me.

- I plan menus by the month. On the evenings when I need to be out, or if I have a heavy afternoon's worth of work, we enjoy Crock-Pot meals. This way, I don't waste time wondering what to feed the family, and meals are served on a regular schedule.

■ I never shop for office supplies. Most office supply stores deliver if you order online or by phone.

■ I have learned to think before making a commitment. My immediate response is "Let me get back to you." I then weigh the time costs of accepting a commitment against the emotional costs of declining, and then I make a final decision.

My children are now 18 and 19. Far from feeling neglected, they have both thanked me for working in my direct-selling business from home and teaching them a strong work ethic. As a result of my working from home, we have always been there for each other.

Today's Actions for Family and Business

Are you treating your business like a business or like a hobby? Gain your family's support by:

■ Taking an action that expresses your appreciation for their support—special toys, outings, or other rewards.

■ Closely managing your calendar and keeping everyone in the family in the loop about expectations and plans.

■ Increasing your productive hours by taking advantage of free and inexpensive services such as delivery and babysitting. ■

■ Elevate Conversations to Connections

By Bonnie Ross-Parker
Teaching the joy of connecting

THE ART OF NETWORKING

Let's face it: as a direct-selling professional, networking is one of the most important business-building activities you can incorporate into your schedule. It gives you a continual stream of new customers, potential recruit leads, and interesting new friends—all essential to your success. For some, networking appears to be a race to see who can collect the most business cards or shake the most hands. For others, it is a nerve-racking, nail-biting experience. ***In fact, networking is an opportunity to elevate a simple conversation into a meaningful connection that offers value to each individual.***

My intention is to help you hone the art of networking by giving you a few simple tips that will make you more comfortable and, dare I say, even learn to *like* networking!

Show Up to Be Remembered

Show up. The saying "You have to be present to win" is relevant, especially when your business success depends on continually meeting new people. If networking is the process of engaging a person in a meaningful conversation to learn about her and assess whether there is a "fit" with what you have to offer, then it requires that you get out and meet new people. Make a point to *show up* at one networking event or more each week.

Be memorable. Can you recall a time when you observed someone who was physically present but mentally elsewhere? She might have been standing alone, far away in thought or quiet and uninvolved. Now think of a time you observed others engaged in conversation, sharing ideas, connecting with friends, and creating new relationships. Which scenario leaves the better impression? People who are engaged and alive are remembered. The next time you attend a networking event, set an intention to be engaged and alive, and notice how your experience is enhanced.

HOW TO START A CONVERSATION

One of the *best* ways to get over any fears you may have about networking is to be prepared with a few conversation starters. Armed with these, you will feel more comfortable making that initial connection, no matter how new you are to the group or the situation.

"I notice from your nametag you're with _____. *What do you like most about your job?"* You'll be amazed at the number of women who don't like *anything* about their work! If the response is positive, it can open a door for you as well. A woman who "loves the people I work with" may want to sponsor a party for her female colleagues or be open to "meeting your team" to build a side business.

"What is the best thing that happened to you this week (last week)?" This question accomplishes several things: You'll begin the conversation on a positive note, you'll learn if she is generally a positive or negative person, and you'll discover something interesting about her.

If her nametag indicates a business or industry, you might ask, *"That sounds very interesting. How did you get involved in* _____?" This also opens the door for her to share her level of satisfaction with what she does and gives you a window into how she came to her current position.

Build On the Conversation

Once you've started a conversation, keep it going by listening carefully and asking lots of open-ended questions. Place the spotlight on the speaker, knowing that when the spotlight turns to you, she will feel a connection and be more receptive to what you have to offer. By offering sincere compliments, being genuinely interested, and recognizing something unique or special about her, you elevate the conversation to a connection.

If you remember that her comments hold vital clues about her life and aspirations, you will begin to discover whether you have something of value to offer her.

Today's Actions for Making New Connections

Set a goal to seek out and participate in at least two networking events where you'll meet other professional women in the next two weeks. Your local Chamber of Commerce; American Business Women's Association (ABWA); Business and Professional Women's Association (BPWA); Business Network, Intl. (BNI); and the Direct Selling Women's Alliance (DSWA) all provide excellent networking opportunities. At http://www.Google.com you'll discover over 402 *thousand* networking associations and organizations. Surely you can find a few in your community!

By deciding to show up, learning simple ways to begin a conversation, and then finding places you can practice these skills, you will soon become comfortable with the art of networking for a flourishing, successful business. ■

■ Conquer Fear of Rejection and Move On to Greatness!

By Marilyn Snyder
Powering up your passion

BECOMING OUR OWN PROGRAMMER

When we were children, we were like little computers. Learning as a child is like being programmed. We were programmed by parents, teachers, friends, and even television! We had no choice about what programs were written into our lives. ***As adults, however, we can*** *choose not only who programs us with which messages; we can even be our own programmer!*

As babies, we are happy or sad in the moment, with no thought about others, or the future, or how the stock market is going. As we grow, however, many of us are programmed to worry a lot about other people and to fantasize about what they are thinking. Such thoughts include:

■ "Why don't they like me?"

■ "What can I do to make them like me?"

■ "I hope I don't offend them—I want them to like me."

Do you see how we have been programmed since birth? This programming teaches that the more people who like us, the better off we are. This affects the men and women entering direct selling in that they *confuse rejection of the sale with people disliking them.* When they get a No in direct selling, they should think, "Great! I am one step closer to getting my next Yes." But many don't think this way. Instead, they waste time thinking "Why didn't she buy from me—she must not have liked me. How can I make everyone like me?"

So how can you make everyone like you? *You can't, and it doesn't matter.*

WRITING YOUR PROGRAM

Although the great salespeople know that selling is all about building relationships, they also know another very important thing. They know that selling is a numbers game. For every three people they get in front of, only one person will buy. If two buy—great! If all three buy, they know the end of the world is coming! Great sales leaders also know this: *rejection is part of the game.* They deal with it, learn what they can from it, and then they forget about it.

Here are three important ideas to remember and use—starting to-day!

1. If you are preoccupied with rejection, you are focused on the wrong person. Instead of focusing on the customer you are trying to help, you are focusing on *you*. Great sales come to the people whose sole focus is on the customer and how to serve her. If you are thinking of *her* needs and how you can help *her*, you won't have room in your thoughts for fear of rejection. Instead, you will be rid of the emotional drag from that fear and will be more successful.

2. Ask questions. Ask questions. Ask questions. I cannot say this enough! If you are asking questions, not only are you finding out what your customer needs and wants and thereby giving better service, *but you are also forcing your mind to focus on her.* Again, fear of rejection has no room to get in.

3. *Do not take a failed sale personally.* There could be any number of reasons your customer did not buy from you, and most of them have nothing to do with you. She has a relative in the business. You look just like her spouse's ex. It's Friday or Thursday or raining. She really doesn't need the product, she doesn't have the money, or maybe you really are not her type of salesperson. Whatever the reason, it doesn't matter. Just learn what you can from it and move on.

Sitting still and saying, "Why didn't they like me?" is not going to help you achieve the goals you want to reach or the dreams you want to fulfill. Fear of rejection is like all of the other fears out there. If you give it power, it will take control. Don't let it. Remember, you are too busy making a wonderful life for yourself and too busy giving and helping others to let any fear stop you.

Adults are like computers too. The difference is that adults can write their *own* programs. I challenge you to program fear of rejection out of your professional life.

Entering Program Code

- Take time to reflect on how you felt when you decided against buying something. It was about the product, right?

- Identify and shut down negative self-talk. ■

■ Know Just Enough

By Kathie Nelson
Equipping busy people to do more business

WHAT YOUR PROSPECT WANTS TO HEAR

You've signed up to represent a product you feel passionate about! You know the opportunity is fabulous, as is the value your company delivers. You roll up your sleeves, eager to learn everything there is to know about your product. After all, you want to have all the answers if you are posed a question, right? *Wrong!* I've found **the two most important things to know are your product's benefits and your compensation plan.**

You may ask, "Is it really that easy?" Yes, it is. Let me tell you why.

- Making money and exchanging value happen when you understand the benefits to your prospect and what's in it for you.

- When you understand how you can make money, you'll be motivated to take action.

- When you are clear about what is in it for your prospects, you'll be more direct, get to the point, and close sales more quickly.

The reality is simply this: your prospect doesn't care *how* your product does what it does. She wants to know *what is in it for her.* How will it make her life better, add value, solve her problem, or make her feel *WOW!* If she does care how a product functions or is made, she will ask. When you think about what motivates *you* to buy, isn't it what the end result will be when you use the product? After all, when a man buys a quarter-inch drill bit, he doesn't want the quarter-inch drill bit; he wants a quarter-inch hole! He's buying the product only to achieve the result.

Advertising agencies have been pushing our buttons for years, dangling the "pain-relief" or WOW! factor in front of us in such a consistent manner that as we browse the aisles of our favorite grocery or department store, we feel we must have *that* product. As a direct seller, you can use the same approach.

THE SECRET FORMULA

Want to know the secret? Lead your prospect through the four stages of learning your product to propel her to the bottom line. *What's in it for her?* Use language she understands, and she'll respond even more quickly.

In new distributor training, you typically learn facts and benefits. They're great—the first two stages of learning about your product— but they reach only *some* of your prospects *some* of the time. To move more prospects to purchase, you must be able to lead them through the next two stages. To prepare for the third stage, look at the benefits of your product and make a list of the solutions, or "pain relief," it provides. And best of all, for the fourth stage come up with a WOW! factor. Your four stages might look like this:

> **Fact:** natural ingredients; **Benefit:** not adding chemicals to face; **Solution:** reduces puffiness and fine wrinkles; **WOW!:** look years younger, recapture youth.
> **Fact:** 50/50 cotton/poly; **Benefit:** looks and feels like cotton but doesn't wrinkle; **Solution:** minimal ironing, looks great, saves time; **WOW!:** sharp, professional, chic.

You might say, "That sounds great, but those aren't my products! I haven't been to new distributor training yet. How do I get started?" It's as simple as asking some questions, taking into account what you already know about your product, and coming up with a presentation that is all your own!

Increasing bookings, sales, or recruiting can be boiled down to this simple process. Remember, most prospects won't care how your product is made, where it comes from, or the process they need to follow to get results. They only want to know *what is in it for them!* Know the solutions you offer or the WOW! factor. Those are enough. Go for it! Get in front of your target audience and share what's in it for them!

Sharing the WOW! Today

Within the next 48 hours, make contacts that get results!

■ Make a list of everything you know about the product. Make another list of the solutions or WOW! it provides.

■ Make a list of those in your target audience. Who would derive the most benefit from the solution you provide or would want the WOW! you offer?

■ Make contact! Call your customers and prospects. Network in groups serving your target audience. Skip your company's history and manufacturing process. Get to the point. Share what's in it for them! Then invite them to check it out. ■

■ Focus On Execution!

By Gary Ryan Blair
The Goals Guy

BRINGING YOUR DREAMS TO LIFE

When your most cherished goal seems to be slipping away, **strengthen your execution.** Having worked with thousands of direct sellers throughout my career, I've observed that success is 10 percent vision and 90 percent execution.

I realize this statement runs counter to the premise that a goal is the most important ingredient of success, and that you succeed or fail based on the merits or worthiness of your goal. Let's examine the relationship between goals and execution.

Unless you properly plan, execute, and remain focused until completion, the goal—and that means any goal—is irrelevant.

By analogy, when they were very young, both Tiger Woods and Serena Williams had grand visions of being champions in their sport. Was it the vision of the goal that made them great performers, or was it their willingness to execute? How many other aspiring athletes had great visions but didn't succeed because they either didn't have a plan or failed to execute a plan?

> **Y**our goals will never fail you. Rather, you fail them, largely due to lack of implementation!

To succeed at the highest level in direct selling, you must value and enforce (with yourself!) the principles of execution and follow that course until you're successful. The good news is that you don't have to be blessed with lots of native talent like Tiger or Serena. The skills required to succeed in direct selling are within the reach of everyone who is willing to remain focused on execution.

DEVELOPING YOUR EXECUTION SKILLS

Consider these questions as they relate to you:

- Have you ever missed a golden opportunity because you failed to develop an idea?

- Have you ever been frustrated by your inability to follow through and execute plans, even after committing to do so?

- Would it be worth a focused effort to permanently fix the underlying causes of inaction?

If you answered Yes to any of these, you'll want to know why execution is the key to greatness, what good execution is, and how anyone can master the art of execution.

Why Is Execution the Key?

Because the execution of your plan is what transforms your dream into your reality.

What Is Good Execution?

It is making good decisions and making things happen. It is reacting well to unpleasant and unexpected events. It is developing characteristics that are critical to your success, such as efficiency and effectiveness.

How Does One Master the Art of Execution?

- Focus time and resources on the core activities necessary for achievement. There are always more things to do than time and resources to do them. Go for the high-payoff activities.

- Hold yourself accountable to deadlines and adjust tasks accordingly. Missed deadlines are a symptom of poor execution and lack of discipline. Establish realistic time lines, then monitor your progress and make course corrections to ensure you stay on track.

- Surround yourself with people, experience, and expertise. Well-trained, experienced people know how to get a job done effectively. Inexperienced or untrained people will simply not be as effective. People who experiment and learn become experienced executors.

- Realize that everything you say, think, and do counts. Consciously pay attention to the small details of core activities, and notice whether each one moves you closer to, or further from, achieving your goal.

The small details are what make the difference between mediocre results and outstanding results.

The success you enjoy depends on many things, but mostly it depends on you and your willingness to execute until the goal is achieved.

Improving Your Execution Today and Tomorrow

Take these steps in the next 48 hours to embrace the discipline and *do* what needs to be done for success.

- Identify your high-impact activities, give them top priority, and get them done.

- Monitor your progress. Are you on track to meet your deadlines? Make any needed adjustments.

- Pay attention to every word you speak and action you take. Everything counts! ■

■ Balance Six Areas Critical to Your Start-up Success

By Jenny Bywater
Known as "Jenny B" in the Party Plan industry

WHERE TO DIRECT YOUR ATTENTION

When you're getting started in the party plan business and feel overwhelmed by all the advice and information available, *focus on the six areas most critical to your success.* I've found that when you master these six areas and develop the habit of covering them consistently, success becomes your happy routine. The six areas are:

1. **Bookings.** This is the lifeblood of your business. When your date book is full, your business keeps moving, and the money flows in.

2. **Hostess coaching.** Your skill in helping your hostess learn and do everything necessary for a successful party also gives her a self-confidence all your guests will enjoy.

3. **Increasing attendance.** This is often overlooked but critical to a successful party. After all, it is easier to sell to a live person!

4. **Increasing sales.** Your ability to apply certain techniques will generate additional sales.

5. **Customer service.** Once you have customers, you have to treat them well to retain their business.

6. **Recruiting or sponsoring.** This is the key to building wealth! Sharing the opportunity comes naturally when you are proficient in the previous key areas.

As you can see, these key areas are the continual cycle of your business. To be successful, you first have to recognize how each of these areas impacts your business. Then decide what you are going to do for *every party* in each of these areas. In reality, you have to address *all six* at once!

FROM PLANS TO HABITS

Balancing the six areas is not difficult when you take a few moments to make a plan. Ask yourself, "What am I doing for my next party to get more bookings, to help my hostess, to increase the attendance, to increase my sales, to give great customer service, and to plant recruiting seeds?"

I often ask this question of my team at trainings: "If you book a party, are you going to go and do the party?" Most give me a puzzled look that says, "Of course I will!" Then I ask: "If you book a party, are you going to do *everything* you can to make it as successful as possible?" Then I begin to see the wheels turning in their minds as they ponder that commitment. Your hostess expects you to do everything possible to make it successful. You need to expect it of yourself.

If you are going to do a party, wouldn't you rather it be a $700 party than a $350 party? When you implement your plan, you'll see your sales begin to climb, your bookings increase, and your team grow! *(Once you have a team, you'll need to add two more areas to your balancing act: coaching your team members and praising their efforts.)*

The best part is that when your plans become habits, it actually becomes easier to balance it all. You become comfortable in knowing exactly what needs to be done—and you do it! You'll be better able to balance your family and your business because you've developed a routine that creates success, and success will motivate you to keep on doing it!

Create an Action Plan Today

Your company provides a training manual. Look in it for six *new* things—one from each category—to add to your plan for your next party. At the party, you'll be practicing something new in each of the areas. When you find techniques that work for you, make them part of your routine. You'll soon exhaust your training manual and be ready to look to other sources for fresh ideas. When you practice a new skill in each of the six areas faithfully at every party, success quickly becomes your habit! ■

■ Work Now, Play Later

By Shirley Tyson
Graciously leading the way for others

GETTING STARTED ON THE RIGHT FOOT

Did you start your business so you could make money while balancing life around a work schedule? The appeal of direct selling is the value of leveraging time. This incredible opportunity allows us to make money and build a business around our true priorities, one of which is our family. Have the discipline to invest in learning right from the beginning to set the stage for an extremely profitable business. Remember this motto, *"Pay the price up front so you can play in the end!"*

I earn a six-figure income that works around my grandchildren and family life from holding fast to this approach. Of course, I have worked with others who want to "play early and pay later." They are still waiting to make money. Which will you choose?

PLANNING A SUCCESSFUL ROUTINE

If you are in business, you have a work schedule. One of the things we love about this type of profession is the freedom it allows. To enjoy that freedom, we must do what it takes to become the best. Instead of letting each day happen to us, we begin with a plan:

■ Get out your calendar. Set a time to work your business. Quit procrastinating. Choose *when* you will do your work!

- Write down 100 names of people you want to call. Don't worry about the No's. The more you call, the better you become. Get calling!

- Hold two to three shows a week minimum. The more you do, the better you get.

Pay the Price Up Front!

It is important to develop your routine. Schedule around your family. You can still be the best wife, a great mom, and yet run a successful business. For example, set aside five hours on Tuesday, Wednesday, and Thursday. Take this time to call, follow up, and get the parties booked! When a party cancels, instead of taking that time off, use it. Make calls and replace that showing. Take a look at your calendar. What days of the week work best for you?

> *Consider finding age-appropriate toys that are special "phone-time toys."*

If you have young children and are frustrated with your phone time, consider finding age-appropriate toys that are special "phone-time toys." When Mommy or Grandma has to be on the phone, it is a treat to play with the toys. Reward your little ones for honoring your time. Keep your commitments to your children too. If you've asked them for 30 minutes of time so you can make calls, stick to 30 minutes. Acknowledge them for helping you do your business!

On many occasions you'll have unexpected time. A nap or a play date might create a window of opportunity to make a few calls. Have that list of 100 contacts ready and available. You will likely fill your calendar before you contact your complete list. Remember, the more you call, the more appointments or bookings you get, the better you'll feel, and the more money you'll make. Pick up the phone!

Two to three parties a week may seem like a lot to schedule. Look at it from this perspective: if one party reschedules, you still have two. The consistency in presenting your product helps you polish your presentation, gain more sales and bookings, and develop recruiting leads. Move from good to better to best!

Will you commit to persevering and working toward your personal best? Working on phone skills, presentations, and follow-up? Leaders compete with themselves. They invest in learning. They pay the price up front so they can play in the end.

Get into Action

Within the next 48 hours, commit to the following:

■ Review and mark your calendar. Set a work schedule. If you have young children, pick out a special age-appropriate toy for each child to occupy them while you are on the phone.

■ Make or update your list of 100 contacts. Keep it handy at all times. ■

2

Booking and Coaching Your Hostess

*I*n the Party Plan segment of the Direct Selling industry, *bookings* are the lifeline of your business—dates on which you meet in the home of a hostess with her friends to share your products and business opportunity. Without bookings, you are temporarily out of business. With bookings, you enjoy a continual source of sales, new customers, new bookings, and potential team members. *Hostess coaching* is your interaction with the person who has scheduled a party. It is the very thing that determines whether the experience is a dud or a delight.

In this chapter you discover the secrets to successful booking and hostess coaching, as seen through the eyes of the people who have built thriving businesses by perfecting these skills. Brace yourself—you may be surprised by what you'll discover, for all these insights share one common attribute that is essential to success. Can you find it?

A word to the network marketer. Even though you may be tempted to skip this chapter, we encourage you to press on. Recently, the line between the party plan and the network marketing world has blurred, as traditional network marketers experience the value of *partying for higher profits.* Be open to the possibilities, and you just might find that this way of doing business suits you better than you imagined.

29

■ Restore Your Business with Bookings

By Sue Rusch
Helping you become more

STAYING IN BUSINESS

You open your calendar and gasp. You have absolutely no bookings! You think, "How did this happen? I know I've been busy with other things, but I really *have* been thinking a lot about my business." If this scene is familiar, you're not alone. *Having no parties booked means you have no paydays scheduled.* **In this condition, while there are still lots of things to do, you are essentially out of business.** Fortunately, your business can be revitalized.

I recall once when I thought I was working my business but was actually preparing for success rather than getting results. When I got ready to call upcoming hostesses, I was shocked to discover that I had no upcoming hostesses to call! My first step was to find support. I felt that this predicament had *just happened.* Thankfully, the person I turned to for support urged me to take responsibility and take immediate steps to get back in business.

GETTING BACK IN BUSINESS

Decide why success matters to you. When you want something badly enough, you find a way to get it. In truth, you probably know *what* to do to restart your business. But is your *Why* strong enough? No matter why you are in business, a clear sense of purpose is essential.

List the reasons why *now* is the best time to host a show. Make a list of the benefits to your hostesses. What makes *now* a great time to do business with your company? What makes this an ideal season to host a show? Be timely and service-minded when you talk to prospective hostesses.

Schedule two evenings and one Saturday to make phone calls. Identify blocks of uninterrupted time during which you will make calls. Make a commitment to yourself to get your business back on track.

Make 100 phone calls. There's no secret here. Success is related to your willingness to stick with your phone until you reach the desired result. The time you spend seeking alternatives is time you're not spending making calls!

Call 100 past customers or contacts. Ask if they'd like to learn about what's new and exciting at your company. Invite them to share the fun of your products by hosting a show. What's the worst that can happen? Some will say No. What's the best that can happen? A few may say Yes.

Call past hostesses and invite them to rebook. Your past hostesses may be waiting to be invited! Ask when they'd like to schedule another show to share what is new and exciting.

Host a show at your home. You can coordinate a successful show in less than a week. Invite acquaintances and friends. Keep the focus on the benefits of hosting.

Participate in a craft fair or exposure event. Hosting a booth is an easy way to meet a number of new people quickly. Concentrate on bookings instead of product sales. Consider running a home-show video in the background to illustrate the fun of hosting a show.

Limit e-mail communication. E-mail is convenient but doesn't allow the personal connect you need in this situation. Your voice and personal touch go much further toward building strong hostess relationships.

Commit to these prevention strategies:

- **Establish a booking goal.** Set a goal each month and stick with it until you have filled your calendar.

- **Set a booking deadline.** Choose one week each month to assess future bookings and make calls to fill your calendar.

- **Make time for phone calls.** Don't allow distractions to divert you from business success.

- **Actively invite people to host.** Relying on door prizes or completed forms is a passive approach to recruiting hostesses. Take a more active approach and personally invite each guest as she places an order.

- **Ask for rebookings.** Invite each hostess to host a future show. You'll be amazed how often they agree.

- **Work consistently.** When you do at least one show a week, you get in a rhythm that keeps your business going.

When you are in business for yourself, there's nothing like the pride of successfully facing a challenge head on. Bookings can change the direction of your business. What steps will you take to restore the vitality of your business?

Today's Actions for Jump-Starting

- Pull together a list of past customers and hostesses to call.
- Block out time for making the calls. ■

◼ Make the Most of Every Show

By Beth Jones-Schall
Sharing the spirit of success

PREPARATION THAT MAKES THE DIFFERENCE

As a direct seller, obtaining both future *bookings* and *recruiting leads* is essential to growing a healthy, profitable business. There's no better place to obtain both than at your in-home parties, where guests can discover your product, your hostess program, and the career opportunity in a fun and relaxed environment. But great shows don't just happen! It takes your ***concentrated efforts before, during, and after every show to reap the greatest rewards.***

Set the Stage for a Fabulous Show

Building rapport with your hostess prior to her show is easy when you follow these simple guidelines:

- ◼ Touch base with your hostess frequently during the four weeks before her show. After giving her a hostess packet that contains the materials she'll need for her show, follow up each week to reinforce her decision and help her take steps toward success. Most important, follow every step of your company's suggested hostess-coaching program and then go the extra mile with personal notes and upbeat phone calls. The more frequent your communication with your hostess, the stronger the relationship you'll build and the fewer cancellations you'll have.

- ◼ Give your hostess a reason to call her guests to gather their RSVPs. A new product debut, a product on sale that month, a reminder to bring a friend, a suggestion of what to wear or bring so they can fully participate in the show—any of these is a reason to make the RSVP call and another reason for the guests to attend. Reminder phone calls made by the hostess will result in higher attendance and higher sales. (If the hostess is too busy, offer to make the calls for her.)

■ On the night of the show and just before the guests' arrival, have a "hostess huddle." Ask her which products she wants to earn with her hostess benefits, which of the guests she thinks are most likely to book a show that night, and which guest would make a terrific consultant. These simple questions can make a significant difference in the results of your show.

Plant Booking and Recruiting Seeds

The best way to share the hostess program and career opportunity is by "planting seeds" throughout your presentation. Seeds are brief, subliminal messages that ease guests toward a decision to schedule a party or consider a business of their own. Here are some proven planting times:

■ At the beginning of your show, thank your hostess and mention how much you're looking forward to treating her to some of her favorite products, which she'll earn with her hostess credits.

■ When you introduce yourself, share your personal story, emphasizing how you have benefited from owning your own business and pointing out how the opportunity fits all your needs and schedules.

■ Midway through your presentation, display one of the items your hostess will be receiving with her hostess credits or bonuses.

■ At some point, share one of your favorite products that you just happened to receive in your starter kit. Describe the generous product discounts you enjoy and the awards and trips you've earned with your company.

■ Provide guests with a Wish List where they can write down their favorites as you demonstrate the product. At the end of your presentation, have guests refer to their lists and say: *"If your list is bigger than your budget . . . don't worry! Simply pick out the items you want to order tonight; then let me treat you to the rest for free by using our hostess program."* You may want to circulate a list of dates you have open, either on the back of the Wish List or on a separate index card. Tell them: *"These are the dates I have available. Select a date that works for you, and we'll get started tonight."*

■ At the end of your presentation, display a career information packet and say: *"It's been _____ years since a friend invited me to give this career a try. I thought I was way too busy but decided I had nothing to lose. I've never been sorry! I'm compensated well for the hours I invest in my business, I enjoy meeting new people, and I really love having control over my schedule and my future. I'm so glad my friend encouraged me to give it a try. I want to encourage each of you to give it a try, too. This information will answer some of your initial questions. Then I would be happy to meet with you personally."*

Sensational Shopping Time

During shopping time, keep your ears and eyes open for clues to your next hostess or team member. Make a mental note of those who are asking questions, have multiple items on their Wish List, are experienced home show hostesses, or have brought a guest. Then privately say: *"Lynne, I notice you* [mention one of the above]. *I would love to treat you to our hostess program."* As you tally each guest's order, recognize and reinforce her selection. Say: *"Lisa, you'll love the* [product]*! Our* [another product] *complements your choice. I'd enjoy treating you to it with our hostess program."* or *"You have great taste; you'd make an excellent consultant."*

Today's Actions for Successful Shows

■ Adjust your hostess-coaching steps to reflect shorter, more frequent contact.

■ Set a goal to plant at least five booking or recruiting seeds throughout your next presentation and write them on an index card.

■ Write "Booking Seed" and "Recruiting Seed" on two small Post-it® notes; then place them in your demo trays or case where you will see them during your product demonstration. ■

■ Quit Asking and Start Offering

By Karen Phelps
Keeping the fun and profits in your business

ARE YOU GIVING OR TAKING?

You've set your goal for the number of bookings you would like to hold per week. You have your script in hand. You make calls to some of your closest friends and relatives to ask them to hold a party to help you get started in your new business, but they turn you down. Why does this happen? How can they say No to you? You soon become afraid to ask, because you don't want to hear another No. If this sounds familiar, relax. Help may be as easy as learning to *offer them a gift rather than asking them for a favor.*

WRAPPING THE GIFT

Each of us is busy. Even close friends and family have things to do besides helping you get involved in a business they may not understand and may not really support. By offering them an immediate reward for their cooperation, you move asking for a party from an altruistic favor friends and family do for you to a business decision they make for themselves.

Remember, it's not about you. When you ask others to book a party to help *you* out, you are leaving *them* out of the picture. We all worry about asking others to do us a favor, so what if you changed it around? What if instead of asking them to do us a favor, we offered them the opportunity to earn free and discounted products? *Simply change your thinking and your question takes on a different meaning.* See if you notice a difference:

> **Example One:** "Hi Susie. I've just joined XYZ Company and I'm really excited, but *I need* people to book parties to help *me* get started. Would you have a party in the next three weeks *for me?*"
>
> **Example Two:** "Hi Susie. I've just joined XYZ Company and I'm really excited. The products are great and *I get to hold parties and give away free and discounted products.* I would love to *offer you the opportunity* to earn some of these products by having a few of your friends and me over for a fun-filled evening. The dates I have available are Tuesday the third and Thursday the fifth. Which one is better for you?"

Do you agree that the second example provides more information in a nonthreatening way? So the first lesson is *don't ask for a party,* but instead *offer the opportunity* to earn free and discounted products.

Remember there are *two winners* with every party: the consultant, who earns the commission, and the hostess, who earns the hostess credits. You need to *truly believe that you are providing a service to your hostess.* You are giving her a way to earn the products she likes at substantial savings. Become a believer in your company's hostess program.

Last, make sure you keep your bookings alive by booking one or more parties at every presentation. Instead of becoming just an order taker, make sure that as a guest is placing her order, you reinforce the benefits of hosting a party. You might say something like, "Susie, you'll love the items you are purchasing tonight, and I know there are *several other things that you liked.* Don't forget that, as a hostess, you can earn a lot of these items for free or at substantial savings. All you need to do is invite your friends and me over for an evening just like tonight. I have Tuesday the third, Wednesday the second, and Thursday the fifth available, and I will bring you a bonus gift. Which date is best for you?"

Finding the Gift

- Learn the benefits of your company well enough that you truly believe you are offering a gift to those you share the business with.

- Learn your company's hostess program well enough that you fully understand the benefits a hostess realizes by holding a party.

Use these surefire techniques, and I guarantee you will keep your calendar full! ■

■ Send Subliminal Messages

By Jenny Bywater
Known as "Jenny B" in the Party Plan industry

ENTICING THEIR INTEREST

When you want to tell everyone about your business but are afraid of being pushy, ***use subtle visual messages to excite your customers' curiosity.*** I've found this is the most effective way to book, sell, and sponsor without feeling uncomfortable.

Discomfort is a dilemma many in the Direct Selling industry feel. You have a great product and a great opportunity, and you want to shout it to the world! But how can you get your message across without acting like the stereotypical salesperson whom everyone makes jokes about?

You need a new way to stimulate interest. For example, how many invitations do you send for a party? The industry average is anywhere between 25 and 40. Let's say you send 30. The average attendance at the party will be six. With these numbers in mind, how many people will hear of your booking or recruiting message? Six, right? The six who attended the party will learn about your products, about the benefits of booking, and about your opportunity during your demonstration. How many people will then *miss* your message? 24! That's right—24 people who might be interested in knowing about your products or opportunity will not even get the chance to know about them or you!

So what can you do? Call all 24 people and tell them? Yes, that is an option but is quite time consuming. Send them a catalog? Yes, but that can be quite costly; yet if someone has shown an interest, it is definitely a good option. However, I've discovered easier, simpler ways to plant seeds of information that can prompt interest and questions.

INVITING CURIOSITY VISUALLY

When you send an invitation or catalog, use *stickers!* Make sure to use attractive and eye-catching stickers that start your customers thinking and asking questions. Here are a few slogans I've found effective:

- "Earn some free when you party with me!"

- "Why pay full price? Free is twice as nice!"

- "When money is low . . . have a show!"

- "Call me anytime to place an order."

- "Gifts for every Holiday."

- "Full-time pay . . . part-time hours! Ask me how!"

- "I love what I do! You can too!"

- "Have you ever thought of doing what I'm doing?"

- "Get paid for having fun!"

Adding stickers with these messages to your mailings can motivate your customers to think about booking, buying more, and joining your team! Without saying a word or being pushy, you are recruiting and booking simply by prompting questions and interest. You can even use the slogans as an opening when you call to follow up. Or a prospect's interest might be kindled and motivate her to attend the party to learn more. Friends have told me: "I know people are reading the stickers because they will come up to me at a party and say, 'Do you really love what you do?' or 'I have thought of doing what you do. Please tell me more!'"

You can entice the interest of potentially anyone you meet when you wear a button that expresses an effective slogan. Buttons are great because you are leaving it up to the people you meet to *ask you* the questions. This puts you in the enviable position of doing "permission marketing" because *they* initiate the conversation. Instead of walking up to someone and saying, "May I tell you about my opportunity?" you could just wear a button that asks, "Could you use an extra $100 a week?" When someone answers, "Yes, I could use that $100," you have the opportunity, and her permission, to tell her about your company!

The benefit of putting stickers and buttons to work for you can be more than you ever dreamed!

Communicating Subliminally Today and Tomorrow

Here are some steps you can take to start your subliminal campaign:

- Locate vendors who specialize in stickers and buttons. My company, The Booster, has been creating these products for direct-selling professionals for 33 years. Visit http://www.thebooster.com for details.

- Begin using stickers and notice the increase in guest attendance, outside orders, show sales, and bookings. Remember the success formula: If B > C = DO IT! (If the *Benefit* is greater than the *Cost*, then *Keep on doing it!*) ■

■ Take Control of Your Calendar

By Delores Douglass
Juggling it all while building a thriving business

THE SECRET OF BALANCING YOUR LIFE

If you started your own business to spend more time with your family or stay home with your children, you must *control your calendar to achieve your goals and maintain your balance.* I've found that controlling my calendar is the key to living the life I want to live, and I'm sure you will too.

The two most important strategies for scheduling success are:

■ Keep only one calendar.

■ Carry it with you at all times.

When you follow these guidelines, you have *full control of your commitments.* Let's look at how this works.

When talking with someone with whom you *want* to share your time, you can open your calendar and set an appointment you are confident you can keep. You look more professional because you're showing that you take your time—and hers—seriously.

Your calendar can also protect you from *time thieves.* Because you "don't work," you're a prime candidate to be asked to volunteer for all kinds of events and activities. Without your calendar, you might be tempted to make a commitment that doesn't take you any closer to your goals. (I feel this is one of the big reasons why many women fail in direct selling.) But when you have your calendar, all you have to do is check it before committing or declining. It gives you the power to say No without guilt.

You can be a tremendous role model for your children in the way you run your business using time control, goal setting, a strong work ethic, and commitment. Once you've mastered the basics, show your children your methods and help them start taking control of their own lives.

SEIZING THE DAY—EVERY DAY

Here are some of the specific methods that have helped me control my calendar, and I'm sure they will get you off to a good start:

- **Buy a calendar you like.** It doesn't really matter what kind of calendar, although it's important to be able to look at a month at a time, as well as schedule days down to the hour. Make sure the calendar is small enough to carry with you at all times. Higher-end systems like DayTimer® or Franklin Covey® allow you to purchase a 12-month calendar that begins with any quarter, so you don't have to wait to get into a new calendar year.

- **Record your commitments.** When you have your new planner with pages covering at least the next 12 months, start by filling in all the fixed activities you are committed to: church, social events, clubs, children's school activities, spouse's work, family functions, and so on. Record every event whose timing you cannot control and that you want to include in your life. Soon you'll see a trend of which days are available to work your business.

- **Mark off time for your business.** Identify days and hours that don't conflict with family or personal activities. Decide how much time you want to devote to your business success and mark off that time as work time. Don't forget to mark off time for preparation, paperwork, phone calls, and so on. You're likely to find that squeezing everything in is a challenge! Remember that inserting a business into your life may require you to drop some other things from your life, at least temporarily.

- **Use highlighters to color the different *kinds* of your commitments.** For example, use green to highlight work hours, yellow for family, blue for social activities, and pink for personal time. Color-coding helps you see whether your life is in balance. At a glance you can see whether you're spending your time as you want or whether you need to make changes.

Remember, you won't always be in balance. In fact, it's okay to have months that are out of balance so long as there is a reward at the end that puts it all back in balance. Also, there will be deadlines, activities, and unexpected events that require your attention. Just remember that you control your calendar, and therefore you control your time and life.

Start Managing Your Commitments Today

- Purchase a planner or calendar that fits your needs and lifestyle.

- Record all activities on one calendar.

- Use highlighters to color-code business, personal, family, and social activities.

- Carry your planner with you everywhere you go—*always.*

- Use your calendar to plan your commitments *every day.* ∎

∎ Hang Up on Your Phone Phobias

By Christie Northrup
The Lemon Aid Lady ™

YOUR CASH REGISTER GOES RING-RING

Are you effectively using the cash register in your home office to keep your calendar and checkbook overflowing? No, not the machine that goes cha-ching . . . the one that goes ring-ring—your telephone! Or *do you suffer from Phone Phobia: fear of using the phone?*

PHONE PHOBIA RECOVERY

Here are the most common Phone Phobias along with their Phone Aid Prescriptions. When implemented, you'll quench your thirst for more customers, hostesses, and new consultants.

You have permission to phone. The number one Phone Phobia is manifested in this fear: "Prospects will think I'm pushy." Guess what? If a prospect gave you her phone number, she gave implied permission to call her! Follow through on your implied promise to keep connected. Develop your permission-based marketing further by asking her, "How often do you want me to keep you updated?" If she requests you to call when new items are released, you have her permission to phone, and she has your promise that you'll do so. Always keep your promises.

Catch her at the right time. Perhaps your Phone Phobia is the fear that you'll be catching the prospect at an inopportune time. This phobia is easy to eliminate. When she answers the phone and you've identified yourself, simply ask, "Am I getting you at a good time to chat for two minutes?" (Don't use the negative language spoken by many: "Is this a bad time?") Giving yourself a time limit of two minutes alerts her that you're respectful of her time. If the prospect agrees the time is right, you've connected with someone who is thankful that you've called and wants to listen to what you have to offer. Keep your promise to be brief and concise.

Keep your promised callback appointment. What if she's glad you called, but she doesn't want to take advantage of your offer right now? For example, when you make booking calls and a potential hostess has a very full schedule for the next three months and doesn't want to add to it, what do you say? Ask her, "When do you want me to call you again?" Never make that decision for her. One afternoon I was making booking calls. A woman said, "This is a bad time; can you call me later?" Until that time, I'd inform a prospect when I'd call her back by stating, "I'll call you in three months." For some reason, I did a *twist* and asked her. Guess what she said? "How about 6:00 tonight?" So I did. And she booked for the next week. Regardless of the requested recall time, always call her back when you've promised.

Assume action. When a prospect agrees she wants to buy or book but wants you to call back at a future date, call back with the assumption that she is ready to take action. "Marge, Christie calling from Northrup Party Plan. I promised I'd call you this month so you can book your party with me [or purchase the new items]." Your confidence in the purpose of your call reminds her of her request for your return call.

Hanging up on your own Phone Phobias. Like many illnesses, Phone Phobias often begin in the mind and manifest themselves physically. You could make yourself physically ill by worrying about being pushy, calling at the wrong time, or not keeping your promises to secure a booking or sale. Here are two points to remember:

1. You should fear—in fact, you should be quaking in your shoes—that instead of saying No to you, a prospect will say Yes to *someone else* who has overcome Phone Phobias and is connecting with your prospect. The fear that a prospect will do business with a competitor should be all the motivation you need to pick up the phone right now!

2. When you take the focus off yourself—forget that you have a booking goal, an incentive trip, or bills to pay—you take the pressure off your prospects, thus hanging up on your personal Phone Phobias and adding gallons of hosts, customers, and new consultants to your business!

Creating a Business Bank of Phone Appointments

So that you'll remember who wants a return call and when she requested it, create a simple Business Bank. Using a paper or electronic notebook, title 12 pages with each month of the year. When a prospect asks you to call back in September, go to that page. List her name, address, phone, and brief notes about your present call and why she wants a September contact. For example, "Going to Europe for the summer; wants to have a party when kids return to school." At the beginning of each month, you'll have bushels of people to call—at exactly the time your prospects want to hear from you! ■

■ Change to Meet the Market

By Joellen Sutterfield
Creatively connecting for higher profits

A NEW CHALLENGE

The September 11 attacks alerted the world and everyone in our industry that "the times they be a-changing!" Many of my top hostesses refocused on family events and personal health. "Busy" became the buzzword. Party plan companies retained their faithful clients, but many consultants across the industry started to experience difficulty in scheduling home product presentations. Working twice as hard for less felt like the norm. Some consultants threw in the towel and blamed slower booking ratios and everything else on 9/11. Some prayed it would all go away and that one day they'd find their calendars magically filled. Instead of taking either approach, I decided to *use this challenge as an opportunity to learn* and to keep my business and that of my team growing. This meant becoming extremely flexible and creative with bookings.

IDENTIFYING WHAT TO CHANGE

Home presentations are the foundation of the Party Plan profession, and the booking is our lifeline. No matter how much you excel in recruiting, your business can't grow unless someone is purchasing your product. Each direct-selling company has a booking formula that works when *you* work. However, adjusting any plan to suit the sales climate just makes sense. Amazingly, I found more doors opening when I began selling what my clients were buying!

What were they buying? Or better yet, because I always tackle a problem from the opposite side, what *weren't* they buying? After interviewing a few key clients, I found these to be the top answers across the board:

- ■ Time and convenience ("I'm too busy to make a commitment.")

- ■ Money ("Everyone I know is out of money or work.")

■ House or location ("I'm never home," or "My house is a mess.")

I used this information to create new bookings by working at solutions for each issue individually.

■ I addressed the money issue with *free* product offerings for the hostess or for a guest who provides referrals. Also, adopting a genuine no-pressure sales attitude is the key! If you are passionate about your product, you know they will love it once they see it!

■ In response to the time and location issues, I developed what I call the *Low-Carb Alternative* party—in other words, I just give them the meat.

Low-carb dining is all the latest rage, and every advertisement you see is now Atkins-friendly. Just as a low-carb meal needs to be *light, flavorful, instant,* and *satisfying,* so it is with my recipe for booking success:

Low-Carb Booking Recipe

Light: Minimize the presentation time and the number of guests required.

Flavorful: Power-pack miniproduct demonstrations tailored to their needs.

Instant: Make it easy to book with you with minimal planning or lead time—book in close.

Satisfying: Cut the time, but don't skimp on customer service.

One nice thing about Low-Carb parties is that they can be done virtually *anywhere!* Before and after presentations are awesome. These are done before the movies, after work, after exercising; in fact, meet them at the gym! One of my best shows was after a square dance contest! Because the Low-Carb party happens without much notice, invitations are informal (a call or e-mail) and the hostess need not be stressed out about refreshments.

Of course, the recipe only works if you make the booking calls and *offer!* Next time you're offering, try a new approach by presenting both menu options. It may sound like this:

> Sally, I would love to host a presentation with you because I know yours would be a success. I offer two options: we can do a full-blown presentation with all the bells and whistles, or I now offer a lighter low-carb alternative! Which sounds most appetizing to you?

She may laugh, but she will certainly ask you to tell her more.

Preparing for the Winds of Change

- Poll some of your valued customers to identify what factors may be diminishing your bookings and slowing your sales.

- If you need a shorter presentation, review your material and determine what features you can take out to cut your presentation to 20 or 30 minutes.

- Review your sales history and see what products sell most, and highlight them in your Low-Carb presentation. ■

■ Deepen Your Relationship with Your Hostess

By Jane Deuber, MBA
President and Cofounder of the DSWA

HOSTESSES FUEL YOUR BUSINESS

Hostesses are the lifeblood of a direct-selling business. They are our temporary business partners, connecting us with new customers, finding potential team members, and sharing their enthusiasm for our product—all in the comfort of their living rooms, dining rooms, and kitchens. Whether you conduct in-home shows three times a week or only occasionally, *deepening your relationship with your hostess can literally transform how you do business and at the same time improve the results you enjoy.*

Think about it . . . what greater honor can a person bestow on you than to invite you into her home, introduce you to her friends and family, and create a supportive environment in which you can showcase your business? Yet so often direct sellers view the hostess-coaching process more as a time-consuming task than as a privilege for which they are truly grateful.

MORE THAN A SOURCE OF BUSINESS

Hostess coaching today is more than a hostess packet, a stack of invitations, and an occasional phone call. In a world where the pace is nearly the speed of light, you must slow down enough to *honor each hostess* for the opportunity she has provided you. *You must shift your thinking from an attitude of expectation to one of appreciation.*

This isn't to say that you throw away your hostess-coaching checklists or disregard the guidance your company has provided you on the topic. On the contrary, it means you do all that *and more* so that your hostess becomes more than just a *temporary* business partner— and instead provides continual referrals, possibly joins your team, and, if you're truly lucky, develops into a dear friend. Practice the following elements of deepening your relationship with your hostess and these results will be yours.

An Attitude of Gratitude

Express your appreciation to your hostess in a genuine and heartfelt way. If her show is helping you reach an important goal, share that. If the income from her show is going toward a new washer and dryer or helping to fund your kid's college education, let her know. Giving the gift of gratitude to another person is like opening up your heart and letting her see the difference she is making in your life.

A Mound of Motivation

Find out why your hostess scheduled her show and then coach her from that perspective. If she is motivated by the prospect of earning free products, help her set a show goal that will result in the free products she wants. If she is motivated to help you build your business, explain how her having plenty of qualified guests who can become long-term customers or top-notch team members will help you achieve your goals. If she scheduled her show to help her friend (your original hostess) earn a bonus, you'll need to dig a little deeper. Although it may have motivated her to select a date, it is probably not enough to keep her motivated over time.

Step-by-Step Instructions

Your hostess can't hold a successful show if she doesn't know how to do it! A survey conducted with more than 100 hostesses revealed that *the biggest frustration for hostesses was a lack of communication from their representative prior to the show.* Be sure to provide *every* hostess with clear, step-by-step instructions, not just in writing, but also in person and by phone. The time you invest will come back in the form of great attendance, high sales, multiple bookings, and potential team members.

A "You Can Do This" Attitude

Like many of us, your hostess will likely become discouraged as she prepares for her show. Make sure that your frequent contact with her is uplifting and encouraging. Become a beacon of light in her life for the brief time that you are working together, so she experiences the fun of being a part of your business and your life.

Actions for Today

Get out your schedule and a piece of paper. Write down the names owf every hostess you have on your calendar for the next four weeks. Answer the following questions for each hostess and watch how your attitude easily shifts from expectation to appreciation:

- What did you like about her when you first met her?

- What do you know about her family?

- How can you make her feel special?

- What will you do to show your appreciation? ■

The Art of Selling

3

What is *selling?* For some, the word conjures up images of used-car salesmen or pushy, polyester-clad scam artists who try to sell us something we don't want. Others believe they "aren't good at it" and avoid it like the plague. This chapter gives you a different view of selling: a kinder, gentler view that you might find acceptable and dare we say . . . enjoyable.

Why is selling so important? Put simply—selling is the *heart* of your business! Without sales, no products are moved, no money is exchanged, no commissions are earned, and no overrides are paid out. Sales are the hub of the direct-selling wheel that keeps our industry churning—28 billion dollars strong and growing!

So we implore you: put those recruiting brochures aside long enough to revisit the ancient art of selling with a modern-day twist. You might discover not only that the sales process can be rewarding and fun but also that perfecting the skills shared here will help you hone your recruiting skills as well, for they are intimately interwoven.

■ Keep On Selling!

By Carla Spurgeon
Balancing sales and sponsoring

LEAD BY EXAMPLE

In 20 years of building a thriving business, I have come to understand that no matter how high up the success ladder you climb and no matter how large your organization becomes, *a leader must lead by example in the area of personal sales.* When products are being sold, team members are making money; and when your team members prosper, they are inspired to continue growing their businesses.

I gained an understanding of the importance of personal sales from my sponsor, who *walked her talk* by maintaining high personal sales throughout her career. She encouraged me to never fall into the trap of thinking, "Now that my team has grown and I'm making a great income, I no longer have to personally sell." This kind of thinking leads to a slow and steady decline and the ultimate failure of your business. If that's not enough, consider these benefits of maintaining high personal sales:

- You'll gain your team's trust and respect for leading by example.

- You'll have empathy for the challenges your team faces every day.

- Your training talks will be authentic, as you speak from experience and share real-life stories of triumph and challenge.

- You'll stay in tune with the needs of the customer and remain excited about the benefits your product offers.

ON-THE-JOB TRAINING

One of the greatest benefits of having plenty of sales appointments on your calendar is the ability to offer on-the-job training to your team. By bringing a team member to your appointments, you create a special bond that comes from her watching you make the best of every situation, sharing a laugh, and growing and learning along the way. She will also enhance her product knowledge and sales skills while watching you leverage your time by blending the activities of sales and recruiting.

WALKING YOUR TALK

Perhaps the best way to lead by example is to follow your own advice. Hold yourself to a new standard of not asking your team to do anything you personally are not doing. I share the following information with my team members to help them remain focused on what's important to their success. These are the actual six steps I do to keep my sales activity high:

1. **Maintain an ever-growing contact list.** I carry a list with the names of everyone that I need to contact by phone, mail, or e-mail about my company and products. I add names to this list every day.

2. **Communicate daily.** I reach out to at least five people daily—new contacts, follow-up calls, bookings, and reorders. You have to speak to the person to have an impact—answering machines don't count!

3. **Make time for personal development.** I set aside 15 minutes or more each day to focus on my personal growth. I do conference calls, leadership training, and product training as needed.

4. **Sell consistently.** I schedule demonstrations, parties, and personal appointments so that sales are coming from multiple sources all the time.

5. **Share your knowledge.** I invest time in training my team in the areas of selling and sponsoring because I know these are the keys to the *team's* success *and therefore my success.*

6. **Keep it repeatable.** With everything you do, ask yourself, "Would I be happy if my team duplicated what I am doing right now?" The example you set as a leader is one that your team members will copy—whether you want them to or not.

Actions for the Next 48 Hours

1. On a piece of paper, rate your level of satisfaction with your actions in each of the six areas, using a scale of 1 to 10. A 10 means you are setting an exceptional example in that area.

2. Select one area in which you would like to improve, and identify three things you will do this week to improve.

3. Share your three action steps with someone who will support you in following through. Arrange to report back on your progress at the end of the week. ∎

∎ Natural Selling—The Magic and Power of Dialogue!

By Michael Oliver
Selling from the Soul

THE DESIRE TO SERVE

The critical distinctions between Conventional Selling Techniques (that are designed to persuade people to do what you want them to do) and what I call Natural Selling® (which comes from a desire to serve and allow others to persuade themselves using The Magic and Power of Dialogue) make the difference between a negative or positive outcome every single time.

The outcome of any sales conversation is mostly dependent on your intent and the process you use to communicate.

If you have the intent or Personal Agenda of "What's in it for me?" and use the Process of Persuasion and Manipulation to get what you want, negative outcomes are more likely than positive ones.

If you have the intent or Purpose of "How can I help?" and use the Process of Discovery through Dialogue based on asking questions, listening, and responding to the *real* needs of others, *every outcome will be a positive one.*

You can achieve this positive outcome by viewing selling as simply a Problem-Solving Exercise and *detaching from your own needs.*

DIALOGUE—PROBLEM SOLVING FROM THE SOUL

Dialogue allows you to discover if someone has a problem and whether your solution might be the correct one. It's based on three principles:

- Asking the right types of questions

- Listening

- Constantly *clarifying by feeding back* what you think you heard

Asking nonmanipulative questions allows your listener to openly and comfortably reveal her present circumstances and, more important, how she *feels* about them. After all, who has the history of her life? Who knows what she wants, why she wants it, and how she *feels* about not having it? She does!

It's important to listen with the intent to understand, not to reply . . . to listen without judgment or interpretation. It's also imperative to listen for, and respond to, what she means (feelings), not just what she is saying (logic). *People make changes based on feelings, not on logic.*

Allow People to Persuade Themselves

When your listener replies to your question, she hears her own response and feels the effect this has on her life. If the frustration in her present circumstances is deep enough, *her own feelings will persuade her to change!* This is effortless for you because *she does* the work! You don't have to do anything except change your intent and trust the process. If you truly listen to her, when you later suggest your solution, she will listen to you.

The Essence of Dialogue: Detachment

There are two keys to making dialogue work effectively:

1. Accept that the Purpose of Selling is not about getting what *you* want; the Purpose is helping others get what *they* want. Doing this without manipulation will get you more than enough of what you want!

2. Detach from the Outcome (making a sale, talking about your product, and so on). Let your Personal Agenda *guide* your Sales Dialogue through Discovery instead of manipulating it to an outcome.

People will feel this detachment and be naturally attracted to you. If there is a sale to be made, you will make it every time. *Let go of the outcome and your income will naturally increase!*

An Exercise

Next time you talk with someone, ask questions without an agenda. Don't interrupt, pass judgment, make statements, or offer your point of view. Just listen and ask questions based on the answers you get to your previous questions. Discover for yourself how the Magic of Dialogue feels! ■

■ Questions Are the Answer

By David Cooper
America's income trainer

WHY ASK QUESTIONS?

When people won't buy or be persuaded by you, you can be sure the reason is one of these five: no trust, no need, no desire, no hurry, or no money. You can build trust, create need, amplify desire, and develop the intensity to buy now simply by smiling, nodding, asking enough questions, and listening. *You can create a positive buying mood using certain kinds of questions in a pattern.* When you understand, learn, and master the pattern and three types of questions I'm going to share with you, your success in direct sales as well as personal and business relationships will be amazing.

When you use only sentences in your presentation, your customer is retaining about 30 percent or less of what you are saying. I've found that by learning the art of asking questions, you can increase that to 70 percent and above! Whether you're selling skin care, jewelry, or clothing, be sure your presentation uses this formula: sentence, sentence, sentence, *question?* Sentence, sentence, sentence, *question?* Sentence, sentence, sentence, *question?* By using a question after every 10 or 15 sentences, you'll build that nodding rhythm, that "yes" atmosphere and buying mood.

THE THREE TYPES OF QUESTIONS

#1: Positive Questions

You'll get Yes answers when you're smiling, nodding, and asking one of the following positive questions in place of every 10 or 15 sentences in your presentation. Ask questions such as:

- ■ Could you get excited about . . . ?

- ■ Do you see the value in . . . ?

- Doesn't it make sense to . . . ?

- Don't you deserve . . . ?

- Doesn't it give you confidence to know . . . ?

The more you are smiling, nodding, and asking all the positive questions, the more effective you will be in any communications. You will then understand the art of building a buying mood.

#2: Tie-down Questions

Questions such as the following help to tie down the sale:

- Having your health is the most important thing in the world, isn't it?

- It makes good sense to take care of your skin and prevent signs of aging, doesn't it?

#3: The Choice Question

Regardless of the product, service, or idea you are selling, or whether you ask "Would you rather have this in black or white?" or "Do you think you would rather have the larger or smaller size?" *always* give them the simple choice question.

Save the choice questions for the end. It is a good idea to use a cushion statement before the choice question to intensify the buying mood. Examples are:

- "You know your situation much better than I do." (This low-pressure statement helps to build respect and rapport.)

- "We only want to do what is in your best interest."

Here is an example of a cushion statement with a choice question: "It really doesn't make that much difference to me, but would you prefer the gallon size or would the pint size be enough?"

Don't let the choice question be something that can be answered by a Yes or No. Your choice question should always contain an alternative that takes the purchase and your product for granted.

After you have used a cushion statement and added your choice question, this is a possible conclusion: "Whichever is better for you is certainly fine with me." When you say this phrase, the customer doesn't feel like she is being "sold." It builds confidence and helps you develop an important trust relationship.

Actions for Today

You want to be successful in your direct-selling career, so please remember this: Care enough to prepare.

Begin today to integrate these questions into your presentation, then practice and rehearse them. It will be fun—making all those trips to the bank fun, too. ■

■ Show the Price Is Right

By Karen Walter
Delivering value at every turn

WHY IT'S WORTHWHILE

Products offered by direct sellers are generally of much higher quality than products available through traditional retail channels, and the prices often reflect that difference. ***Learning how and when to address the issue of price is key to overcoming price resistance,*** particularly in a society where discounting, or at least the appearance of discounting, seems to be the lowest common denominator of virtually all commerce.

I've learned that it's best to speak directly to the issue of price *early* in my presentation, so my guests can stop worrying about it and concentrate on the education I'm there to provide. I assume the sale from the outset by telling them the product they will be taking home is more expensive than competitive products, but they will proudly pay the price when they learn why it's more expensive.

I also promise them the product *will* be affordable. I make a point of telling them how I will demonstrate the value—through durability, functional advantage, unique benefits, and so on—so they know where I'm going. By taking away their fear of the unknown up front, I help them relax and enjoy the balance of the presentation. This often results in their having a certain eagerness to help me establish the value.

CLIENTS, NOT CUSTOMERS

The secret to bringing people along as you demonstrate benefits and create value is *chemistry*. It would be difficult to overestimate the importance of rapport in the direct-selling process. The simple fact is that *people buy from people they like.*

I always recommend to members of my team that they get to their shows early enough to be fully set up before people begin arriving. This not only reflects professionalism, but it allows them time to chat with their guests as they arrive. This is the time to get to know your guests. The conversation may not have anything to do with what you'll be offering, but by learning a little about who the guests are and what's important in their lives, and sharing the same things about yourself, you'll be creating clients rather than just customers.

Of course, you should always present yourself as a professional, but I think it's also important to let your prospects see you as "one of them." The best way to do this is to find common threads in your respective lives. Take time to create connection. Let them see you not so much as a salesperson but as an educator. If you love what you do, believe in your product, and genuinely get excited about sharing it, people will find it easy to trust you, and you will have very little problem with price.

Feel, Felt, Found

There is a time-honored method for handling customer objections that works especially well for dealing with concerns about price. It's called "Feel, Felt, Found," and it goes like this: A prospect raises an objection or concern, and you reply with "I understand how you *feel.* When I first saw this product I *felt* that way, too. But what I *found* is . . ." I recommend that you incorporate this method into your presentation on a proactive basis. Anticipate your clients' feelings and beat them to the punch.

You can also use this method to handle objections from prospective members of your team. For example, someone might say, "I don't think I could sell such an expensive product." And your answer would be, "I completely understand how you feel. I felt the same way when I first looked at this opportunity. But then I found that there are lots of people out there buying this product, and I realized I might as well be the one selling it to them."

Creating Packages

One technique I use is to group packages of products together. The purpose of this is not to discount but rather to make it easy for my clients to get what they need. The emphasis is on convenience and building a solid foundation in our products rather than on reducing the price. Discounting sends the message that the product isn't really worth the price, so I always avoid price reductions. Instead, I focus on *value,* and my clients do, in fact, *proudly* purchase the products.

Today's Actions for Conveying Value

Review your product presentation. Does it address the issue of price early and put your clients at ease? Does it convey the product's value and show that it's affordable? Revise your presentation to include these factors. ■

■ Make It All about You

By Mike Russell
Creative Branding and Communications Synthesis for Direct Selling

PERSONAL BRANDING STARTS WITH YOUR *ATTITUDE*

The Direct Selling industry is laser dependent on relationships. That's why personal branding—your unique personal ability to stand out among your 14 million direct-selling colleagues—is hyperessential! There's no magic formula! Branding is your *total* reputation—*earned* by you, not bought or demanded—that makes everyone *want* to be in your presence and stay there.

> **B***e enthusiastic in every possible way. People love being with enthusiastic people!*

Your personal *brand* is the enthusiasm that makes you choose a company, product, or service that truly appeals to *others* instead of just leveraging their efforts to earn you an income. It's what inspires you to learn the products and compensation plan inside and out. It's the continuous application of personality and prowess that makes your retail and recruitment prospects say Yes. It motivates your team. It defuses your prospects' objections—even before they think of them. And it permeates your entire home-based business experience with better-designed e-mails, stationery, and Web sites; a consistently proud and capable voice in those business overview calls; and heightened credibility in those one-on-ones. In short, it shows the world that you avoided the path of least resistance and invited business in effortlessly. In the end, you'll enjoy a far better living.

In the corporate world, branding is about the *customer*, not about the company—and it's far more than just a logo. It's the feeling, memory, and emotion that "impulse" the customer to do business with you in the first place. So why should it be any different with *personal* branding? And what does that mean to you—the direct seller? By now, that's obvious: *Everything!*

Personal branding is more of an attitude than a checklist of action items. But it's an attitude that *leads* to action. Here are my top six personal branding criteria. Use them enthusiastically!

1. **Be enthusiastic in every possible way.** People *love* being around enthusiastic people! It influences everything from your general optimism to your business card design to your willingness to do just one more three-way call. *Real* enthusiasm is obvious—and it permeates your entire direct-selling experience. Over time, it will be the one aspect of your business life that makes you—and *keeps* you—more successful than anyone else.

2. **Be brief.** People "get" things quicker than you think. Get in, get out. Enthusiastically say what you came to say and stop there.

3. **Be expectant.** This is tried and true. When you enthusiastically expect the best, it happens. So *expect* it. Be *known* for expecting it!

4. **Be visible.** Success comes from showing up. So *be* there. *Be* visible. Show up . . . enthusiastically!

5. **Be fearless.** Okay, you don't have to actually *be* fearless, but if you take action in spite of your fears, you'll *wind up* fearless. And it's easier to be fearless if you're enthusiastic.

6. **Be consistent.** Finally, when it's all said and done, *keep* doing it. Then do it again! Then again. Enthusiastic consistency is the mark of a true pro. A *personally branded* one!

Today's Actions for Building Your Personal Brand

Review how you express your enthusiasm—on the phone, in your presentations, while networking, in your personal life. Imagine how you might express more enthusiasm; then *do it!* ■

■ Keep Parties Fun for Higher Sales and More Bookings

By Karen Phelps
Keeping the fun and profits in your business

FOR HEFTY EARNINGS, KEEP IT LIGHT

Whoever first described our business as a party plan knew what she was talking about! Home parties should be *fun!* In fact, **you'll sell more and book more when you keep your parties fun.**

All of us have probably attended parties where we have been bored to tears. The well-intentioned consultant went on and on and *on* about the company, product, and opportunity; forgot that she was leading a *party;* and failed to involve the guests in fun activities. Are you leaving your "fun side" at home? Do you believe you have to be serious to be professional? Nothing could be further from the truth!

BRING ON THE FUN!

Even if your product needs some explanation, your guests aren't willing to sit and listen while you teach them for a couple of hours. We are *all* busy! Your guests need to be rewarded in terms of fun, relaxation, and socialization. If you don't *pay* them, you'll *lose* them.

Guests want to learn as well as relax and enjoy the party. This means involving them in your presentation. Make sure they know that they, too, can offer suggestions on how to use a product. We may not know everything about the product, but we *do* know how to have fun. Here are specific ways to build up your entertainment value:

Teach guests about your products by telling stories. You will quickly lose your guests by describing your products in long, boring detail. Use picture stories to describe a product instead of just the facts. Share stories of how to use your products, or demonstrate how your products make a difference; and they will remember you and your products much better.

Play quick and easy no-brainer games where everyone wins.
Begin with a fun introductory game or icebreaker so your guests can
learn about each other. This will start your party off on the right note
by putting your guests at ease with you and each other.

Play a booking or sponsoring game. Use a game to introduce
the business opportunity rather than rattling on and on about bookings or the opportunity. By introducing the ideas of bookings and
sponsoring in game format, you can learn about the guests, book
more parties, and present the opportunity in a nonthreatening way.

Learn people skills. Greet each guest at your party with a smile
and a handshake. Adopt the motto "Guests that arrive as strangers
will leave as friends." When you involve the guests and joke with
them during the party, you swing them over to your side. I often
tease guests about having a party, and as I explain everything they
can earn by being a hostess, I close with "... *plus you'll get me for another couple of hours. Isn't that exciting?*" I actually have had guests book
a party because I was so much fun!

Today's Actions for Increasing Amusement

- Think about your last party, put yourself in your guests'
  place, and ask yourself if you would have had any fun. If the
  answer is No or Not much, then you need to *plan more fun
  into your parties.*

- You may need to move outside your comfort zone to
  implement new ideas. Consider joining Toastmasters or
  some other organization that encourages you and builds
  your confidence when you're speaking in front of a group.
  When you are relaxed, you *and* your guests will have more
  fun.

- Remember to bring the kid in you to every party. Make a list
  of little games you enjoyed as a child and be willing to use
  them in a pinch.

■ Invite a special guest (friend or spouse) to attend a party to see your product presentation and then let you know if you've been a stuffed shirt.

Remember, if you and your guests haven't had fun in the past, it's time to lighten up and party down! Your bank account will thank you! ■

■ Overcome Prospecting Fears

By Pat Pearson, MSSW
Unlocking the secrets to success

NO BRAG, JUST FACT

In 30 years of working with direct-selling professionals, I've learned that one of their greatest fears is that people will think they are selling themselves. Fear of self-promotion is a major block to success in the field of direct selling. Overcome your fear of self-promotion by *sharing examples from your business to help others* see the opportunity rather than by self-aggrandizing. Overcoming your fear prepares you for a recruiting explosion. After all, how can you help someone else see the opportunity if you don't share your own success?

Self-promotion is seen as a form of ego-tripping—of focusing attention and admiration on oneself. If that were the objective, it truly is not a very attractive attribute. But presenting your successes in a way that involves sharing, giving, and creating opportunity is not self-promotion at all. It is the gift you give to those who want a better life.

REVEALING YOUR BUSINESS

Think back to your own recruitment. Did the person who recruited you seem egocentric, or did you listen to her because she seemed eager to share an exciting opportunity that could change your life? I predict your answer is the latter. Someone approached you with a gift—the opportunity to create something wonderful in your life. Others will respond to you the same way as you responded to the person who gave you the opportunity to start your business.

When you approach your business from the perspective of sharing a wonderful, exciting gift that can change lives for the better, the fear of self-promotion just disappears. No more will your head be filled with such thoughts as "They won't like me" or "I don't want people to think I'm *selling* something!" Instead of focusing on yourself and how you feel, you are totally focused on the person in front of you, on her hopes and dreams, and on how you can share with her a way to achieve them. Sharing a gift of a better life is the most wonderful thing you can do!

What happens when you decide to share instead of "sell"? People open up to you. They share their own dreams, their hopes for helping their families and their children. They are accessible and interested, and want to know more. The words flow between you, and you have the opportunity to paint a picture of their future that is colorful and bright. When the focus is off you and on them, it is impossible to be self-centered.

Starting Your Story

How do you get from fear to fearlessness and become someone who shares your story? When faced with the fear of sharing your opportunity with others, try these three simple steps to move from fear to excitement:

1. Think of the person who recruited you and how happy you were to find something capable of bringing personal growth and abundance into your life. Write down some of the words she used that caught your attention. Ask yourself how those words allowed you to open up to her story, and record what you remember.

2. Make a list of all the positive changes that have occurred in your life as a result of starting your direct-selling business.

Reflect on what a gift it is and how grateful you are that your sponsor shared her business with you.

3. Now think of a person *you* want to welcome into your business and write her name at the top of a piece of paper. List all the ways you believe the business will positively impact *her* life as you envision her as happy and successfully building her business.

With this image in your mind, pick up the phone and make the call. Much of our role as a sponsor is to see the wonderful things in another that she might not yet be able to see in herself. ■

■ Heart to Heart

By Carol Garvey
Appreciating the privilege of leadership

WHAT REALLY MATTERS

You can win all the awards, achieve all the titles, and have all the financial success, but what do you really have when all's said and done? I believe ***what's* truly *important is the quality of the life you create, and that is profoundly affected by the depth of your relationships.*** Fortunately, we are in a relationship business.

When I first got into direct selling, I saw the value of the product and soon recognized the income opportunity. But it took me a while to see the bigger picture. What many people find surprising is that it's not about money. Don't get me wrong; I'm not saying money isn't important. But it's not the real reason people succeed in this business. There's always a more important and profound Why than just money. Make it your passion to help people find their Why and the money absolutely will follow.

For some, it's about freedom. This business allows people to call their own shots, to determine their own future. But for many, it's even more fundamental. I've found that most people really just want to be somebody. They go through their whole lives not believing in themselves and not having anyone else believe in them enough to encourage them to take a chance on themselves. What we do in our industry is create an environment where it's emotionally safe to take risks, where even if you fail to meet a particular goal, you know people will still care about you and still be there to support you, because they've failed too, and it didn't stop them.

I try not to categorize people or make assumptions about anyone. I don't really care where someone is in her life at this particular moment. What I care about is the person she's willing to become.

The nature of our business is to be transparent. In other industries, people don't talk about how much money they make. But in direct selling, you're always quick to tell people where you came from, where you are, and where you're going. That kind of honesty lets people know it's okay to open up and really connect with you.

THE CONNECTION *IS* THE REWARD

This business is about connecting. It's about building relationships, one-on-one. When you ask someone to consider your business opportunity, aren't you really inviting her into your life? To provide the support she'll need to become successful, you must be willing to go through the fire *with* her, and that means sharing her ups and downs, celebrating her victories, and understanding the emotions she will have gone through to get there.

I've come to realize that the greatest opportunity this industry provides is one that can't be found in any compensation plan or awards program. By working closely with each person on my team and getting to know each one personally, I've had the privilege of building a "family" made up of hundreds of people who are taking a journey together. We tell people our goal is to walk the beaches of the world with them, and we've done just that.

My wish is that you witness the magic of this metamorphosis: To see someone who has been beaten down, and stuck in a mental cubicle her whole life, not *knowing* what she's capable of, and then to watch her overcome whatever gets in her way and free the champion that's always been inside. Once you've seen that happen, you'll know deep inside like me—that's what our businesses are all about!

Start Connecting Today

If you want to increase the quality of relationships in your business, follow these three steps:

1. Look very carefully at your own Why. Is money or prestige really your primary motivation, or are you actually seeking the feelings of acceptance and admiration you associate with being successful? Become clear about what's truly important in your life, and recognize that you will have whatever you choose to create.

2. Make building quality relationships your *first* priority. Treat everyone in your organization (and in your life) in a way that supports that priority.

3. Help others find their true Why and support them in learning to make relationships their first priority too. Help them connect to a goal that's bigger than they are, and watch them grow into the people they were always capable of being but never believed they could be.

By following these guidelines, you will not only build an extended family of your own; you will also unleash powerful success forces in your business. ■

■ Automate Your Reorder Business

By Jeff Shafe
Demystifying business software for improved profits

YOUR EASIEST PROFITS

One aspect of direct selling that attracts many people to the profession is the promise of residual income—money that comes to you with little or no effort on your part. Visions of earning an income in the comfort of your own home, having more time and freedom, and being your own boss are the fuel that keeps the fire burning.

Although there may be some exceptions, nearly every successful business is built on repeat business, because *the process of selling to an established customer is less costly than selling to a new customer.* In the direct-selling business, this means that the more comfortable your customers are—with your product, with you, and with your personalized service—the more money you make with less effort.

If you offer a consumable product, your reorder business can be a substantial component of your residual income. But it won't just happen by itself. *You must take the time to establish the system and habits that make the reorder process as automatic as possible.* A strong reorder business requires that you make customer follow-up a nonnegotiable business habit. Even though your particular system can be anything from a tickler file to software custom designed for direct sellers, the key to success is that you use the system consistently.

Realistically, how do you add customer follow-up to everything else you're already doing to build your business? The answer is . . . you automate it! Automating customer follow-up doesn't mean depersonalizing it. It means consistently staying in touch with people based on what you already know about them, something I like to call "intelligent communication."

CONNECTING MORE FREQUENTLY, MORE RELIABLY

Let's say that you found several new customers at an event last weekend. A nice follow-up would be to send each of them a personalized e-mail thanking them for their purchase and offering your assistance. Of course, if the e-mail starts out "Dear Customer," it's not going to be very personal. Your e-mail broadcasting system should include the ability to merge contact information into each e-mail as it's being sent—such as, "Dear Sue," "Dear Lynn," or "Dear Craig." That way you can create e-mail templates that become personalized each time you use them.

Now, that takes care of the thank-you message, but what you really want to do is continue following up regularly until a customer either places another order or asks to be removed from your mailing list. To do that automatically, you need a software feature called Schedules.

A schedule of activities can contain mail-merge e-mails like your thank-you note, appointments that show up on your calendar, and tasks that show up on your to-do list. Rather than just sending a single thank-you e-mail, you might instead create a Customer Follow-up schedule containing the following:

- A thank-you e-mail sent the next day

- A just-checking-in e-mail sent one week later

- A follow-up call reminder on your to-do list for two weeks later

- A reorder e-mail or call reminder one month later, and each month thereafter

The actual content and timing of these activities should be based on your products and your personal style. The important thing is to create a schedule that provides you with a consistent and easily implemented way of following up with each and every customer.

Here's what to look for in the business management software you need to make this happen:

- Mail-merge e-mail broadcasting for selected groups of contacts. You can use this to stay in touch with your team too!

- Mail-merge letter writing and labels for people who don't have an e-mail address

- Integrated contact and financial management so you can easily find and communicate with people based on their previous purchases

- The ability to create follow-up schedules to automate the follow-up process

Anticipating questions, sharing tips, and checking to see how a customer's purchase has worked out are all good follow-up topics. You'll be surprised how many people will thank you for your personal touch and then call you up to reorder their favorite products.

Today's Actions for Automating Follow-up

Research the kind of follow-up or tickler system that would work best for you. Find up-to-date information in the DSWA store at http://www.mydswa.org. ■

■ Build Repeat Business

By Grace Putt
Still going strong after 45 years in business

THE KEY TO LONGEVITY

If you want to build a business that lasts, reorders are the name of the game. And if you want to know the secret to getting reorders, here it is: *Treat every customer exactly as you would want to be treated if you were the customer.* Following this simple rule has allowed me to make a wonderful living and have a wonderful life for over 45 years.

The beauty of this rule is how easy it is to apply. No matter what the situation, you can always ask yourself, What would make me feel special if I were the customer here? Then do precisely that. These are questions that can guide you:

- Are you choosing a product to represent? What product would you choose if you were the customer?

- Are you trying to decide how much inventory to carry? What kind of availability would you like if you were the customer?

- How willing are you to answer questions about how to use your product? How much information would you want?

- When and how will you ship your orders? How soon would you want to receive something you ordered?

- How will you handle a referral? How would you want your best friends to be treated by someone you referred?

SMALL GIFTS CREATE BIG OPPORTUNITIES

Whenever I ship an order, I always include a little sample of some product I know my customer is not using yet. I also put in a short, handwritten note that explains how to use it and lets her know I'll call her in a week to see how she likes it. My clients know they can expect that little something extra from me, and it's a great way to introduce new products.

I also make a practice of sending a gift product to anyone who refers me to one of her friends. It's a way I can say "Thank you," and of course it's also a good way to introduce new products. It certainly works—after 45 years of serving my customers, 99 percent of my new business now comes from referral customers, and I am consistently one of the top producers in the company.

Over the years, I've had the privilege of meeting and associating with quite a number of lovely people. I've always made a point of treating them with care and letting them know I think my clients are the most special people on earth. As a result, I've been able to travel the world and experience things I would have never dreamed possible.

Today's Action for Building Repeat Business

If you want to make your dreams come true, I would advise you to make excellent service and extra thoughtfulness synonymous with your name. If you take extra good care of your customers, you'll find they'll take good care of you! ∎

4

Sponsoring and Building Your Team

The key to survival in direct selling may be making sales, but the key to generating a huge income is building your organization through *sponsoring*. You see, no matter how good you become, you can only be in one place at a time, doing one thing at a time. But what if you *could* clone yourself? What if you could be in two or more places at once, generating more sales, seeing more people, and providing more service? When you sponsor others, you do just that.

Today you'll find a new way of building a team that is a far cry from the outdated, manipulative, bait-and-switch tactics of years gone by. The new millennium requires that we adopt a new view of sponsoring that puts *people* before profits and the emphasis on *service*. Some have adjusted their efforts and business practices to the point that they now enjoy what so many are aspiring to achieve. They have done it in spades and have the toys, the lifestyle, and, more important, the *perspective* on what it truly takes to sponsor successfully for a thriving direct-selling business. In this chapter they share their wisdom to guide you on your quest for success.

79

■ Build Credibility for the Profession

By Delbra and Tim Lewis
Leading by example

LEARN TO OVERCOME SKEPTICISM

You are committed to building your business, and you love your company, your product, and sharing your great business opportunity with others. At some point in your career you will come across people who look at direct selling with skepticism and may do so because of a lack of education about the industry. Some have heard negative feedback from someone who started a home-based business and wasn't successful. This individual may blame the company, the business model, or her upline. She may use terms like *scam, pyramid,* or *rip-off.* While building an organization of over 2,000 in just one year, we have experienced firsthand similar criticisms and have learned how to build credibility for the industry.

We feel skepticism creates a real opportunity to educate others about what an illegal pyramid is and why a legitimate direct-selling company is not a scam but an amazing method of marketing that financially rewards the individuals who distribute the products for the company.

ATTACKING THE ROOTS OF SKEPTICISM

When discussing the issue, keep in mind that your listener's skepticism may be a result of fear—fear of success or fear of failure. She may have attempted to work with a direct-selling company previously and either the company failed or she did. Ask her questions about why it didn't work. What kinds of things could she do differently this time? Was it the business model or something else that she found challenging? Has she heard of anyone who has been successful in direct selling? Is she aware that there are over 44 million people in the profession worldwide? Ask questions and listen, so she can discover the possibilities and look at direct selling in a new light.

No matter what the question, be sure to listen intently and show no sign of defensiveness. Find words that build a bridge between her comments and yours. For example:

> *Prospect:* I have heard that many people spend a lot of money on inventory and never make any money.
>
> *Distributor:* I understand what you are saying and have heard some very similar stories. It is just smart business to purchase only as much inventory as you feel you can sell. Our company has an outstanding training program in place to educate us about marketing strategies and skill development so that products are sold and solid commissions are earned. May I share with you a little about how we market our products to earn great commissions?

CREDIBILITY BUILDERS

- We have been in business over *x* years.

- We are a publicly traded company.

- Our products are well known for . . .

- We have over *x* distributors in the company.

- Our team is made up of professionals, stay-at-home moms, full-time and part-time women and men who believe in the company as I do.

- Our company has expanded into *x* number of countries over the past few years.

- The company requires little or no inventory.

- The company has an outstanding training program.

Practice Makes Permanent

Do role-playing activities with a member of your family or team so you can practice how to overcome skepticism of the profession. Ask your partner how she felt throughout the exercise. Did she feel you became defensive, or did you indicate an educational viewpoint with a desire to share your passion for the profession? If she felt you were defensive, ask what made her feel that way. Was it your voice, the words, or your body language? Obtain clarity on how you can get your point across while engaging the prospect with a desire to understand. ■

■ Become a Recruiting Powerhouse

By Joan Nilsen-Robison
Master team builder

IT'S ALL ABOUT THEM

Recruiting is the cornerstone on which you build your direct-selling organization. In my experience, the key is to *identify the needs of each prospect.* By learning to listen and really *hear* what our prospects said they needed, we grew our team by more than 1,000 members in just three years.

The truth is that you're surrounded by qualified prospects every day. The trick is to listen to each one, hear what she really wants, and then offer your opportunity when it can meet her needs. Keep the focus on her needs rather than your own, and come from a place of caring and compassion. This creates a foundation for a strong ongoing relationship.

KEEP IT SIMPLE

There's a hard way to recruit and an easy way. You could go out and talk to six or eight people a day but chances are that would take your whole day and then some. Or you could do two or three two-hour classes (shows) per week, each with 10 to 15 friends of the hostess, at which you would make retail sales, set bookings for more classes, and have the opportunity to recruit. In both cases, you would talk to about the same number of people. One way is just a whole lot easier than the other.

Make no mistake, recruiting is very definitely a numbers game but not in the way most people think. It's not about blowing through large numbers of people to find out who will stick. Instead, it's about giving *everyone* the opportunity, then working with the ones who choose to work with you. I realized very early that most people won't come to you and ask you to sponsor them. You must ask every person in every class, making no assumptions and no prejudgments.

How to Ask

Use specific words when you ask prospects to consider your opportunity. For instance, ask prospects if they would like to take some information about your opportunity home with them. That way, you avoid triggering their defenses. Then ask each one individually if it would be okay for you to contact her in a day or two, to answer any questions she might have. Schedule it close, so she will still have some excitement left from the class.

It's best to do the follow-up in person because this process is all about connection. But it's fine if she chooses to do it by phone. When discussing the appointment, let her make all the choices—when, where, and so on—again to eliminate any defensiveness. When you do connect, ask a question such as "What excited you most about this opportunity?" or "Tell me what makes you feel like you'd like to work with this program."

Always assume she's in, and ask questions to uncover her needs and motivations. It's critical to listen carefully and ask clarifying questions. In fact, I train all my team members to remember that

"Questions are the answer!" and "When in doubt, ask a question to figure it out."

Also make a point of telling her that you don't make a cent from signing her up. The only way you make anything from the relationship is if you help her succeed. That way, she understands your commitment to train and support her. This is often a deciding factor.

The Art of Listening

If you listen carefully, most people will tell you what they really want. For instance, the wife of a successful dentist might not be motivated by the income opportunity, but she might be looking for a good reason to get out of the house and connect with other women in a fun setting.

The most gratifying thing is watching someone you've helped become successful and seeing the person she becomes as she gets there. I remember one woman who couldn't even look me in the eye when she first signed up. Her self-image was so low that she just kept staring at the floor. Today when I see her walking proudly across the stage to collect her awards, I love the sparkle in her eyes that sums up what this business is all about!

Plug into Your Recruiting Generator Today

Review your recruiting methods. Where, when, and how do you currently share your business opportunity? Using the new ideas you've just read, identify three ways to improve the way you ask and the way you listen. Implement your new methods and watch your team grow! ■

■ Recruit and Build with Style

By Stephanie Frank
The Accidental Millionaire

THE CONCEPT OF STYLE

Have you ever left a recruiting discussion with a potential new team member filled with frustration and thought to yourself: "She would be so good; I answered all of her questions and she still said No; why?" Maybe you're developing new leaders in your team and they seem, well, so *different* from you. How can you be an effective recruiter, developing teams faster and stronger than ever? *Learn about personal styles, and begin aligning yourself with the styles of other people.*

Your personal style is the way you approach people, tasks, and surroundings. It forms the foundation for all your interpersonal, parenting, decision-making, learning, management, recruiting, and leadership styles. One particular style is no more *right* than is another, and all styles can be used to succeed. Understanding and matching another person's style will skyrocket your recruiting, retention, group sales, and overall growth.

Maybe you can relate. How do you react to a challenge? Do you become more outgoing, energetic, detailed, focused, or frustrated? Do you become less patient, diplomatic, creative, reliable, or trusting? It's probably a combination of all of these things. How does the other person respond? Does she double her efforts or give up?

Intrinsic personal style differences create conflicts between you and team members, which slows your business. There is a simple catalyst to explosive growth: Recognize the personal style of each team member and give each one the information and kind of treatment that make her feel most comfortable.

UNDERSTANDING PERSONAL STYLES

There are four main styles of behavior, although infinite combinations make individuals unique. Through my work as a business development coach, I found that every person has the capacity for exhibiting all four styles in varying degrees. Learning to communicate by using the strongest styles helps each of your team members achieve superior results in a minimum of time.

To use this technique, you must understand the basic styles and their characteristics:

Behavioral—Task Oriented

- Wants results now

- Seeks authority

- Tactical, strategic approach

- Acts rapidly

- Driven to achieve goals

Self-assured, driven, and extroverted. Meets challenges with fearlessness. Prefers planned methods to achieve goals and results. Sometimes seems oblivious to others' feelings. Makes decisions quickly based on summarized facts.

Affective—People Oriented

- Loves people

- Seeks to influence

- Intuitive and creative

- Idea filled

- Large contact network

Intuitive, creative, and influential—often through speaking or writing. Believes in the value of people and likes to sell others on themselves, ideas, or products that they believe will be helpful. Relates to people better than to tasks and makes decisions based on intuition and emotion.

Cognitive—Task Oriented

- Quality oriented

- Acts cautiously to avoid errors

- Engages in critical analysis

- Seeks to create a low-stress environment

- Follows directives and standards

Quality conscious, introverted, avoids being influenced negatively. Cautious and pays attention to details, while being alert for inconsistencies to maintain security and control. Makes decisions based on detailed facts.

Interpersonal—People Oriented

- Reliable worker

- Seeks to help others

- Promotes balance

- Sees things that others miss

- Easygoing and warm

Highly adaptive, seeks to promote harmony and comfort for herself and others. Practical, friendly, and naturally warm. Introverted. Balances both logical and intuitive modes of operating. Makes decisions based both on intuition and logic.

Homing In on Style

Start today to get a better understanding of how people's style affects your recruiting.

- Determine which style you are most comfortable with, and understand that you may have to make yourself uncomfortable to most effectively communicate with others in *their* style.

- Listen carefully for clues to a person's style before you start presenting your business opportunity. A few carefully chosen words from the lists above will strengthen your communication position with your new recruit or team members and catapult your success rate.

- Ask questions to promote understanding of the other person's style. Here's an example. After presenting the business opportunity, you ask, "Do you have any questions?" You may get several answers like these:

    - "I just need the facts." *Behavioral*
    - "This looks like fun, how many people are on the team?" *Affective*
    - "Do you have any more material I can take to review?" *Cognitive*
    - "Do you think I'd be any good at this business?" *Interpersonal*

Giving people information while matching *their* style can double your income and help you develop deep, meaningful relationships. Practice this daily and reap the rewards. ■

■ Teach Them to Fish

By Janet Wakeland
Tenaciously training others to be their best

TRAINING FOR GROWTH

"Give a man a fish and he'll eat for a day, but teach him to fish and he'll eat for a lifetime." Never was this principle more aptly applied than in direct selling. If you want to build a strong organization, ***train your team members to be powerful recruiters.*** The best way to do this, of course, is by example. *Show,* then tell. Become passionate about recruiting, and you'll soon find it's contagious.

Approach the question of recruiting from a business mind-set. Learn every single benefit you and your company could possibly offer someone who may be a candidate. I encourage members of my team to write down at least 30 benefits on a piece of paper to carry with them at all times. Then, when the opportunity to discuss their business arises, they're prepared to help the prospect find what would motivate her.

Help each team member recognize that what the business opportunity offers could be an extraordinary *gift* in the life of the next person she meets. Invite her to think, "Who can I help today?" Encourage her to listen to the conversations around her and watch for flags. Is the woman standing in line at the post office frustrated with her job? Does the clerk at the grocery story wish she could spend more time with her kids? Is someone in her church struggling to make ends meet? Help her focus on the difference direct selling can make in the lives of those around her.

Whenever anyone in your organization recruits someone, you have a responsibility to train that person to the best of your ability. One of the first things to help her understand is that *it won't be easy.* *Easy* is a word she should remove from her vocabulary. Few people expect their regular jobs to be easy, so why should they expect direct selling to be easy? Yes, it offers more freedom, more satisfaction, and more financial potential than most jobs, but it is *not* easier. Help your team members develop realistic expectations so they won't experience disappointment and disillusionment.

Although it's important to provide your trainees with the basic skills of booking, selling, and recruiting, it's even more important to help them set standards of excellence for themselves. Encourage them to see the possibilities all around them, to come from a belief in abundance. Get them past the idea of trying it for a few months. Again, how many of them would *try* a new job for a few months?

TRAINING FOR ALL LEVELS

Give everyone at all levels of your team the same opportunity for quality training and let them choose to what extent they are willing to avail themselves of that opportunity. Divide your team into three groups:

1. Those you have personally sponsored

2. Those at all levels who have stepped forward as leaders

3. The entire team as a unit

Communicate with each group in an appropriate manner. For example, you will have a different agreement with your personal sponsors about your availability and their accountability than you will with the group as a whole. You will also have self-feeding information mechanisms for your leaders, so they can move at their own pace. But you'll also want to make sure the leaders get the message that you'll support them in developing the skills they need for whatever level they've achieved. If someone is just stepping into leadership with three or four people in her group, she needs to know she isn't expected to have the same skills as someone with a 100-person group.

Finally, it all comes back full circle to this: Be a role model. Set an example. Book, sell, recruit, and train exactly the way you want the people on your team to do. Walking your talk is the most effective training and inspiration you can offer them.

Today's Actions for Training "Fishers"

- Develop a list of every single benefit you and your company could possibly offer someone who joins your team.

- Challenge members of your team to write down at least 30 benefits on a piece of paper to carry with them at all times.

- Encourage team members to share their lists with each other and with you. Find out how many benefits you can identify when you put your heads together. ■

■ Build Your Business by the Numbers

By Sarah Janell White
Passionately pursuing her dream

CONSTRUCTING METHODICALLY

Do you hold a vision of yourself walking across the stage at Convention, lights shining, your team cheering, and your being honored for your outstanding accomplishments? Whether you are building your business full-time or investing just a few hours a week, if your dream is to advance to a higher level of leadership within your company, you simply must learn to *build your business strategically rather than by accident.*

As the youngest person to ever achieve the top leadership level with my company, I've been fortunate to sponsor hundreds of people throughout my career. Because of this, I am often asked how I am able to consistently sponsor so many people onto my team. What's my answer? *"Keep your focus on the numbers and the results will take care of themselves!"*

Now, many direct sellers will share that they would rather do just about anything than crunch the numbers, because by nature we love people, *not* numbers. But if I were to tell you that building your business by the numbers will result in higher sales, more bookings, and consistently welcoming new recruits to your team each month, would you consider the possibility then?

WORKING THE NUMBERS

What does building your business by the numbers really mean? It means making sure that every day, week, and month you make a connection, share your hostess program, or talk about the business opportunity with enough people so that you are assured recruiting and booking success. How many is enough? If we look at the industry average, we discover that for every ten people we talk to about our business opportunity, we can expect to sponsor about one new person onto our team. (The same ten-to-one ratio holds true for bookings as well.)

But wait! We are busy women. We have very full lives and other obligations. Right? How in the world can you get in front of that many people each week? The answer lies within the very thing that puts money in your pocket and shows on your calendar . . . your in-home parties! The in-home party gives you a room full of happy, prequalified customers who are interested in your products and accepting of the way you do business. The people you meet at your shows often like to meet new people and love something new. Does this sound like the kind of person you would like on your team? You bet!

Looking at the statistics, it would stand to reason that if

- you consistently worked with your hostess to have at least ten people present at each show,

- you include compelling sponsoring seeds throughout your presentation, and

- you offer each guest the opportunity to learn more about having a business of her own, *then* you would potentially *find one new recruit from every show.*

Just imagine the possibilities of presenting your opportunity to 520 people simply by holding one show per week for an entire year. With a one out of ten closing ratio, that would result in approximately 52 new, quality people added to your team! How would your bonus check look then?

Let's Review Your Strategy

- Consistently hold one show a week for a total of 52 parties a year. Remember, you'll need to book more than four shows per month to allow for postponements and cancellations.

- Work closely with your hostess to have ten guests present at each show. If your guest average is fewer, you'll need to hold more shows to reach your ten qualified contacts per week.

- Include compelling recruiting seeds throughout your product presentation. Don't forget your hostess. She is by far your best prospect at the show!

- Offer the business opportunity to every guest at the show.

What's wonderful about *building your business by the numbers* is that it is simple, repeatable, and keeps you focused on your efforts rather than on the results. As you become more skilled at sharing the opportunity, your closing ratio will improve and your team will grow even faster.

Today's Actions for Getting Started

- Focus on filling your next four weeks with one or two shows each week.

- Review your hostess-coaching strategy and create a checklist for every show on your calendar so that you never miss a single step.

■ Write out how you will incorporate recruiting seeds into your product demonstration to pique guests' interest and set the stage for you to offer the opportunity one-on-one. ■

■ Lose the Hype!

By Jeri Taylor
Top income earner telling it like it is

WHAT TRUTHFULNESS ATTRACTS

Recently, I was asked how I have been able to build such a large business and personally recruit so many people into my organization. The answer that came was so natural, so true for me that it took no thought or contemplation. "Tell it like it is," I said. "People who are looking at your business opportunity want to be told the truth, not sold on a dream! *When you tell the truth, you set your recruits up for success.* When you exaggerate or talk only of the successes of the top 1 percent of your company, you set them up for disappointment."

I believe that sincerity and honesty are key characteristics in building relationships and essential to becoming a master recruiter. In fact, prospects will not only join your team when you tell the truth, but you'll find they become loyal team members who are willing to do what it takes when the going gets rough. It's the prospects who are sold on a dream who come in, become disillusioned, and leave.

The truth is that direct selling works! It is a proven business model no longer on trial. Why then are so many people compelled to exaggerate a viable, proven opportunity with so much hype? Excessive or false claims only build false expectations and damage the reputation of your business and the profession as a whole. I think that most hype is the result of insecurity about the company or the industry.

REPLACING HYPE WITH INTEGRITY

So how can you eliminate hype from your business opportunity presentation? First and foremost, you must know your compensation plan and which behaviors the company pays you for. Explain that people will only be successful if they are willing to do the work that the company is rewarding. This is no different from a job except that a job pays you to attend, and direct selling pays you to perform. Here are a few things I tell my new team members:

- I always tell a new distributor to be consistent in the hours and effort that she puts into her business. If she works a full-time job, her time is limited. If she is only able to put five or six hours a week into building her new business, tell her that she has to do it consistently. No excuses allowed! Just do it!

- Be honest about what it will take to be successful. Give her a realistic time line based on her lifestyle and hours available to work so that she can set achievable goals.

- When you are sharing your business with a potential recruit, listen to what her life is about! Ask:
  - "Where are you in this journey called life?"
  - "What are your interests and beliefs?"
  - "What do you want for your future?"
  After discovering these things, tell her about someone in the business who is like her and is succeeding—someone she can relate to and who will motivate her to say, "If that woman can do this, then so can I!" Sharing real stories of *real* people who have succeeded gives credibility to you and your company. If you are new in the business and don't know any stories yet, ask your upline for their stories and read your company newsletters and other literature to learn of others.

- Remind new associates that they are indeed starting a *business.* Be honest about the start-up costs in their entirety. Don't just mention the initial sign-up fee, but detail all other expenses they will need to cover such as business cards, personalized literature, and so on.

If you are honest and drop the *hype,* your business will grow in the right way. This business is about duplication, so be the kind of person in business that others want to duplicate. Be the image of your business—the image of honest success that people want to be!

Today's Actions for Building Integrity

Think about the last time you presented the business opportunity. Were you clear, complete, and accurate in your description of the benefits and costs? Identify three ways you can make your business opportunity presentation more open and honest. Review the lifestyles of the last five prospects to whom you've presented the business opportunity. Did you have success stories ready to share that matched their lifestyles? Research success stories of your company's distributors until you find several that fit the lifestyles of the prospects you meet most frequently. ■

■ Recruit to Retain for Long-Term Success

By Terrel F. Transtrum
The Retention Expert at ServiceQuest®

KEEPING THE CONNECTION

What is the secret to your success? Ask most direct sellers and they will tell you it is to constantly recruit. Although growing your organization is essential, *the truly wealthy in this profession are focusing on something called retention.* Retention is the length of time a customer or team member remains with you. When you have high retention, people stick around longer, your business is more stable, and your sales volume is less susceptible to the dramatic ups and downs caused by customer and team member dissatisfaction.

Recent studies show that the majority of direct sellers enter into the business to receive a discount on their personal consumption of a product or service. Therefore, it makes sense to *recruit to retain.* Give every newcomer the red carpet treatment, making sure she gets exactly what she wants out of the business, whether it is discount pricing or a flourishing business—both groups are essential to your long-term success. This is the secret understood by retention leaders who build their business one person at a time for lifelong volume.

Attributes of a Retention Leader

So what inspires customers and team members to stick around? You! A retention leader is someone who exhibits the following distinct attributes:

- **Nurturing.** Nurturing is the key attribute of a retention leader. She fosters respectful and trusting business relationships that protect and preserve the bonds of trust and loyalty. Just being in her presence makes a person feel valued and deepens her sense of self-worth.

- **Service-minded.** Leaders who retain their people live by the creed "Seek to bless, not to impress." Rooted in a Golden Rule philosophy, the degree to which you serve reveals your thoughts, actions, and motives. A service-minded leader forges a bond between herself and her team that leads to long-term relationships.

- **Honorable.** Though it's an overused buzzword in the business world, *integrity* is nonetheless an attribute of true retention leaders. They do what's right, they do what's honorable, and they do what they say they will do. When you make integrity your internal compass, you inspire others to stay the course even during tough times.

- **Committed to the wealth formula.** A retention leader enthusiastically embraces her company's wealth formula (compensation plan) and helps others see the long-term benefits of working the plan.

Key Practices

In addition to developing the attributes above, I offer the following daily practices that will help you become the leader who builds a strong organization for long-term success:

- Understand, manage, and exceed the expectations that others have for their business. Don't trade short-term gain for long-term wealth by inflating what's possible. Let others know that they can expect to succeed if they are willing to do the work.

- Build strong relationships with *all* your team members—customers and team builders. You'll see team builders remain committed to their goals, develop long-term customers who order each month, and see business builders emerge from your pool of loyal customers.

- Discover the needs and wants of each person you encounter. First seek to know what she wants, then help her to get it. Some of the most successful retention leaders go so far as to maintain a profile of each new recruit, detailing personalities, desires, and personal information.

- Strive to help others get off to a fast start, which will help them withstand the onslaught of external negative forces. Help each new team member develop three short stories: Why this company? Why these products? Why this business system?

- Study your retention data, which hold clues to how you can improve. As much as you study your enrollment and sales reports, study who is staying, who is leaving, and the reasons for both.

- Make a point to reward longtime customers and team builders to foster an environment of loyalty.

Take Actions That Retain

- Review the four attributes of a retention leader and notice where you are strong and where you could be better. Write down how you intend to strengthen one attribute in the coming week.

- Make time to look at your retention record. How long are your customers and team members remaining with you? Begin to track this over the next six months and watch the magic happen. ■

■ Defeat Low Self-Esteem to Boost Recruiting Success

By Lisa Kitter
Personal Empowerment Specialist

GETTING OUT OF YOUR OWN WAY

Are you finding that your prospects fail to follow through after they say they will enroll or look at your opportunity in more depth? Could your low self-esteem be the culprit? Low self-esteem is unconsciously broadcast through body language and word inflections. Prospects shy away from doing business with, or trusting, you if they subliminally pick up on these signals. ***When you develop greater self-esteem, you're making the best possible investment in your own success.*** No matter how confident you are, there's always something wonderful waiting to be discovered within yourself.

The power of self-esteem is arguably the most important factor in reaching our full potential in business as well as in the rest of our lives. Before we can develop or improve our prospecting, leading, training, and recruiting skills and fundamentals, before we truly can start to achieve, we must believe that our value is worth improving.

As a business builder and confident prospector, you help people develop and follow their dreams. In direct selling we have the opportunity to dream big and to actually achieve that vision with effort, persistence, consistency, and self-development. We work in an industry where we can realize extremely high incomes, but only if we truly believe in ourselves—if we understand ourselves and accept that we are worthy of great achievement.

DISCOVERING SELF TO FIND ESTEEM

Direct selling challenges us to delve *deep* inside ourselves and find out who we really are. We must acknowledge and expand our good qualities. For many of us, these are uncharted waters and can be frightening. Finding ourselves is hard because our society is so distracting and allows us to live outside ourselves without ever really coming to grips with who *we* are.

Many people get started in their own home-based opportunity, and soon such issues as deserve, leadership, prosperity, and self-esteem begin to surface. Prospecting and influencing others become frustrating experiences because these people lack the assurance that comes with acknowledging the verity of their personal worth. Here are some ideas that can help you to more fully come to grips with yourself and allow you to succeed:

- **Focus on the abilities you *do* have** instead of strengths you don't have. List as many of your strengths as you can think of. Post this list where you will be able to review it daily. Sometimes others can see our strengths more easily than we can. Ask some of your closest friends to list three or four things they like most about you. You may be surprised at the things they come up with that you entirely miss.

- **Think about a time when you felt really empowered.** Next time you're ready to prospect, prepare by visualizing yourself at that special moment when you knew you were awesome! Feel the feeling, remember the moment, place yourself mentally and emotionally back in that time of personal success.

- **Place a full-length mirror in your office or near your desk.** Practice getting comfortable with yourself. Look into the mirror and give yourself four sincere compliments every single day.

- **Pay attention to your internal communication—your self-talk.** Are you thinking positive, empowering thoughts that will build your self-esteem, or are you constantly putting yourself down?

- **Pay attention to how you interact with others.** If you are negative with them, odds are you are being negative with yourself.

- **Immerse yourself in an environment of self-confidence.** Associate with successful, self-confident people. Read books and listen to speeches by people who have a track record of helping others develop high self-esteem.

When I began implementing these few, easy suggestions I'm sharing with you, my business exploded in a good way! Keep sticking to your plan of action, focus on your many great qualities, and have patience with yourself. Continue to develop your skills daily and realize that transforming your life is a marathon, not a sprint!

Be Good to Yourself Today

- Sit down *tonight* and make a list of your good qualities. If you want to work with friends, meet together and list not only your own good qualities but each other's as well.

- Post the good-qualities list in a place where you will be forced to see it daily. Commit to reviewing the list each time you see it.

- Identify a positive person who loves you and builds you up, and commit to spending more time with that person. ■

■ Apply the Secret Science of Sponsoring

By Marcy Koltun-Crilley
Living the life of her dreams

APPLYING SCIENCE TO EVERYDAY EXPERIENCE

One of the most common problems distributors have in building their business is the inability to sponsor people they can work with and who want to work. I am asked almost weekly, "What's your secret to sponsoring?" The *secret* is actually a *science*. Mastering it has allowed me to effortlessly sponsor wonderful partners, triple my income, and buy a million-dollar house on Maui without hard work or struggle. ***The secret science is in understanding and using the law of attraction and intention.***

Recent research by Dr. William Tiller, professor emeritus at Stanford University, captured the attention of physicians and quantum physicists. Dr. Tiller scientifically demonstrated that humans can raise or lower the pH of water and even shorten the time it takes for fly larva to develop, *all* by the power of human intention—by concentrating on it and *willing* it to happen! The law of attraction simply states:

> Everything, including human thought, is energy and is always pulsing a vibration, similar to radio waves. Since like attracts like, whatever you get in your life *always* matches what you are vibrating, or broadcasting.

Here is the tricky part. Your vibration and what you attract is not about your words and your thoughts. It's about how your words and thoughts *feel* to you.

- ■ If you *say* "I have money," but what you *feel* is "I am broke," then what you are actually broadcasting is *scarcity*, regardless of the words you thought or spoke. Consequently, you will attract *scarcity*, because that is what you felt and broadcast.

■ If you feel as though you *need* to sponsor to make money, you're going to attract people who perceive you as someone who needs *them* so *you* can make money. They will perceive you as a *user* of others, and the people you attract will be *users* also.

The trick is to match your intent or desire with how you *want* to feel. Decide how you want to feel ahead of time, and spend energy convincing your soul to feel the way your mind wants it to feel. When you match up your intention (mind) with the corresponding feeling (soul) without conflict, by universal law your intended result *has* to come to you.

The way to attract the type of people you want in your business is to become a resonant match to that type of person. In other words, *become* the kind of person you want to recruit.

CREATING HARMONIOUS RESONANCE

The following is a simple three-step process that utilizes the law of attraction to sponsor people into your business. Commit to doing it for one week, and you'll see the results!

1. Each day, write down what you want (related to sponsoring), why you want it, and how you want to feel. Make this your dominant intention by repeating to yourself until you feel congruity of thought and feeling. For example, "I want to attract the perfect partners for myself with ease and in the perfect time. I will have fun, be happy and abundant, no matter what!"

2. Before you start calling prospects, write down your intended results. For example, "For these calls, I will attract *only* the perfect partners for myself with ease and at the perfect time. I will have fun, be happy and abundant, no matter what!"

3. Write down one experience you would like to have that you believe possible today. For example, "I want to find someone with whom I will instantly connect because we share something in common. I will have fun, be happy and abundant no matter what! This will happen at the perfect time."

It is important that you *feel good* regardless of the actual outcome from your calls; and be sure to include "This will happen at the perfect time." Although you may not connect with anyone during your call session, four hours later you may make a fantastic surprise connection while grocery shopping!

If you practice this method daily, you will soon have the business you want with the people you want.

Be Scientific Today

1. Write down the characteristics you want in team members and how you want to feel about them.

2. Repeat your intention to find them until you feel congruity between thought and feeling.

3. Know you will find them with ease and in the perfect time.

4. Take action to find them with complete confidence and unlimited patience. ■

■ Shorten the Success Curve with Leads

By "Motivated Mike" Lemire
Helping direct sellers think huge, work hard, and succeed!

INCREASING YOUR EXPOSURES

The key to success in our industry will always be to talk consistently with more people every day. Whether you do it on the phone or use the Internet, a good-quality lead program can help your business explode on a local, national, or international basis.

Here's the bottom line. The number of people you talk to determines the number of exposures. The exposures determine the number of people sponsored, and the number sponsored directly affects your income. Lead programs accelerate your *success curve* because you talk to more people who have *requested* information about starting their own business.

Not all lead programs are the same. Among the many lead companies and lead systems, I suggest you find a lead *consulting* company. Personally, I built my business with one such company and to this day, it is the only lead company I link to on my Web site. Why? I had a wide variety of leads, lead services, and options to fit *my* needs. Any lead program is like an investment or becoming physically fit; it requires *time* and *commitment.* You are experiencing a new learning curve, so *give yourself one year.* Prospects who don't join today might in six months—*following up always pays off!* You will improve with time, and that means your ratios of exposures to closes will become *smaller.* Ratios will help you in becoming more profitable with your business. The end result is just incredible: you'll be able to *map* your progress and income!

Here's what top money earners do when working leads:

- They see their lead program as an *investment* in their success.

- They develop and understand their *ratios.*

- They focus on *systems* instead of themselves.

- They ask questions to uncover the prospect's *hot buttons.*

- They *follow up* until they get a Yes or a No.

- They *sort* rather than convince.

- They sell the *dream and the team.*

- They *weather the storm;* some leads *will* work and some *won't.*

- They *focus* on all aspects of training and personal development.

- They *promote* lead programs to enhance their team's activity and income.

CHOOSING YOUR MEANS FOR SUCCESS

Is there a formula to determine whether buying leads is the right choice for you? No. *You* must decide how fast you want your business to grow. *You* must decide if you'd rather sort through people who have indicated no interest in starting a business or if you'd rather talk to people who have requested information.

Remember, a lead program is another *tool* that is available to build your business. Deciding *how* to build your business is your choice. But I will say this: If you are *serious* about your *business* and *serious* about "firing your boss," a lead program will help you accomplish that goal *in a shorter period of time.*

Determining the quality of a lead can sometimes be difficult also. Many distributors can be furnished with the best of the best and still not have success, because they lack the communication skills and the work ethic required to obtain the success they seek. Both of *those* areas can be improved through personal development and *practice.* To get better at anything takes time and effort. Why not improve your skills while talking to people you *don't* know?

Remember: "If it sounds to good to be true . . ." and "You get what you pay for." *Use common sense.* An offer of 10,000 leads for $100 should tell you something. On average, a quality lead should run between $2 and $5 each. Usually, the more qualified the lead, the higher the cost. Many teams lower the cost of leads by participating in a co-op lead program, whereby individual expense is lowered through volume and shared cost.

No matter what you do, don't idle too long wondering about what to do—just do something! *Imperfect action is better than perfect inaction.* To do is to learn, and *repetition is the key to learning* everything.

Afraid to contact people you don't know? *Success can be found only outside your comfort zone.* The most successful people in our industry were, at one time, exactly where you are and feeling exactly as you feel. The only difference is they consistently talked to more people, and they probably did *that* with the help of a good lead program.

Today's Actions for Starting a Lead Program

Life is full of choices, and this is one of them. The most successful people in this business have used *all* the tools available to them at one time or another and have determined which works *best* for *them* . . . and most decided early on to consistently and persistently *work with leads.*

Decide Do you want to use a lead program and, if so, what kind?

Commit You must commit to lead training, personal development, and all that's required to get the most from the leads you receive.

Learn You can find many free training ideas regarding leads and sponsoring archived at http://www.Motivated Mike.com . . . use them! ∎

∎ Be More Committed to Your Dream Than Your Reality

By Marcia Wieder
America's Dream Coach

SEEING WHERE YOU'RE GOING

Successful people in direct selling (and in life) have big dreams and pursue them. You have many that you passionately share and that inspire others to join you. Yet on the road to realizing your personal and professional dreams, life often provides distractions. People, places, and things get in your way. If you are serious about living a dream-come-true life, it is essential that you *learn how to stay more committed to your dreams and goals than to your reality.*

As a leader, you serve as a model of integrity by saying what you mean and meaning what you say. If you have a dream of growing your organization, promoting up, or walking across the stage to be recognized for an achievement, what you say and do is essential. Demonstrate to your team, family, friends, and community that when you say you are going for your dreams, *you mean it.*

The road to making your dreams come true starts with where you are now. Try stretching a rubber band between the thumb and the middle finger of one hand. Then imagine the tension inside the rubber band as you pull on either the top of the loop or the bottom of the loop. Tension resolves itself in whatever direction there is more focus, or the side being pulled on. If you imagine the top of the rubber band is your dream and the bottom your reality about this dream, whichever one you are more committed to is the direction your life will move.

PLAYING THE BALL WHERE IT LIES

Your challenge is to make an *honest assessment of where you are now.* For example, where are you currently with respect to building your team and your income? What concerns do you have in these areas? Do you worry that going for your dream will take more time than the time available? Perhaps you don't believe it's possible to make your dream come true. The fact is that you will never be able to get to a place you want to go until you *evaluate where you are and what needs to change.*

As you look at your reality, you may hear an inner voice whispering all your limitations—all your attitudes and beliefs, concerns, fears, worries, and tales about why you can't have what you want. Fortunately, your positive attitudes and beliefs also will arise—that is, you *do* believe your dream is possible, because it's something you've always wanted, something to which you're committed, something you know you can have, something you are worthy of.

People frequently sabotage themselves by putting their negative attitudes, beliefs, or fears into their dream. If you're putting your concerns into your dream, your fears will become bigger and seem more real as you move closer to getting what you want. Your concerns don't belong in your dream; they're part of where you are now, not where you're going.

Here is a simple process to avoid sabotaging your dream. On a sheet of paper, draw a line across the middle. Label the top your dream, the bottom your reality. Now fill it in with detail. Write down your attitudes, accomplishments, relationships . . . anything that describes either the dream or the reality. Fears, doubts, or concerns go into the reality section. Don't kill off your dream by projecting your fears into the future.

After all is said and done, ask yourself this direct question: "Which do I want more, my dream or my reality?" If the answer is your dream, prove it. Demonstrate that you are serious about achieving your dream by taking action today.

Today's Action for Living Your Dream

If you have not already done so, create a clear picture of your dream life. Be clear and specific, and create it on paper or in the computer—someplace where it won't be easily lost.

Now get that piece of paper, draw a line across it, and use the process you just learned to remove negative feelings and factors from your dream. Now is the time to commit to your dream— more than to your reality. It *is* achievable! ■

■ Craft Your Recruiting Story

By Maria Dowd
Leading with heart and soul

OPENING YOUR SOUL

When you're recruiting a new prospect, **be prepared to share your experience in a polished, captivating story.** In my work with hundreds of new distributors, I find the stories that deliver the greatest impact—that constantly cultivate prospects—are *not* shared on a whim. Rather, they are a result of searching your soul for the story within.

Your personal recruiting story is a vital component of your recruiting success because it

■ solidifies in your own mind your Why, your reason for being in the business;

■ attracts others to your business and helps them identify their own Why; and

■ reinforces your commitment to your business with each telling.

In crafting your personal recruiting story, it's critical to speak to and from your soul. Your story must be heartfelt and must strike a chord in the hearts and minds of your prospects, as you share why you came to be involved with your company and how your life has been enriched along the way. Your story must first excite *you*, because you will be sharing it again and again, and then it must ignite your prospect's pilot light of desire.

Today, your personal recruiting story may strike a chord with someone who's in the midst of a divorce. Tomorrow, it may offer hope to someone who just received a pink slip. The next day, it could motivate a woman who's just finished reading a great inspirational book. Next week, your message could touch the sensibilities of someone who came up a few hundred dollars short when paying bills, and a few hundred dollars could have made the difference. When your story reaches into the heart of a person at the right time and that person is ready to hear it, she'll know it and will reach out to you.

SHAPING A SPELLBINDING STORY

So how do you craft your recruiting story? Here are guidelines I use to help others craft their personal story.

Start with your real-life experiences. Use the stuff that makes us want to cry, scream, crawl into a hole, or move to a deserted island somewhere in the South Pacific. Being mindful not to sound self-absorbed, your story might begin with the feelings of exasperation or doubt you once felt. It then reveals your journey from that point to where you are today. Open your heart to your prospect and let her share the breathtaking journey your business has afforded you.

Blend realism with unyielding optimism. To spark your prospect's desire for a better quality of life, your story must be honest, yet triumphant; real life, yet magical.

Reveal your immense passion for the products or services you offer. Let your prospect see the sense of pride you feel for your outstanding business opportunity and the excitement you feel for the company and its culture. When your passion for your company comes alive in your story, you spark your listener's curiosity to learn more.

Make an irresistible offer. Your story must show prospects how being a part of your company can lead them to the same experience of delight, self-confidence, even unbridled exhilaration you feel as a result of your journey.

Start Crafting Your Story Today

Begin by writing on index cards or Post-it notes where you were at the beginning (emotionally, financially, and so on) and contrast that with where you are today. Then list what you love about your company, the products, your upline, and your team. Identify how being in business for yourself has affected your life, hopes, and dreams. Now place your cards or notes on a wall and arrange them into clumps of ideas that fit together. Order the clumps into a compelling sequence of events and thoughts, and then you can begin writing your story.

Once you have crafted your story, practice sharing it with others. Ask them: "How does it make you feel?" "What images does my story conjure up?" "What does it make you want to do next?" Then, continue to refine it.

You'll need more than one version of your personal story, each to appeal to a different audience. One version may appeal more to our innate, tribal, or community needs. Another may hone in on lifestyle desires, whereas a third may focus on personal and professional growth and empowerment.

Yes, this process takes a little soul-searching, but the results will bring you a greater appreciation of your business and a compelling story that will help you build your team. ∎

∎ Master the Art of Sponsorship

By Jim Britt
Success Builder in Network Marketing and Direct Selling

DISCOVERING DEEPER VALUES

When you measure the success of your sponsoring program, it's not how many people you enroll or how much money you make; it's *how many people you empower, how many lives you help change, and how many people you help to live life more fully.* These are the results that make your work truly rewarding.

Every new associate you sponsor is looking for reasons to stay on your team; she is also looking for reasons to leave! That's because people find comfort in their old ways and fear change. Leaving our comfort zone summons our deepest fears—"What if it doesn't work?" "What if the opportunity isn't real?" "What if I can't do it?" "What will others think of me being in this type of business?"

Sponsoring can be defined as looking out for another person's interest or well-being. It is a *learned* art! On this journey of self-discovery for both you and your associate, you can help her learn what in her past has not worked for her, where she is now, how she envisions her future, and what changes she needs to make to create that future. When you connect your business opportunity to her vision, she will become a long-term business partner.

BUILDING BONDS OF VALUE

Prospects and team members ponder everything you say and do. Each one is influenced by your commitment, your goals and plans, your ability to follow through, and your willingness to do whatever it takes to help her become successful. All these things create value. If you create enough value, she will stay on your team. Your job as a leader is to remove the doubt and add value.

Successful networking is founded on relationships. The more you help someone discover and realize her dreams, the stronger the personal bond you develop and the stronger your relationship becomes. Strong emotional bonding between your team members and you is the biggest factor in long-term success.

Building strong emotional bonds opens up worlds of possibilities. As you create a bond with one person, she will want her friends and associates to know you too. She will, in turn, follow your example and create strong bonds with individuals on her team. That is the beauty of networking. Your good work can multiply and affect many more people than you can personally know.

Build a Valuable Relationship Today

Pick a day to spend with a prospect or someone on your team. Forget about your business and make it your objective to get to know that individual as a whole person. Ask questions. *Listen* to her cry for help. Discover her current circumstances, what she wants in life, what's missing, and what's important to her. Ask about her family, her job, her health, and her concerns. Find out what excites her and makes her happy. At the end of the day, ask yourself, "How can I help my friend?" Then act boldly to reach out to her. ■

■ Build a Multicultural Team

By Nick "Keeper" Catran-Whitney
Innovator in Entertainment Marketing

REVIEWING MARKETS

I was at an opportunity meeting in 1998 for my direct-selling company. One of our top distributors was there. I had heard a lot about this woman's ability to recruit people into her organization, and I wanted to know what made her so successful. When I finally got a chance to speak with her, I said, "I'm looking to get more minorities into my organization, but it's just not going as well as I'd like. What do you recommend?" Her answer shocked me: she claimed she would never recruit minorities. Her perception seemed to be that minority markets had nothing to offer her business. The fact is, *so-called minority markets are currently expanding while the so-called majority market is shrinking.*

INCLUDING OTHERS FOR FUN AND PROFIT

The lack of diversity in direct selling is an issue that has largely been ignored. For example, the network marketing segment of the Direct Selling industry is 80 percent white, 10 percent black, and 10 percent everyone else. This is an unfortunate oversight because by 2007, minorities in the United States will spend over $2 trillion dollars per year: Hispanics $925.1 billion, African Americans $852.8 billion, and Asians $454.9 billion. Not only that, over the past ten years the white population in America has shrunk by almost 10 percent and continues to decline, all the while minority populations are increasing rapidly.

The bright side of these statistics is that this huge untapped market is a gold mine for the wise distributor. Many white direct sellers have told me they want to build a multicultural team, which, especially in light of the changing racial demographics in the United States, seems like an important strategy to adopt. The problem is that these direct sellers don't know how to go about building multi-cultural teams; and, in fact, most companies don't have the infra-structure in place to help them go after the minority markets and don't yet have the tools and skill sets necessary to develop them.

The phrase by Brian Tracy comes to mind here: "If you think education is expensive, you should try ignorance."

If you are a distributor wishing to build a diverse team, then you *know* that recruitment and retention of minority markets is key for the continued success of your organization. What do you do? How do you move ahead of your company and develop the necessary tools to go after the minority markets?

Here are a few tips that can help in building a multicultural team:

- **Know your market.** You must be willing to learn about the minority market you are targeting.

- **Learn the language of your target minority.** Even well-integrated minorities have their own unique language uses, and it pays to be comfortable with their language.

- **If you already have minorities on your team, learn from *them*.** Don't be afraid to tell them you are looking to expand your business to their minority market and that you need to learn more about their culture.

- **Read minority magazines and newspapers, and watch minority television shows.** You will gain a greater understanding of that market. Do this without judgment. Remember this market's view of life is much different from yours.

- **Tailor your message to the market you intend to serve.** Your business opportunity must be one in which those in that market can picture themselves succeeding. If you have minorities in your organization, ask them to help you with your presentation.

- **Attend job fairs geared toward minorities.** You can find these in minority newspapers.

- **Visit colleges that have a large minority population.** Go to the shops surrounding the university. Student organizations, beauty salons, and barbershops are great places to make contacts.

- **Advertise in minority and college newspapers.**

- **Follow up on your contacts.** Show the same commitment to minorities as to anyone else.

- **Treat everyone with respect.** Don't lower your standards when approaching minorities.

Planting Diversity Seeds Today

- Study the diversity issue and determine for yourself whether diversity makes sense to you.

- Target a minority market that you want to penetrate and include in your team profile.

- Select three of the strategies presented above and start incorporating them. ■

Coaching
Your Team

*I*magine this scene . . . It's your first month in business. You've signed the distributor agreement, received your start-up kit, perused the training manual, and are using and loving your company's products. You're excited about your business and can't help talking about it with friends, relatives, and co-workers. You're not exactly sure what you're doing yet, but you're having fun in the process. A friend at work happens to notice, and she too falls in love with the products. Before you know it, she's signing on the dotted line, just as you had done only weeks before. Yikes! You have your first team member!

Yes, sponsoring is where the long-term money is in direct selling, but to many, what comes after you sponsor is what's intimidating. It doesn't have to be that way! In fact, the act of coaching and supporting your team to success can be the most rewarding aspect of your business—free from stress, feelings of obligation, and doubt.

In this chapter you discover a unique and enlightened approach to coaching your team, called Principle-Centered Coaching.™ The professional coaches and top-performing leaders who share their insights here use these skills every day to support others in achieving their dreams. They can work for you too.

■ Detach from the Outcome

By Jennie England, PCC, CPCC
The DSWA Coaching Center Director

LETTING GO OF WHAT IS NOT YOURS

As I coach direct-selling professionals, I find many who are experiencing stress and anxiety as a result of failed expectations. Whether expressed outwardly or not, many people have this viewpoint: "If I've put a lot of effort into something, I want to get something in return." However, the fact is that we really don't have control over many circumstances in our business and our life, and we can become disappointed when things don't turn out as we had hoped. *These expectations often fail to materialize as a result of events totally outside our control. As we learn to let go of responsibility for these kinds of events, we find that we can be happier and experience more joy.*

Here are some possible scenarios:

■ You set a party date; your hostess invites 12 guests, but only 2 show up.

■ You have three phone conversations and an in-person meeting with a potential recruit, but she decides "not now."

■ You see great potential in a new team member and look forward to her advancement, but she doesn't come through as you had hoped.

If this sounds at all familiar, and you're ready to experience less disappointment and anxiety about outcomes in your business, then read on!

GIVING AWAY RESPONSIBILITY

Let's take the example of the promising new recruit. Imagine yourself in the picture. You are excited about her potential. She seems to have all the qualities, work ethic, skills, and commitment to build a thriving business. How can you be a supportive upline while avoiding the pitfalls of disappointment?

First and foremost, make no assumptions! Talk with your new team member to find out what *her* business goals are by asking *You're the Expert Questions,* one of the five skills of Principle-Centered Coaching.

Questions you might ask:

- "What future do you see for yourself and your business?"

- "What is your dream and what is your commitment to achieving it?"

- "What time are you able to devote to your business each week?"

- "What first steps will you take to move toward your dream?"

- "What support would you like from me?"

By learning what your team member wants from her business, you remain focused on *her* goals—not yours. With *her* goals in mind, you can better serve her needs as she learns and grows her business.

Second, practice *Heart-Centered Listening,* another Principle-Centered Coaching skill, by being totally present in the moment. The business and what she will do with it is *up to her.* Your role is simply to support and guide her as appropriate.

Finally, detach yourself from the outcome. This doesn't mean that you stop caring, but it does mean that *you no longer take responsibility for the success or failure of your team members.* Release yourself from the stress and anxiety that result when you want so much for her that you lose objectivity.

Once you have helped your team member identify her goals and shown her the path to success, responsibility for her success lies with *her,* not you. Even though her success is part of your success, *she* is responsible for seeing it through. Let go of your attachment to what's down the road and trust that if you are clear in your intention as her leader and do your very best to support her on her journey, the outcome will be as it is meant to be!

As you gain the skill of detaching from the outcome, you find you are able to maintain your inner state of optimism and service, and not take things personally or feel responsible for the success of your team. With this internal strength, you can support team members in going for their dreams with a light heart—no longer anxious about the outcome.

Actions You Can Take

- If you are not familiar with each of your team member's dreams, schedule a time to talk with each one of them.

- As you listen to each one's dreams and desires, be careful not to lead her to what you believe is possible for her. Instead, just keep asking "And what else?" and watch where her imagination takes her.

- Write down your team members' dreams and goals, and refer to them often so you don't project your own ideas onto them but simply support them in achieving all that they want for themselves.

■ Listen—and Give the Greatest Gift

By Jennie England
The DSWA Coaching Center Director

AT THE HEART OF SUCCESS

One of the things I love about the people attracted to the Direct-Selling profession is their desire to support other people's efforts to be the *best* they can be. This industry is all about relationships, helping people grow, and offering service, don't you think?

Through my experiences of training and coaching thousands of people, I have come to understand that *the fastest way to build relationships is to genuinely care about the other person.* This is true in both your personal and business life. And isn't it true that this is what your team members want to know—that you *really do* care about them as individuals, not just as salespersons in your organization?

Perhaps the best way for you to demonstrate that you care is to apply the coaching skill of *Heart-Centered Listening*. This skill is at the very core of your coaching relationship with your team. As you use it, you create an environment of respect, trust, and safety among your team. As one leader in the industry recently told me, "I just can't believe how much stronger my relationships are with my team members just by listening to them with my heart."

BECOMING A BETTER LISTENER

Some of the most basic of human needs are to be heard and understood and to have a connection with others. We give these gifts to one another through Heart-Centered Listening. Here are some points to keep in mind as you develop this trait:

- First, shift your focus from your own thoughts to what the other person is saying. Listen with an open heart to the words of the speaker. Beyond listening to the words, listen to the feelings, needs, and energy of the speaker so that you can truly understand them. This comes quite naturally when you listen with your heart.

- At the same time that you give 100 percent of your focus to the speaker, quiet your own internal dialogue so that you do not interrupt, judge, interpret, advise, or read your own experience or feelings into what the speaker is saying.

- Express interest by using body language—making eye contact and sitting in a receptive posture. As you practice this, you will see that Heart-Centered Listening is not passive—it's very active.

- When you practice Heart-Centered Listening with a speaker, notice the dreams, vision, goals, and challenges expressed through her words and demeanor, and don't take lightly the trust she demonstrates by sharing them with you.

When you find yourself discouraged or doubtful about her abilities, shift to listening with empathy—without judgment. Watch how acceptance and understanding move her to a more positive outlook.

When your team member shares a triumph, listening reinforces her joy and celebration.

Once you have truly listened to your team member, you might try using a subskill of Heart-Centered Listening called *reflecting*. This involves summarizing and saying back to her what you've heard and understood her to have said. It lets her know that you have "gotten it" or gives her a chance to restate concepts you might have missed. Once she knows that you understand her, you'll find she doesn't feel the need to repeat herself and can more readily move forward. Consequently, listening and reflecting actually saves time because team members spend less time explaining a challenge and can move more quickly to finding a solution.

Make a decision to learn about and practice Heart-Centered Listening—the first core skill of Principle-Centered Coaching. The result: Your team members will feel validated, understood, and accepted—all of which leads to greater self-esteem, confidence, and success in their business and personal life!

 Today's Actions for Heart-Centered Listening

- Choose at least one phone call a day to truly listen and understand a member of your team.

- For the next 24 hours, avoid giving solutions or attempting to just fix a situation. Instead, support the team member in finding her own way, which builds her confidence and increases accountability.

- Practice Heart-Centered Listening with a family member each day, and see how positively she responds!

Giving the gift of Heart-Centered Listening can enrich and transform the lives of others. Most important, giving this gift will transform *your* life! ▪

■ Ask Inspiring Questions

By Carly Anderson, MCC
Member of the DSWA Coach Referral Network

THE MAGIC OF SINCERE INTEREST

When you want to inspire a person to greater success, **ask questions that tap into her wisdom and sources of natural talent.** Through my work as a leadership coach, I have found this is one of the best ways to move a low-income team member to a higher level of business activity.

Inspiring questions come from the heart. So before I tell you how to ask inspiring questions, let me ask how you *feel* about your team members. How you view their capabilities will have a huge impact on your ability to support and lead.

Do you believe your team members are capable of finding the right way to build their business based on their strengths and skills, or do you think they need to be shown what to do every step of the way? Which of these two statements comes closest to your belief?

- ■ My team members need to be constantly reminded of what they must do next to build their business. My role is to direct them and keep them on track as they build their business.

- ■ My team members are resourceful and complete people. I trust they have the resources within them to find the best way to build their business. My role is to find out what they need from me in order to reach their full potential.

The philosophy expressed in the first statement is based on control and command, whereas the second is based on *service.* When you choose to serve your team members instead of command them, you'll discover your ability to *inspire* them. Consider the well-known adage, "Give enough people what they want, and you'll also get what you want." It expresses the age-old wisdom that a philosophy of service positively affects your ability to lead others to success.

AWAKENING HER INNER WISDOM

Once you have shifted from directing team members to serving them, the types of questions you ask will change considerably, from closed to open-ended:

- **A closed question** requires only a Yes or No response; for example: "Have you followed up with those leads you got from the Web site?" The answer can only be Yes or No, and your team member might feel she needs to justify herself if she hasn't.

- **An open-ended question** encourages your team member to come up with her own creative answer; for example, "How are you doing with those leads from the Web site?" Open-ended questions usually begin with What, How, or What if.

As your leadership skills improve, you'll ask more and more open-ended questions that help others tap into their inner wisdom. These are referred to as *You're the Expert Questions* and they are one of five essential skills of Principle-Centered Coaching. Here are some empowering questions to ask:

- What's the vision you have for how you'd most love to live your life?

- How does building this business support that vision?

- What inspires you about your business?

- What might be the fear that stops a person from becoming a top performer?

- What will you do differently the next time you encounter an obstacle?

When you encourage a team member to find her own answers, she's more likely to implement the ideas and follow through, which inevitably leads to greater success. Furthermore, encouraging team members to access their own wisdom frees you from feeling as though you must have the answer when they encounter a challenge.

Team members soon see you as a support rather than a crutch and gradually begin to take responsibilities for their actions and the results they are creating. All of which enables you to enjoy your role as coach at a deeper, more significant level.

Actions for Today and Tomorrow

Take these three steps in the next 48 hours to shift toward service and inspiring leadership:

1. Evaluate your personal philosophy. Make sure it's coming from a place of service.

2. Think about your team members. Identify the wonderful qualities each member is not seeing in herself.

3. During the next week, practice asking your team members open-ended questions that help them identify these qualities and tap into their own wisdom and talents. ■

■ Make Friends with Your Inner Critic

By Jennie England, PCC, CPCC
The DSWA Coaching Center Director

HEARING VOICES

We each have an inner critic that often keeps us from making changes, such as starting a new career in the Direct Selling industry, meeting new challenges, or learning new skills. *If we are not careful, that inner critic zaps our energy, creating self-doubt and low self-esteem.* The inner critic is like an overprotective mom who wants the best for us but clips our wings in the process. Do any of these scenarios sound familiar?

- You're about to interview a potential team member and offer your business opportunity, when in the back of your mind you hear a voice that says, *"She's already successful in her current career; why even bother?"*

- You've just started to make calls to invite friends and relatives to hostess a party or take a look at the business opportunity, when the inner critic says, *"Your friends are already busy with their lives. You'll just make them feel obligated and uncomfortable!"*

- You've built a successful business, and you're ready to leave your day job when you hear, *"That's way too risky—you'll never make it in this economy!"*

This voice in your head that squelches your good ideas and has you doubting yourself has various names. In Principle-Centered Coaching, we call it the *inner critic*. It's a voice that is with us throughout our every day. It tells us who we are and how we are doing, and defines and interprets our every experience. In fact, it works very hard to get us to accept *its* interpretations as *our* reality!

A LEADER'S VIEW OF THE INNER CRITIC

As a leader, you'll want to practice noticing when the inner critic shows up for you—that is, which events trigger its arrival. Recognize how it makes you feel and how it influences your decisions to go forward or to pull back from what you truly want. Then, after observing your own reactions, begin to recognize when the inner critic shows up for your team members. For example, when a new team member starts, gives her first demonstration, or conducts her first business opportunity presentation, her inner critic is probably right there!

It is important for you, as her leader, to be able to identify the arrival of the inner critic and help her understand how to deal with it. By sharing your understanding with your team member, you will be able to support her in observing and moving past the fears and doubts created by this inner voice.

The truth is that your success and the success of your team are determined by your ability to transform the inner critic from foe to friend! Follow the six steps below and learn how to do this.

SIX STEPS TO TRANSFORM THE INNER CRITIC

1. List three messages that you hear frequently from your inner critic, and describe how these messages make you feel.

2. Personify the inner critic through naming, drawing, or describing; have a little fun with this step!

3. Choose your response. Between every stimulus and response, *there is a moment of choice.* Choose to disconnect from the inner critic so you can *distinguish fact from illusion.*

4. Affirm your true strengths, accomplishments, and qualities to reprogram the inner critic's negative messages into positive, affirming messages.

5. Have a dialogue with your inner critic to understand it and create a healthy relationship with it—one that supports your reaching your potential.

6. Be the observer of your thoughts without judgment so you can become proactive rather than reactive.

As you practice these six steps, you begin to develop a more lighthearted relationship with your inner critic. As you take responsibility for responding to it in the way that serves you best, the inner critic will quiet down, recognizing that you are safe and capable of taking care of yourself!

It's been said that we have 60,000 thoughts a day—and most of them are the same as yesterday's thoughts. Because our thoughts create our experience of life, it's important that we *choose* them wisely.

Actions to Befriend the Critic

- Take time *today* to identify your inner critic's three most debilitating messages, and tag each message with how they make you feel and act.

- Now, tag each of the three messages with how you *want* to respond, and commit to responding *that* way instead of following your conditioned response.

  Remember, if you don't do something different *today*, *tomorrow* will look pretty much like *yesterday*. ■

■ Reveal Her True Self with "I See You" Acknowledgment

By Cheryl Walker, PCC
Member of the DSWA Coach Referral Network

SEEING THE GREATNESS IN OTHERS

We all like to hear praise and compliments from others. It feels good when someone says "Great work" or "Good job." As a direct-selling leader, you probably find yourself recognizing an accomplishment or praising progress nearly every day. What I have noticed, however, both in myself and in my team, is that the power of a compliment is short-lived, often disregarded, or forgotten in minutes. It was not until I became a professional coach and learned the skills of coaching that I came to understand *the true difference between recognition and acknowledgment and the impact that acknowledgment can have on our relationships with others.*

When we give a compliment, we are speaking about what the person has *done.* An example of a compliment might be "Great presentation!" or "You ran a good meeting yesterday." Acknowledgment, on the other hand, goes much deeper and has a more powerful impact on the person receiving it. In Principle-Centered Coaching, we call this *ICU Acknowledgment* (as in "I see who you are!") because it goes beyond the person's action to recognize the qualities and characteristics *that enabled her to do what she did*. ICU Acknowledgment recognizes her inner character—who she is—and meets her basic need to be "seen." Here is an example of the contrast:

> *Recognition:*   You ran a good meeting yesterday, Laura.
>
> *ICU Acknowledgment:*   Laura, as I watched you run your team meeting, I saw your ability to deeply listen to your team. Your openness and patience allowed team members to speak honestly, which in turn helps them grow.

Looking for positive qualities in your team members rather than looking for problems to be fixed creates a significant shift in the interpersonal dynamic and establishes an environment of trust and mutual respect. Often, a team member is not aware of her own strengths and capabilities. As a leader, you have an opportunity to reveal to her the strengths, qualities, and capabilities she displays. When you acknowledge her, you hold up a mirror and say, "This is the person I see in you!" Often for the first time, you awaken in her an awareness of qualities she might not have noticed or accepted before. This new self-knowledge builds self-esteem and empowers her to keep learning, growing, and doing her best!

There is a gift here for you as well. For a leader, nothing is more rewarding than watching someone light up as she recognizes her own greatness and then moves forward with new enthusiasm to reach her fullest potential!

LEARNING TO REVEAL HER CHARACTER

ICU Acknowledgment takes a bit more time and thoughtfulness in the beginning, but with practice it becomes very natural. There are three basic steps:

1. Identify the qualities that enabled your team member to do what she did. Some qualities to look for are patience, dedication, commitment, perseverance, caring, thoughtfulness, creativity, initiative, enthusiasm, clear communication, or wisdom.

2. Keep your acknowledgment simple and to the point. I have found that a shorter statement delivers a greater impact.

3. Be honest and speak from the heart. When your team member can feel your authenticity, it deepens the impact and creates a lasting effect.

As you internalize the practice of ICU Acknowledgment, you find that your team members follow your lead. Soon ICU Acknowledgment will undergird your fellowship, and you'll find yourself in another kind of ICU: an intensively caring unit!

I hope that you can see the transformative impact that ICU Acknowledgment can have on your relationships with your team and your business. When used with the other four skills of Principle-Centered Coaching, it helps you support your team members in taking powerful actions toward their dreams as you experience the joy of making a significant contribution to another person's life!

Today's Actions for Acknowledging Others

Study the list of characteristics in step one above. Commit them to memory. Today and tomorrow, practice identifying at least one of them in someone who describes an achievement to you—and watch her light up! ■

■ Agree on Action Plans and Accountability

By Augusta Horsey Nash, MCC, CPCC

Member of the DSWA Coach Referral Network

THE POWER OF OWNING THE ACTION

As a leader, you already know that individuals who commit to, and take responsibility for, action are a rare find. Most often you find yourself juggling your business, team members, customers, and prospects—simply trying to keep all the balls in the air—all the time, every day. *Equipping team members to take action, commit to a time frame, and take responsibility* allows you to step into "leading" rather than managing tasks and teams.

FROM MANAGING TO LEADING

When you combine the powerful principle of *Agreed Action and Accountability* with the other four Principle-Centered Coaching skills, your bottom line benefits. The less time and energy you spend following up and managing productivity, the more time you can spend leading, coaching, and modeling. What do I mean by the coaching skill of Agreed Action and Accountability?

- ■ *Accountability:* Use open-ended questions to guide your team member to define what she will do, when she will do it, and how both of you will know it's completed.

- ■ *Actions:* Design tasks aligned with her vision of success within a strategic business plan.

- ■ *Agreed:* You and your team member see the actions as specific, measurable, ethical, realistic, and timely. She chooses the actions she is willing to take because they are doable, beneficial, and, ultimately, her choice.

Envision the impact of applying this principle when working with your team. When each team member has a goal, agrees to the action necessary, and commits to a time frame, it frees everyone, including you, to do more!

Engage your team members. Clarifying the steps or specific tasks to reach a particular goal can be fun! But at the beginning, you might find it frustrating. You might have so much experience and expertise that you know exactly what she *should* do. And for time's sake, you might be tempted just to tell her and be done with it! But if you take this approach, she will keep coming back to you for specific instructions *every* step of the way. Be aware that investing a little time now will free more of your time in the future.

Let's look at an example of how Agreed Action and Accountability might work for you. Imagine you're a team leader with a brand-new team member. Your success is founded on your expertise in cold calling. Your new team member says she wants to host one sales event by next month; it's in her business plan. You ask her some "You're the Expert" Questions. "How might you do that? How else?"

If she doesn't bring up cold calling, you might suggest it as a possibility. You might want to go on and tell her to make 45 cold calls next week, but you don't! Instead, you ask how many she would feel comfortable doing. Once she commits to a number of calls, share a few things that worked for you and also what didn't so she can get a sense of what might work best for her, too.

You've reached an agreement for the actions to reach her goal. Now you create the accountability. In this scenario, you might ask, "How would you like to be held accountable for this action?" or "How will I know you have completed the action?"

Once you agree to a time for checking in, encourage her and express your confidence in her ability to reach her goal. Be aware that sometimes she might be unable to complete the action by the set date. When you allow for this possibility, you build trust and reliability in your relationship. In the event of a missed deadline, help her design a new action plan and ask the same questions as those in the original conversation. She is learning her own limitations and strengths, and gaining trust in your leadership.

Finally, affirm your commitment to your team member's success by asking, "How might I support you in this activity?" Now is the time for a truthful "I See You" Acknowledgment. Share the wonderful things you see in her: her heart, her courage, and her sense of adventure. This is the best possible way to tell her *she can do it!*

Get Out of Frustration and into Action

Ready to move from managing into leadership? Create powerful conversations with your team, conversations that are clear, clean, and empowering. In the next 48 hours, take these steps:

- Connect with your team members to revisit their goals.

- Apply the principle of Agreed Action and Accountability. ■

■ Catch the Spirit of the Pareto Principle

By Gale Bates
Succeeding strategically in business

USING THE 80/20 RULE

In 1906, Italian economist Vilfredo Pareto created a mathematical formula describing the unequal distribution of wealth in his country. He observed that 20 percent of the people owned 80 percent of the wealth. This has become known as Pareto's Principle, or the 80/20 Rule, and has applications in many areas. Applying this principle to direct selling, 20 percent of your people usually do 80 percent of the sales on a consistent basis. *The key to using the 80/20 Rule is to focus on the 20 percent who are presently producing while not forgetting the 80 percent who may produce in the future.*

As I manage my team, I find the value of the Pareto Principle is to recognize the high-performing 20 percent and focus on the important actions needed to help each of these women build and develop a strong business. Use the following steps to lead with the spirit of Pareto:

- Identify the high-performing 20 percent by *assessing their consistent activity.*

- Communicate on a regular basis with each high-performing team member.

- Coach and encourage each high performer through weekly telephone appointments during which you give her solid action challenges; for example, help her focus on getting bookings.

- Create small *action groups* to teach women how to win national incentive awards by focusing on action steps and profit. Again, the 80/20 Rule predicts that 20 percent of your customers generate 80 percent of your revenues. Achieving the goal of a national incentive award promotes confidence and self-esteem.

- Create a daily *hot line* for women to phone in to hear a tip on developing their home-based business in addition to a positive, motivating message. Even though this valuable training is available to all team members, it's typically the 20 percent who use it.

Every team member needs self-discipline to run her own home-based business. My goal is to work closely with the high-performing 20 percent to help them make as much of the opportunity as possible. At the same time, I try to recognize the value of the 80 percent who, at any time, may catch the spirit and move into the 20 percent group.

As you use this principle, you'll find the rewards of helping women build their own successful business is your *own* biggest reward.

Today's Actions for Living by the Rules

- Decide whether *you* are a 20 percent worker or an 80 percent worker, and *make a conscious decision about which you want to be.*

- If you decide you're a 20 percent worker, get the attention you deserve from your upline.

- As you build your team, remember to *work* with the 20 percent and *offer* to the 80 percent. ▪

■ Transform Relationships through Coaching

By Linda Wiseman-Jones
Leading with Principle-Centered Coaching

CONNECTING PEOPLE WITH VISION

Have you ever felt that as a leader you always have to have the answers? Do you hold a vision of *your team members taking greater responsibility for their business and being more accountable?* If your answer is a resounding *Yes,* then you are like I was before I discovered the incredible freedom and empowerment that comes with learning the "right" way to coach my team.

Because most of us in the Direct Selling profession are self-motivated, optimistic, and somewhat driven people, we naturally carry with us the inclination to tell people what to do. After all, it is easier and faster and usually produces results. However, when we take the position that *we* have all the answers, whether indirectly or directly, we inadvertently take upon ourselves the responsibility for each team member's success or failure. Then when her business "doesn't work," whom does she blame? *Her leader!* That's the problem. Our goal therefore is to steer others to their own answers, prompting them to take responsibility for their reasons and choices, and building their businesses with a sense of ownership.

PASSING THE TORCH

The good news is that coaching is a set of learned skills. These skills increase our ability to communicate effectively with our team, inspire members beyond what they thought possible, and develop other leaders within our organizations to continue the dream. The skills enable us to develop relationships of mutual respect, trust, and integrity. Modeling ourselves to incorporate these skills, we empower our team members and give them ownership in the solution.

The next time a team member contacts you because she is frustrated in her efforts to get bookings or sales or to recruit leads, *pause* before you reply. Being the leader you are, you might be tempted to jump right in and tell her what she needs to do. That simple pause allows you to implement the Principle-Centered Coaching skills that increase your team member's confidence and self-esteem, and empowers her to take action.

As you *listen* with your heart to her situation, you will be able to *acknowledge* specific efforts and character qualities, and respond with open-ended *questions* that help her tap into her own answers.

For example, after she shares her struggles to get bookings at parties, you respond with an acknowledgment. In the past you might have given her a compliment: "You're awesome!" This time, you *acknowledge* her by saying, "Your desire to serve your customers is clear!" When you notice and highlight the specific strengths of her character, she understands that "I see you." In pointing out *who* your team members are as individuals, you help them see themselves as they truly are, which increases their confidence and self-esteem.

Resisting the urge to tell her what she needs to do, you can move into *open-ended questions*. These questions illustrate your confidence in her ability to solve her own problem. She will gain clarity and insight, and begin to shift to seeing herself as the expert. In this example you may ask her a few questions to help her come to a solution that works for her:

- "What would you do differently next time?"

- "How would you ask differently next time?"

- "If your guests have similar reactions at your next party, how will you respond differently?"

You'll be amazed at the freedom you'll feel and the wisdom that can come from the answers you receive. It won't always be easy to stop simply providing solutions. However, you will find that it becomes easier as you practice—especially when you observe what happens to your team!

As your team member solves her own problem, she gains confidence and ownership of the future action. Watch her professionalism, activity, and demeanor build as she practices and gains the positive results of her own solutions.

Your Action Plan

Can you see the difference between "telling" and "coaching?" Do you think your results and relationships might be different if you used coaching skills? It is a paradigm shift. I recommend that you start to make the transition by using these skills in the next 48 hours.

Begin with "I See You" Acknowledgments. Practice identifying at least two character traits in your team member that led to her achievement.

Next, practice the "You're the Expert" Questions. Resist the urge to tell her what to do. Instead, ask what *she* could do or how she could do it to change the results. ■

■ Shower the People You Love with Appreciation

By Donna Marie Serritella
Industry consultant, speaker, and author

APPRECIATION—WHAT'S YOUR PREFERENCE?

One of the most meaningful ways to deepen your relationship with others is to express your heartfelt appreciation for all they do. But how do we do that? Do we send a handwritten note, a bouquet of flowers, or a box of chocolates? The truth is that people's preference for the way they like to be appreciated is unique to them, and when we hit the mark, it has a lasting and significant effect. *There-fore, the art of knowing exactly what makes people* **feel appreciated** *is important to your ability to build lasting relationships.*

Knowing exactly what appreciation style someone values most creates a win for everyone. The receiver feels wonderful and the giver experiences the satisfaction of having made someone feel special. How do you practice the fine art of showing appreciation? You learn to discover a person's *appreciation language.* Appreciation falls primarily into three categories:

- *Auditory appreciation* is expressed by telling someone how much you appreciate her and describing specifically the impact her actions had on you personally. Some prefer this expression be done privately while others want it done in front of a crowd.

- *Visual appreciation* comes in the form of something tangible, such as flowers, a picture in a frame, or a note card.

- *Kinesthetic appreciation* is a hug, a pat on the back, or even a massage.

Showering someone in the wrong appreciation language can be as frustrating as speaking French to someone who speaks only English. It simply doesn't get the point across effectively and leaves both the giver and the receiver feeling misunderstood.

KNOW HER LANGUAGE

Because we tend to show appreciation in the manner in which we most like to receive it, make an appreciation language survey of each of your team members. Identifying someone's preference is as simple as asking! Inquire what makes her feel special or ask her to recall a time she felt totally appreciated. Then make a note of her style for future reference.

For example, my appreciation preference is visual. I love receiving flowers or a handwritten note or spending some quality time together—these make me feel tremendously appreciated. Perhaps you have a team member who prefers verbal recognition. Call her out of the blue one day to share something you truly appreciate about her. Still others may yearn for a pat on the back or a heartfelt hug to feel deeply appreciated.

Appreciative Action for This Week

Take time to notice the appreciation preference of your team members, family, and friends. Clues will surface if you just observe and listen to how they most often show appreciation to others. Notice their environment, ask questions, or ask people who are close to them. Take note, and the next time you want to shower that person with appreciation, speak her appreciation language—not yours! ▪

■ Open Your Heart to Coaching

By Jane Deuber, MBA
President and Cofounder of the DSWA

LEADING IN THE SPIRIT OF SERVICE

If you're a leader with a growing organization, you've probably been told that you should be coaching your team members. Perhaps you're wondering, "Be a coach? What does that mean and how can I expect to coach others when I'm just figuring it out for myself?" *The answer lies in something called Principle-Centered Coaching—a way of working with your team that opens your heart and expands your capacity to lead in the spirit of service.*

To Coach Is to Serve; to Serve Is to Succeed

The foundation of Principle-Centered Coaching is built on five core principles that present an image—a model if you will—of the kind of coach you want to be. Using the following five principles, you will cultivate a supportive, safe environment in which your team will flourish:

- **The Principle of Trust.** An environment of trust is defined by faith, confidence, and belief in your team—and to keep a confidence. Trust is the basis of meaningful, healthy relationships and must be present to create openness, learning, and growth.

- **The Principle of Respect.** When you show respect for another, you interact with dignity and kindness. You honor others no matter their accomplishments or perceived abilities. Giving and receiving respect builds self-esteem and confidence.

- **The Principle of Service.** When we serve others through our actions, we express the essence of leadership. By helping others get what they want, we experience the joy of making a difference.

- **The Principle of Integrity.** Do you do what you say you will do? Integrity is when our thoughts, words, and actions are the same and we follow through on our commitments.

- **The Principle of Authenticity.** An authentic leader is comfortable being herself and does not put on appearances. Strive to be natural, genuine, and honest in your dealings with your team.

RICH REWARDS

Once you weave these five principles into the fabric of your interactions, you will see shifts at many levels. Some are subtle, some obvious, but collectively they are transformational. Here is just a taste of what you can expect. You will:

- enjoy coaching your team so much more when you call to support rather than to fix;

- sense a deeper connection with your team as the members see your willingness to serve and support; and

- see your team grow as you see each new team member as a gift instead of more work and responsibility.

Your team members will:

- feel confident in their ability to build their business;

- be accountable to themselves and their goals;

- be true to their word because the team values integrity; and

- remain clear, focused, and on track toward success.

Ways to Explore the Five Core Principles

Beginning today, hold yourself to the standard of keeping the five core principles at heart in all team interactions. At day's end, review how you have lived these principles and then marvel at the magic that results. ■

Developing Leadership Skills

*T*his chapter is devoted to exploring what makes a leader in the Direct Selling profession. No matter how far up the ladder you climb, no matter how many award pins you display on your jacket or incentive trips you earn, your title does not make you a leader—*you do!* Within these pages you'll find many practical tips on topics such as handling tough conversations, motivating your team, and creating a proactive team culture. However, the essence of what you'll learn here isn't about the "doing" of leadership; it's all about the "being" of leadership.

Perhaps you are new to the business or have chosen not to build a team. You may be saying to yourself, "I can skip this chapter; it doesn't apply to me." May we suggest an alternative perspective, one that just might bring you greater results and fulfillment? Read the chapter anyway, and apply these concepts to other areas of your life. You might be surprised that leadership comes naturally to you.

A word of advice: As you read these insights, put yourself in the picture and avoid passing judgment on your upline, which blocks you from receiving the message each insight holds for you. Instead, take a good look at *yourself* to see what steps you can take to find the leader within.

■ Keep the Desire Alive

By Richard Flint

Moving people toward their dreams

RETAINING BEYOND EXCITEMENT

Building a direct-selling team is like filling a bathtub with water. If you don't have more water (or recruits) coming in than you have going out, the tub is never filled and the sales team never built. So when you're building your business, *keeping team members on board and active is at least as important as recruiting and probably even more so.* In fact, for most of the direct-selling leaders I've talked to, this is their number one challenge. After you work so hard to sign up a recruit and then invest time, energy, and resources in training her, she might become one of the many who leave. Why?

You might not realize that a recruit makes the decision to join your team because of *excitement.* Unless her excitement matures into *enthusiasm,* your new team member cannot become internally motivated. When she is merely excited, she has to "plug in" to you for energy; she has no internal motivation and might become an emotional welfare case. When her excitement matures into enthusiasm, she becomes self-motivated and begins to "own" her business.

Excitement is an externally driven emotion. Enthusiasm, on the other hand, originates internally. In fact, the word *enthusiasm* derives from the Greek for "inspired by a god" or "God within," indicating the power to create.

So how do you take your recruit's immature excitement and turn it into enthusiasm? Let me offer you some simple, yet challenging, practices.

SPARKING HER CREATIVE POWER

Set realistic expectations. I'm not just talking about hers; *your* expectations also must be realistic. After all, in the beginning your expectations *are* hers. If you paint a picture that isn't real, that is what she will work to achieve; the result: her emotional death from frustration.

Ask X-ray questions. You can't assume she knows why and what she's doing. Use *Why* and *What* questions to keep her focused. X-ray questions center on *thinking* and *problem solving* rather than on simply expressing emotions. Here are two examples of X-ray questions:

- ■ "What are your real expectations for your business?"

- ■ "Why do you think it is important to follow the networking process we have been talking about?"

Set a realistic pace! Excitement often prompts a recruit to move faster than she can manage. You must keep her moving at a challenging, but achievable, rate. If you don't, the result might be burnout or an emotional collision with herself.

Educate her. She might think she can "just do it." That thought will destroy her. You must become her leader as well as her teacher. Just sending her to training sessions is not enough. She needs to see *you* doing it!

Communicate with her. Too many times we recruit and abandon. Your presence in the beginning creates a big part of her excitement; if you disappear, you create a big part of her disappointment.

Take her by the hand. Leadership is about your *walking with her,* not her running with you. Don't do it for her, but guide her with patience.

Allow her to fail. If she doesn't fall down, she won't learn how to get up. So let her fall, but be there to help her get up.

Tap into her dream. Constantly connect her back to why she wanted to start her business. Fear will cloud her dream; when that happens, she will feel confused. Remind her of her dream to help dissipate fear.

Hold her accountable to implement what she has learned. She might go to training and never do anything with the information. Guide her into integrating new skills successfully.

Offer direction; don't direct her. When you offer direction, you are leading. When you direct her, you are doing it for her. Make her personally accountable.

Never make yourself responsible for her success. If you allow her to attach herself to you emotionally, she will never become independent. She must be responsible for her own success. When she feels ownership, the result will be *enthusiasm.* She'll be a self-motivated business partner and part of your team for the long haul.

Today's Actions for Increasing Retention

Identify any team members who are still driven by excitement rather than by enthusiasm. Choose one, and create a plan to spark her creative power and take ownership of her business. Set your own realistic pace for implementing your plan for her and for creating and implementing plans for any others you identified. ■

■ Prospect for Hispanic Gold

By Camilo Cruz, PhD
Empowering the Hispanic market for a prosperous future

TREASURES IN YOUR BACKYARD

As a direct seller, you've probably been told that you can build a business that expands all over the world. People get excited about the possibility of international expansion and call their teams to action by inquiring, "Who do you know from Mexico or Argentina?"

Although an exciting proposition, this vision of international expansion ignores the fact that the ***Hispanic market in the United States represents $600 billion in purchasing power by a population of more than 40 million people.*** In truth, the Hispanic market is a bountiful source of potential clients and distributors right here in our own backyard, not to mention a way to step off into the international market.

THE GATEWAY TO EXPANSION

Over the past 15 years of working with numerous direct-selling companies in the U.S. Hispanic market, Spain, and Latin America, I've come to understand what keeps distributors in the United States from paying due attention to the incredible potential that it represents.

The following five straightforward points will help you recognize this potential, eliminate false stereotypes you may have regarding other markets, and point you in the right direction to build a business that expands all over the Americas.

Expand the limits of your business. Most direct-selling companies operate in many Latin American markets. In fact, for many companies, sales and sponsorships in Hispanic markets domestically and abroad account for their greatest growth.

Plant the seed of globalization. Although most direct sellers know their business could go international, most never consider it because they don't know where to begin. "I don't know anyone in Argentina." "I don't speak the language." "I couldn't travel to all of those places."

Get to know your market. Okay, let's say your company decides to take the plunge and take your business global; what next? Despite a heavy accent or your lack of knowledge regarding their culture, customs, or language, keep in mind that other people's dreams, needs, and desires are probably the same as yours. We all want to improve the quality of our life, achieve financial security, and reach our goals. In fact, the desire to achieve these goals is probably what brought them to the United States in the first place.

Erase any preconceived notions about the market. Moreover, don't make the mistake of prejudging an entire market based on false stereotypes or limited experience. Remember that shortcomings are found in every culture, and most are individual based, not culture based. Nevertheless, the difference between building a great business and having an average business is what you focus on. Are you going to focus on people's strengths or their weaknesses?

Don't forget you're in a duplication business. Sometimes, in trying to attract new prospects, particularly trying to be sensitive to those from other cultures, we inadvertently deviate from company guidelines for building our businesses. Remember that those guidelines are there to help you build a big business. Make sure that you maintain and teach a system that can be duplicated. Keep it simple and make sure *anybody* can duplicate it.

Your First Shovelful

- Go back to your prospect list, add some Hispanic surnames to it, and commit to contacting them.

- Check your company brochures to find out which other countries are open to you. Remember, each year 300,000 new immigrants arrive in the United States from all over Latin America. You are bound to bump into someone from one of those markets.

- Encourage Hispanic team members to allow you to help sponsor foreign contacts *they* know. You can't imagine the number of times I've heard stories like this: "I sponsored my manager, who is from Mexico, and two years later I had an organization of 500 people in Guadalajara."

There are several good reasons to consider expanding your business into other markets. Sure, people are different. Sure, not everybody conducts his or her business the same way you do. It's true that distributors who build big organizations need to exemplify a true entrepreneurial spirit and dare to dream big. Some of them will just dream in a different language. ■

■ Talk Her Down off the Wall

By Debi Agee
Leading with compassion

LETTING CRISIS OPEN YOUR SOUL

The phone rings, and it's a recent recruit. "I can't do this anymore," she says. "Maybe I'm just not cut out for this business." When you hear this heartfelt cry, ***respond from your heart to rebuild her courage and confidence.*** At some point, nearly every member of my team has felt like this, considering nothing less than the destruction of her dreams. So my ability to "talk her down off the wall" has made a big difference in my success.

Before you can help your struggling recruit, you must be ready to share your soul with her, to be open and accepting of her feelings, and willing to share your own.

■ ***Listen with your heart—***What is she really saying? Is she afraid and unwilling to risk rejection? Has she suffered a recent discouragement? Has her personal life changed, causing her to question her commitment to her dreams? Know that her greatest need is simply to *feel heard.* It's like the old saying, "No one cares what you know until they know that you care." It's not your job to judge her feelings. Whatever they are, they're real to her. If she experiences your genuine compassion, she'll likely talk herself through the issues.

■ *Be vulnerable*—Leadership is not all about inspiring enthusiasm or being the cheerleader. Sometimes your recruit needs to see that you've faced fears too. By sharing your experience, you'll help her envision overcoming her own obstacles.

REBUILDING HER COURAGE WITH COMPASSION

After the recruit has let off enough steam, and you are confident she feels she's been heard, use these tools to help her reconnect to her potential and her dreams:

■ *Build her self-esteem*—Recognize that feelings of inadequacy are usually at the root of self-sabotaging behavior. Help her find some successes to build on. Remind her of what she's done right, if only believing in herself long enough to sign up. Offer to work with her through her struggles. Your willingness to assist is a tangible demonstration of the value you place on her.

■ *Help her reconnect with her Why*—What inspired her to join your business in the first place? Was it the hope of creating a better life? Was it a chance to leave her job and be more available for her kids? Or was it about getting out of the house and connecting with other people? Whatever her reason, it's probably still important to her.

■ *Rekindle her passion*—What does she really love about your business? Products? Get her to tell you about her favorite product experience. Financial freedom? Ask her what that means to her, and have her describe how it would feel to be free. Owning her own business? Have her explain why that's important to her.

■ *Support her choice*—Stepping back from the business now may be valid. Whether or not it seems reasonable to you, ultimately it's her choice. But remember that No often simply means Not Now. If you've done all you can and she still chooses to leave the business, bless and release her. Ask if you can stay in contact, and maybe send her inspirational messages from time to time. If she never comes back, at least you've treated her with respect and retained a friendship. If she does come back, she'll be more focused and dedicated than ever.

- ■ *Celebrate her success*—Whenever she has come "down off the wall," chances are she will embrace the business with renewed enthusiasm. One woman came to me, ready to quit because her sponsor had become inactive. I worked with her in the ways I've described above. For the last two years, she's been in the top 10 percent of our company. Watching her walk across the stage and collect her awards is one of my greatest joys! Anyone in your organization could end up being just like her.

Preparing for Crisis

Take these actions to build your ability to "talk her down from the wall":

- ■ Evaluate your feelings toward your team members. Can you open your heart to each of them?

- ■ Remember the obstacles you've faced that challenged your resolve, what you did to overcome them, and the results of your perseverance. Prepare yourself to share these stories when needed. ■

■ You Don't Have to Like It, You Just Have to Do It!

By Terra Larsen
Telling it like it is

WHEN DISCOMFORT BLOCKS YOU

In the course of building your business, are you ever required to tackle a task or project that challenges you to step out of your comfort zone or do something that quite frankly . . . scares you to death? Welcome to the world of entrepreneurship! The truth is that even though I have six years of experience in direct selling and have achieved nearly every top award my company offers, I still have those days when I'm faced with a task, a phone call, or a product presentation that makes my heart pound and tempts me to run for the hills. I figured out early on, however, that it was completing these very tasks—the ones that made me uncomfortable—that often had the biggest positive impact on my success. So what do I do when faced with a challenge? I call upon a phrase that has become my personal success slogan and helped me get through many unpleasant tasks. *"You don't have to like it, you just have to do it!"* It's short, sweet, and speaks the truth about achieving success.

I came upon this personal slogan one day while I was recalling an e-mail from a distributor about the fact that she didn't like making business phone calls. As I pondered her challenge, I remember thinking to myself, "Well, to be perfectly honest, business phone calls are not at the top of my list of likes either!" Then I wondered, "Why can I get them done while she and other direct sellers continue to put them off?" Into my head popped the phrase, *"You don't have to like it, you just have to do it!"*

Through the course of building your business, no matter what level of success you attain, you will be faced with tough tasks that need to be completed. Each new level of leadership brings with it new challenges and new tasks that test your courage and commitment. Herein lies the beauty of this profession—the fact that you can build a business, earn an income, and be transformed at the soul level all at the same time! These magic words, *"You don't have to like it, you just have to do it!"* can literally change your life!

COMING TO GRIPS

You may be thinking, "This is just too simple; how can these words really impact my business?" The answer lies in what's happening in your subconscious mind when you speak these words. It breaks the pattern of procrastination by stopping you from lamenting and over-thinking, which can keep you from getting to the task at hand.

Consider this: every day you probably do things for yourself that you don't particularly like. You may exercise, drink lots of water, clean your house, and the list goes on. Now, despite the fact that you don't particularly like these tasks, you do them without a lot of worry, stress, or procrastination. Why is that? You are focusing on the *outcome* rather than on the effort. You want to be healthy and understand that drinking eight glasses of water a day promotes good health. You enjoy a clean, orderly environment and know that picking up and cleaning regularly creates that environment.

Now let's relate that to your business. If you are like many direct sellers, you don't necessarily like to make phone calls for your business. However, you do like the bookings, orders, new recruits, contest prizes, trips, and money that result from making these calls! Am I right? The truth is that making customer calls is an absolute necessity if you want to enjoy all the wonderful things you love about your business. Finishing the hard tasks reduces stress and anxiety and gives you a feeling of satisfaction and pride that you are honoring your commitment to your dreams.

So the next time you feel like you just don't want to do the task at hand, borrow this success slogan and get the job done. *"You don't have to like it, you just have to do it!"* Imagine the endless positive outcomes that await you on the other side!

Today's Actions for Overcoming Blocks

List the tasks that challenge you along with the positive outcomes you expect as a result. Put *"You don't have to like it, you just have to do it!"* at the top of the page and hang it where you can see it when faced with a difficult task. ■

■ Plan for Success!

By Lorna Rasmussen
Leading with style and grace

EXPECTING ACHIEVEMENT

Successful people plan their success because they know that a failure to plan is a plan to fail. The fact is that I've yet to meet a person who has reached the top position in her company, or any pinnacle of success in her life, who didn't plan to be there. **More important than planning to succeed, however, is that these successful people expected to succeed.**

When I joined my first direct-selling company, I expected to reach the highest position, and I developed a strategy to do it. I expected success because I looked around and saw that other people with the same product and the same compensation plan were successful, so I knew it could be done. I also understood, and had the confidence to believe, that if others were capable of being successful in that company, then I was as well.

Many people approach life as though they have no control over outcomes. The opposite is true. You control your own destiny. When I learned that and internalized it, my life changed. Yours can as well. I am not talking about wishful thinking. I am talking about expectancy. To quote from Paul J. Meyer in his program *The Dynamics of Goal Setting* (Success Motivation® International, Inc.):

> Expectations held over a period of time, either consciously or subconsciously, affect attitudes—and attitudes affect actions. Expectations function relentlessly, whether you create them for yourself or someone else holds them for you.

WORKING YOUR PLAN

Planning is easier to do in direct selling than it is in most other ventures. For one thing, it is realistic to expect to reach high levels of income and achieve high levels of success. Also, the plan is often provided for us. We need only adapt it to ourselves, follow it, work hard, and apply a few simple success principles.

- **Develop confidence in you.** The formula: Confidence comes from know-how, know-how comes from experience, and experience comes from getting out there and doing it.

- **Develop a strategy to reach the top position.** This is where the planning comes in. Sit down with your sponsor or a trusted, successful leader in your company and ask her to help you put together a step-by-step, month-by-month plan to reach each level of your compensation plan. But don't feel that you need to know everything in detail. Ask your sponsor to provide you with the information you need on an as-needed basis. Get the big picture and a basic understanding, but don't become bogged down in the details.

- **Treat your business like a business.** Understand it and work it with attention to how you earn money. Take personal responsibility to grow in your understanding and to be in control of your business.

- **Expect to be successful.** Rather than wait and let what happens happen, develop an expectation of success and do everything in your power to make it a reality.

- **Use the "act-as-if" strategy,** whereby you *act as if* you are already a leader. You do this by first observing leaders in your company and then doing the things they do. Take every opportunity to act as a successful person would act. Ask yourself: How would a leader in my company approach someone? How would a leader in my company show up at a meeting? How would she dress? What time would she arrive? How would she greet people?

You may not be earning the income, but you can buy one professional outfit and attend the weekly briefings dressed professionally. You can show up on time, greet people with confidence and a smile, volunteer to support the local briefing, and work with your organization in a professional way—*as if* you were already a leader.

Starting Your Plan

- Set an appointment with a trusted, seasoned, successful person in your company to help you develop a plan of action.

- Imagine how a successful leader in your company would approach others, help others, and attend meetings. Prepare to behave as if you were that successful leader.

- Determine to follow the plan you develop to succeed.

- And believe that it will happen! ■

■ Hold Successful Crucial Conversations

By Ron McMillan

Getting results without losing relationships

IDENTIFYING CRUCIAL CONVERSATIONS

What determines whether you'll stay active in your business, whether you'll reach your true potential? There are many keys but one I know for sure: you have to be able to hold *Crucial Conversations*. *Crucial Conversations occur when three elements come together:*

1. High stakes

2. Opposing opinions

3. Strong emotions

As a direct-selling professional, you have these conversations every day! You run into objections from prospects, conflicts with a non-supportive spouse, resistance from a member of your team who isn't keeping commitments—the list goes on and on.

The sad truth is that when it matters most (as in Crucial Conversations), we tend to do our worst. The good news is that we can learn skills to help us do better—*even be highly effective*—during Crucial Conversations. These skills allow us to achieve the results we're looking for, *without compromising the relationships* that are the lifeblood of our business. Let's take just one common example: dealing with a sensitive issue with a team member.

Suppose you enrolled a new team member two weeks ago. You provided solid initial training and helped her make a list of her top ten prospects. You talked about each prospect and provided coaching so the best possible approach could be used with each prospect. Your new team member committed to you (and herself) that she would contact five prospects in the first week, call to let you know how things went, and get some additional coaching. The week came and went. No phone call. You called her, e-mailed, left messages. No response. The phone is ringing, and this time she's going to pick up. This is going to be a Crucial Conversation! What do you do?

STRUCTURING EFFECTIVE CRUCIAL CONVERSATIONS

- First, *before* you open your mouth, *check your motives*. Do this by asking yourself a simple question: "What do I *really* want?" Do I want to be right; to set her straight; to win? If so, you need to ask the question again—emphasizing what you *really* want. I hope what you really want is to help your new team member be successful and meet her goals, by giving her the coaching she needs. *With good motives, good communication is more likely to follow.*

- Next, *check your story*. What story are you telling yourself: "She must be lazy; this is why I have to enroll ten to get *one* good one." Notice how these statements make you feel. What kinds of emotions, and therefore behavior, will likely follow from these negative stories? The fact is, you don't really know why she didn't call until you ask, so why assume the worst? Ask yourself, "Why would a reasonable, rational person do this?" What if she's been sick, had a death in the family, or came up against unexpected objections? Master *your* story, and you'll master your emotions. Again, good communication is more likely to follow.

■ Okay—*now* you can open your mouth. When you do, *don't lead with an emotion:* "You've really upset me." *Don't lead with a story:* "I thought you were committed to success, but I can see this isn't all that important to you." This makes the other person feel unsafe and unwilling to share. You can't find out what's going on and do what you *really* want, which is to help! *Instead, just share the facts and ask for her input.* Compare what was expected with what was observed. It might sound something like this: "When we spoke last week, you said you'd contact five people about the business opportunity and give me a call. It's been a week, and I haven't heard from you. What's been happening?" This approach will create a nonthreatening environment and hopefully allow you to have a productive dialogue, so you can help your new team member be successful.

Beginning the Conversation

There are many more skills we could discuss and many more types of conversations to which they could be applied, but for now, practice the three you've just learned:

1. Get your motives right by asking yourself, "What do I *really* want?"

2. Master your story—and your emotions—by asking yourself, "Why would a reasonable, rational person do that?"

3. Begin the conversation by sharing the facts—*compare what was expected with what was observed, and ask for her input.* ■

■ Practice the Art of Listening

By Carol McCall, MA, MCC
Performance Coach and Communications Expert

THE GIFT OF YOUR ATTENTION

Communication is at the heart of making or breaking relationships. When you want to strengthen your relationships with every prospect, customer, and team member, *practice conversation as an art.* The art of listening is not only a familiar phrase; it is also a skill to be mastered.

The physical concept of "no two objects can occupy the same space at the same time" applies to listening as well. When you're listening effectively to a speaker, listening is the only thing you're doing at that time. You cannot effectively listen while mentally commenting on what is being said, interrupting, finishing sentences for the speaker, or doing anything else that is distracting. When these distractions occur, you "hear" only about 25 percent of what the speaker has said. The other 75 percent is masked by the distractions.

The art of listening requires that you give your undivided attention to the speaker and tune out the distractions. After many years of listening to thousands of people, I've found that what passes for listening is really just "hearing"—meaning that people only halfheartedly pay attention to what others are saying. This is illustrated by the exchange: "Are you listening to me?" followed by the response "Yes, I hear you." The question is actually asking if the listener understands the concepts. The response is often accurate. The listener heard the "noise" but perhaps not the message.

Although many communication techniques imply the practitioner is listening, the very word *technique* indicates there's a gimmick in such a communication. There are no techniques for effective listening. The art of listening requires not only that you give your complete attention to the speaker but that you also *speak* clearly to complete the communication process.

ELEMENTS OF LISTENING STYLE

Here are five fundamentals of good communication in the art of listening:

1. **Brevity:** summation, making the point concise and clear. Brevity provides you more time to listen because your ideas are shared in short bursts. Also, concisely stated ideas are generally easier to understand.

2. **Acknowledgment:** a style of speaking that verbally recognizes the listener's contribution. Encouraging your listener builds energy and the ability to sustain that energy throughout the process, project, meeting, or day.

3. **Boldness:** being authentic. Authenticity in the art of listening is being "true to the moment, the event, the circumstance, and life's conditions." Good communication requires boldness to speak responsibly with respect and honor. No one should ever have to wonder where you're "coming from." Boldness is not rudeness. It is speaking the truth so that the facts are on the table. It enables teams to take appropriate actions based on the facts. Boldness promotes team trust and strong relationships.

4. **Completion:** satisfaction for now. Completion means that you have received all the information you can for now.

5. **Nonlimiting language:** words that keep a conversation open and honest. Good communication requires that your words keep the interaction flowing. Words like "problem," "but," "wish," "perhaps," and "probably" limit communication because they limit possibilities. Replace them with "challenge," "and," "will," "do," and "don't." These alternatives keep ideas going and add fluidity to the conversation.

Effective listening is a gift, because it affirms to the speaker that she has ideas that you consider are worth your time. Economy and honesty of speech show your listener that you value her time and trust her enough to be honest with her. This is the way effective relationships are built.

Today's Action for Better Communication

Take on one of these fundamentals of good listening and practice it for the next 30 days. Experience the shift in effectiveness this will make in your communications and relationships! ■

■ Make Meetings Work Person to Person

By Linda Lucas
Training, learning, and celebrating others' success

VALUING THE HUMAN TOUCH

When I hear someone say "Live team meetings are a thing of the past—they just don't work anymore," I reply, "You obviously haven't been to the right meeting!" In fact, *meetings can be your number one tool for spreading recognition, delivering education, and fostering sisterhood among team members.*

Ours is a relationship business, not just between a distributor and her clients, but also among everyone on your team. Meetings not only save you time on individual phone calls and e-mail, they build your team's self-confidence, professionalism, and camaraderie, which keeps attrition low and enthusiasm high. Here's a blueprint for holding team meetings that make a difference.

A MEETING NO ONE WANTS TO MISS

Invite everyone: your personal team as well as those who don't have a local upline. Send invitations in advance that announce the theme of the meeting, build anticipation, and encourage everyone to bring guests.

I've found that by starting registration at 6:30 PM, my team has a half hour to network and enjoy the refreshments and displays before the meeting starts at 7:00. Keep the meeting to just 90 fast-moving minutes, so everyone can be heading home by 8:30. Here are a few guidelines for structuring your meeting:

- **The welcome** uses the theme to build anticipation and set the tone for an entertaining, informative evening. Include a get-acquainted exercise, such as a new game consultants can use at a party.

- **The sharing segment** gives members about ten minutes to offer quick tips, describe new ideas that have worked for them, and share recent triumphs. A little advance planning can keep this moving quickly: know who you are going to call on and make sure they're prepared.

- **Recognition** is the time to honor outstanding performance in the areas of sales and sponsoring. I've found I can give *everyone* a chance to shine by offering three levels of recognition: (1) *casual,* for those who have up to three parties a month; (2) *consistent,* for those with up to seven; and (3) *career,* for those who hold eight or more. This gives part-time builders a chance to be recognized for consistency and results.

- **Announcements** should be limited to *local* events, such as craft fairs or opportunities for public service. You can display information from the company newsletters or Web site on a poster or notice board for review before the meeting.

- **Testimonial time** builds belief by having a distributor or two share how they got involved with the business, and how their life is better for it. Again, identifying and coaching contributors beforehand keeps this segment on target.

- **Education** is the core of your meeting, so choose a topic that addresses the needs of the team and then weave in a theme that makes it fun. Put a leader and her team in the spotlight by asking her to prepare a 45-minute education segment. Encourage her to educate and inspire using a handout, an interactive activity, and your amusing theme. Even though you delegate, re-member it is still up to you to make sure the education is appropriate.

■ **Aha time** lets attendees share immediately the one thing they learned in the education segment that they can commit to put-ting into practice over the next two weeks.

■ **The challenge** motivates attendees to apply what they have learned by offering prizes for taking an education-related ac-tion over the next month. Choose a goal that 30 or 40 percent of your team can achieve, so everyone feels like a winner!

■ **Rewards** let you acknowledge those who met the challenge from last month, spoke during the sharing or testimonial seg-ment, or performed a good deed you want to recognize. Prizes can be inexpensive when presented with lots of praise!

Be available to talk to people after the meeting—your best oppor-tunity to build strong relationships. And when you get home, write a thank-you note to each guest and everyone who contributed.

Building Your Benefits from Meetings Today

Take the action that best fits your current level of success:

■ New to the business? Clear your schedule to attend team meetings and volunteer to help.

■ Building a team of your own? Set a date to hold your first team meeting.

■ Already holding meetings? Select two new ideas that you'll incorporate into your next meeting. ■

■ Walk Your Talk

By Lisa Wilber
Making millions while walking her talk

LIVING YOUR ADVICE

"I know I can do it, too, because I've seen you do it." Have you heard these words from your team? It doesn't matter if you just started in direct selling or if you have been in the profession for years and are very successful; you need to constantly be aware that your team members and your customers look to you to be an example. Your customers look to see if you use your company's products. Your team looks to see if you use the ideas you talk about or if you are just paying them lip service. *The validity of the things you say are borne out in the way you act.* If you don't use your own products or follow your own advice, then they must not be very good.

LEADING FROM THE FRONT

Make sure that you set the example of what you want your team to do and achieve. Are you in a party plan company and expect your team members to do three shows a week, but you are only doing one? Does your company sell shampoo, but your bathroom is filled with shampoo purchased at a salon or store? It *does* make a difference! "Do as I say, not as I do" doesn't work for children, and it doesn't work for customers or your team either. If you truly want to be financially independent in this industry, start today to change your habits and set a great example. You will probably not tell your team to do anything that will hurt their business, and what is good for their business will also be good for yours.

Here are a few suggestions:

■ Review your product line and inventory your house. What products that you sell are you not buying from yourself but from somewhere else?

- Collect all the noncompany products and donate them to your favorite shelter. Restock with your company's products.

- When you leave your house, make sure that your company affiliation is obvious. Wear a name badge and promotional button.

- Give company products as gifts for special events, holidays, and whenever possible.

Next, take a look at how you want your team to perform. Do you feel that six qualified recruits per month is a realistic goal for your team members to achieve? Did *you* recruit six qualified team members last month? Do you *routinely* find six qualified recruits every month?

Constantly review your actions and the results that you are getting. One of the best examples that you can set for your team is to always be growing and improving.

Watch for books, seminars, and organizations (like the DSWA!) where you can learn and grow. Start building your own lending library today. Read and listen to books, tape sets, and CDs about our business and profession and then loan them to your team members. Put into practice what you learn. There are so many topics that are relevant for our business: sales, management, bookkeeping, marketing, finance, networking, coaching, image, public relations, and customer service, to name a few. You need to believe with all your heart that the most important factor to your success is *you;* not your company, not your products, not even your team. Building yourself as an asset gives you the assurance that you can rebuild your success in another area, if necessary. This is true peace of mind.

Research your specific company and the direct-selling profession. The more knowledge you have about your company, product or service, and profession of choice, the more your customers will view you as an expert. The same is true of your team.

Living the Values

- Clean out competitor products from your home and replace them with your own products.

- Identify those basic activities of success in your business that you preach to your team, and make sure you are consistently doing them, no matter what stage your business is in.

Model the behavior you want your team members to duplicate. As you climb the ladder of success, *make setting a good example the activity that never goes out of style.* ∎

■ Build a Business, Not an Orphanage

By Richard Flint
Moving people toward their dreams

AN INDIVIDUAL RESPONSIBILITY

Have you ever felt that the majority of your team members expect *you* to make *them* successful? Or that *you* are somehow liable for what they do or don't do to build the business? Or perhaps you've felt guilty when, despite your best efforts, a team member stumbles, fails, or quits. The truth is you are not alone. The truth is that you honestly can't control very much outside your own skin, and **your team members are responsible for their own success or failure.** Sadly, the truth is also that you may well have set yourself up to have your organization depend too much on you.

Many leaders inadvertently mistake the building of a business for the running of an orphanage. In other words, these leaders are filling their teams with people who depend on *them* to build *their* businesses instead of filling their teams with people who are self-motivated and self-directing.

The reasons for these leaders attracting dependent people cover a whole range of concepts. The reasons don't really matter; the results do. The good news is you can repair the situation by making some important changes in the way you view and lead your team.

WEANING THE DEPENDENTS

Many leaders recruit people and then try to *make them successful*—an impossible and frustrating task. The result is that you build an orphanage of resentful people rather than a team of effective business partners. What makes the difference? Personal responsibility—both theirs and yours. As a leader, you have the responsibility to *lead*, not to participate in mass confusion. Your role is to create an environment in which those who want to succeed have the tools to do it. To become the leader who brings leadership to your team, you must:

- **Listen to people's behavior as well as to their words.** The true essence of any person is revealed through her behavior, not her words. Hear what people *say*, but *study what they do.*

- **Detach from the outcome.** What your team member does with her business is out of the realm of your control. Certainly you can guide and coach her on her journey, but whether she arrives at the destination is up to her.

- **Empower yourself with leadership skills and experience.** In truth, you can't lead another person past the point where you are. Neither can you lead another unless you have the credibility and skills to do so. The truth is that most people respect the scar tissue of a veteran more than paper on an "I love me" wall.

- **Always speak the truth.** You can't help people by playing games. You *cannot* care about being liked; you must *always be honest* with what is or is not.

- **Develop people; don't drag those who don't want to grow.** This is so important. You spend too much time begging people to "do it" rather than cutting them lose and working with those who are committed to experiencing their dream.

- **Emotionally, don't cross the line.** You offer people an opportunity to live their dream; you are not adopting them. If you adopt them, you have crossed the line; if you adopt them, they will make *you* the reason *they didn't.* The line is drawn; this is a business, not an orphanage.

- **Recruit people who emotionally like your story and mentally want to know more.** Does it make sense when I say you are a storyteller? Recruiting is about telling your story and finding those who are emotionally ready to listen and mentally ready to take the risk to live life larger than they are presently.

Building your business is not about finding *lots* of people; it is about recruiting the *right* people who are inspired by your success story and want to write their own.

Today's Actions for Ending Dependence

- Accept that you cannot be responsible for anyone else's success.

- Review your presentations to potential team members and avoid any intimation that you will do anything for a team member beyond training her and modeling success for her.

- If you have a team member who is dependent on you, have a candid, truthful conversation with her to determine if you have met your obligation of training her. If you have, give her a recipe for success and invite her to call you when she has implemented your training and wants more. ▪

■ Become the Leader You Would Follow

By Nicki Keohohou
CEO and Cofounder of the DSWA

SHARING THE LIGHT WITHIN

Leadership is more than a title. It has less to do with what you say than with who you are—the core of your *self* that shines through in all you do and say. The character and values of a leader shine through brighter than what she does or says. A great leader has integrity; she is congruent in her words and actions, is honest, compassionate, trustworthy, and authentic. ***To be the leader others wish to become, you must become the leader that* you *would follow.***

Following are a few simple concepts to keep in mind as you summon the leader that is already within you.

A Leader Knows—It's All about the People!

Be focused on the people you serve and what they desire. Do less telling and more asking. Learn to listen more and support rather than tell and give the answers. And remember, *you lead from the front.*

A Leader Inspires Trust

One of the greatest honors in this profession is the privilege to share in the goals and dreams of our team members. By leading others through actions as well as words, you earn your team members' trust and inspire them to build their business and develop their skills. This trust you earn is sacred and must be honored at all times.

A Leader Offers Hope and Inspiration

When you decide to be a leader who makes a positive and significant difference in the lives of many, you will see a transformational shift in your own life as well. Begin today to offer hope to those who have lost faith; offer encouragement to those who are fearful; and inspire others by helping them discover their brilliance.

A Leader Helps Devise a Plan for Success

At the beginning of every journey, you must decide where you are going and how you will get there. Leaders teach the art of goal setting and help their team devise daily, weekly, monthly, and annual action plans to help each member achieve her dreams.

When you live the life of a true leader, you will not only reap the financial rewards of greater personal success, but you will also see how your actions create a profound response that empowers the people around you.

THE RESPONSIBILITIES OF A LEADER

A thriving leader is one who takes responsibility seriously yet enjoys the process. Your team counts on you for words of wisdom, coaching, support, motivation, and so much more. The team looks to you to lead by example.

These are some of the responsibilities of a leader:

- Maintaining a positive mental attitude

- Demonstrating a good work ethic—personally selling and holding shows, interviews, and meetings

- Training your team on success principles and skills to develop their business and personal life

- Supporting your team through Principle-Centered Coaching

- Attending all company events—leadership training, conventions, and conference calls

- Maintaining balance in your life so that you can be a positive example for others

- Empowering your team rather than creating dependency

True leaders can help develop strong, successful individuals and teams, as well as a company culture that reflects integrity, character, quality, and excellence—one that is God-directed and a blessing to our families, communities, and each other.

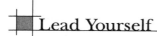 Lead Yourself

Take these three steps to become more of the leader you may want to be:

1. Start a journal and write in it the leadership qualities and skills that you currently possess and recognize in yourself. Take the time to think about those that others see in you that sometimes you don't acknowledge, such as inspirational, compassionate, giving, good communicator, enthusiastic, teachable, ability to instill confidence in others, and supportive.

2. Next, write the leadership qualities that you are committed to developing in yourself. Include as many areas as possible that you wish to improve. This is not an opportunity to beat yourself up—it is a chance to focus on your strategy for future success.

3. Finally, write a list of the people currently on your team whom you will commit to coaching over the next year. Note how many additional team members you will personally coach as your organization grows. Remember, this is *coaching,* not managing! Managing people can create dependency on you. Coaching ensures people are empowered and know how to create their success with or without you. ■

7

Managing Business Finances

Y ou know that *managing* the money side of your business is vital to your success. You might have heard that you could save between $3,000 and $9,000 in taxes each year just by managing your business finances and maximizing your home-business deductions, but you just can't seem to find the time.

In this chapter we give you a glimpse at how some of the most prosperous direct-selling leaders think about and manage their money. You'll learn from those who've made millions how to get control of your money and keep control of it, so you can reach your financial goals, whatever they might be. And if you are among those who think you can't afford the time to take care of your money—the truth is you can't afford not to! Read this chapter and find the peace of mind that can come only from knowing that, once and for all, you are taking care of your finances.

■ Get On the Fast Track to Freedom

By Teresa Romain
Teaching others to access abundance

FUELING UP FOR FREEDOM

I'll bet that *freedom*—especially *financial freedom*—is something you, as a direct seller, value highly. If so, then **eliminating debt is one of the greatest gifts you can give yourself on the road to financial freedom.**

Far too often, direct sellers think that the fast track to freedom requires them to do more and have *more:* more phone calls; more sales; more money; a bigger team; a bigger home; more clothes or vacations; a faster or fancier car; more time. What you may not realize is that your emphasis on *more, bigger,* and *faster* could be detouring you *away* from freedom!

WILL YOU WIN, PLACE, OR SHOW?

Being on the fast track to freedom is really a function of how much money you *keep*—not how much you *make.*

Imagine this scenario. You're driving a Porsche down the road and run over an object that punctures one of your tires. You don't have time to change the tire, so you get out and start pumping air into it. When nothing happens, you pump faster. Nothing changes. No matter how hard, fast, or long you pump air, your fast and powerful sports car won't take you anywhere—until you fix the hole.

Like the Porsche, your business is a fast and powerful vehicle that could transport you to greater levels of freedom and abundance. However, if your business has the flat tire of debt, it won't matter how hard, fast, or long you work. Until you fix the debt hole, your progress toward financial freedom will be slowed or completely stopped—just the way the flat tire stopped the Porsche.

In truth, the fast track to freedom (especially financial) is not a function of *more*—it's a function of *less.* When you have *fewer* expenses and *less* debt (or no debt), you will have more *money, time,* and *freedom.* Consider this example:

John is a direct seller making $5,000 a month. At the same time, he has a monthly mortgage and car and credit card payments totaling $3,000. Beth is another direct seller. She's making $3,000 each month and has no debt. Who is experiencing the most *freedom?*

Now consider this:

Did you know that if you had a $150,000 30-year mortgage and $23,500 in other debt, you could be completely debt-free in seven years with $1,000 in additional income from your business? Then, in the time it would have taken to pay your mortgage, you could create investments exceeding $2 million! Once you fix the hole in your financial tire, you can pump it up quickly and get going on the fast track to freedom!

Revving Up Today and Tomorrow

■ Review your financial picture and become clear about your *income,* your *expenses,* and your current *debt.* It is impossible to get where you want to go if you don't know your starting point. In the process, remember the following:

IAMNOWHERE

Notice that it says either "I am nowhere" or "I am now here," depending on how you see it. Instead of judging where you are today (I am nowhere), let go of your judgment (I am now here) and determine your next step.

■ If you're leaking money, then start repairing your financial hole. *Simplify* your business and lifestyle. Reduce your expenses—temporarily.

■ As you reduce expenses, instead of feeling restricted, remind yourself it's really a fast track to *financial freedom.* Creatively build your business so you can make more money with less expense.

Artist Magaly Rodriquez writes: "Creativity is not being able to use every color in the spectrum. It's about having only two and making miracles with them. Art is discovered by restrictions. Use restrictions as an impulse to creativity."

You, too, can use restrictions—as an impulse to creativity and freedom! ■

■ Get Control of Your Business Finances

By Jeff Shafe
Demystifying business software to improve profits

RECORDKEEPING STREAMLINED

Ever wonder how you're *really doing* in your direct-selling business? How much are you making? How much are you spending? If you're like most direct sellers, you pile up receipts all year and then drop the stack on either your accountant or your spouse at tax time—which can cost you either cash or goodwill.

The good news is that it doesn't have to be that way. *The right business management software program makes it easy to keep up with your recordkeeping and reduces the task of tax preparation to a simple click of your mouse.* You'll feel more in control, encounter less family stress, and have a greater understanding of your business once you've put your system in place.

Good recordkeeping also helps legitimize your deductions in the eyes of the IRS. This is especially important if your business is not yet profitable, because a hobby classification can result in a disallowance of all of your claimed business expenses.

So what features should you look for in your business management software? First and foremost, you'll want to make sure you pick a program that's specifically designed for direct selling, which is very different from running the corner grocery store. Bills for materials and payrolls aren't important aspects of your business, but promotional samples and product trades are. A generic program can leave you sifting through features you don't need and wishing for features you really want.

Second, look for a program that's easy to use. Finding one that's pre-loaded with your company's products and business specifics can save hours of setup time and helps ensure that the program will work well for your business. You'll also want to make sure your system has tax-ready reporting that pulls all of the pieces together for you at tax time.

Third, look for a program where you're able to easily use the financial

> **Y**ou'll want to make sure you pick a program that's specifically designed for direct selling.

information you enter to help build your business. Financial record-keeping is something of a necessary evil, but it gets a lot more exciting when that information becomes the basis for new customers or repeat orders. Being able to automate customer follow-up and identify clients based on their previous product preferences saves a lot of time and helps build long-term relationships.

Making the transition to software-based business management doesn't have to be difficult. Like any new system, you'll want to spend a few hours getting familiar with it and rethinking how you handle things. But once you're up and running and letting your computer do the math, you'll wonder how you ever got along without it.

Today's Actions for Automating Your Recordkeeping

Visit the DSWA Store at http://www.mydswa.org to check out the latest offerings in business software especially designed for direct sellers. ■

■ Get Ready to Come Home

By Barb Pitcock
A Powerhouse of Prosperity

SAFEGUARDING YOUR SECURITY

So you want to quit your job and focus 100 percent of your time on your direct-selling business? Yes, the American dream of coming home is certainly in the hearts and minds of many direct sellers today. Happily, over the past ten years I have had the privilege of seeing many people achieve that dream and move successfully to working their businesses full-time from home. Sadly, I have also witnessed many people who, in their haste to enjoy a better lifestyle, **make the fatal mistake of going full-time too soon, only to experience financial setback and disappointment.**

Having successfully navigated the path from employee to full-time business builder, I'd like to share some of the valuable lessons I learned along the way so that you can become one of the success stories others aspire to emulate.

THE RIGHT REASONS AND THE RIGHT WAY

Your decision to go full-time *must* be based on your commitments and financial desires and not done out of spite. Even though it's natural to want to vindicate yourself to those who refused the opportunity or predicted your demise, that cannot be your motivation. Or perhaps you believe that others will join you once they see you quit your job and enjoy financial freedom. In my experience, they usually don't care. Those who do notice may explain it away by saying "You just got lucky" or "It was a fluke." No, your *real* motivation needs to come from inside—a deep-rooted desire to build a better life for yourself and your family.

Work Ethic

Avoid the common misconception that if you have twice the time, you will double your results. I have watched people who sponsored like crazy while they were busy but who stopped dead in their tracks once they came home to work. With too much time on your hands, it's not uncommon to experience a productivity slump until you develop the discipline to work on your business every day.

Reduce Financial Pressures

If you are under financial pressure during your transition to working full-time, you will not be at your best mentally, emotionally, or physically. Take the following five steps to make a smooth transition for long-term success:

1. Find out exactly how much money you need to live comfortably each month. Be sure to consider hidden expenses that you pay quarterly, semiannually, and annually.

2. Build up your savings so that they can support you for six months to a year in the event of an emergency.

3. Pay off your credit cards before going full-time. You don't want the added stress of monthly payments and exorbitant interest rates.

4. Reduce your spending. There will be a time to enjoy fancy dinners, exotic vacations, and impressive toys but not during your transition to full-time business builder.

5. Set a goal to replace your job income with your direct-selling commissions, overrides, and bonuses *before* you take the leap.

If you are used to being an employee, the transition from job to home is one that requires some emotional adjustments as well. You no longer have an employer who is obligated to take care of you. You'll need to take your business seriously and commit to learning everything you can about the business. As you hone your skills, engage the support of an upline leader who has successfully transitioned to being a full-time business builder. Be relentless about building a solid base of distributors and customers so that you can weather occasional setbacks. And, finally, spend a week of vacation working from home to see if it is all that you expected. Find out if you like having *you* as a boss.

Financial Power Gives You Prospecting Power

Perhaps the most important reason you want to approach your transition to full-time wisely is that it will give you the peace of mind and confidence *to prospect with power.* Just imagine the satisfaction of saying to a prospect, "I am offering you the chance of a lifetime to create a lifestyle you have only dreamed of," and know in your heart that you are a living example of the lifestyle this business can provide.

Actions for Transition Planning

- Seriously discuss this aspect of going full-time with your spouse and come to an agreement. This is no time for a house divided.

- When you decide to go full-time, create a complete transition plan and manage the change with confidence! ■

■ Go Ahead—File Your Taxes!

By Vicky Collins, CPA
Member of the DSWA Prosperity Center Panel

PROCRASTINATION REPELS PROSPERITY

Whenever Jennifer went to the mailbox, she feared she would find an IRS letter asking for her back tax returns. Jennifer, a direct seller for 15 years, had a dark, 10-year-old secret. Overwhelmed, she had stopped filing tax returns and even managed to hide this from her husband. The couple moved a lot for his work, but Jennifer knew it was just a matter of time before the IRS found her. She feared owing thousands of dollars in taxes and feared her husband would leave her in anger if he found out. She knew she was in a mess, but she just couldn't figure out how to make things right. This bright, attractive woman, a company leader with an active and growing team, carried a secret burden that drained her energy and enthusiasm.

Luckily, a light went on for Jennifer during a tax-training workshop I conduct for direct sellers. She called me shortly after the meeting. Sobbing, she shared her dilemma and asked for my help. She was scared yet relieved to finally have confessed her dark secret. I told her she would be okay—that we could fix her situation *if she committed to a game plan.*

Over the next two months, Jennifer found all the records she could. It wasn't perfect. Because of elapsed time, many deductions were just "gone." We focused on working with what we had. We decided to prepare all the returns before telling her husband or the IRS.

As it turned out, all Jennifer's stress about owing money to the IRS was wasted energy. Each return showed overpayments of taxes ranging from $500 to $5,500. Sadly, her procrastination caused her to lose the majority of her refunds. Jennifer's husband, upset initially, calmed down and realized that he could have been more supportive and paid more attention.

The surprise benefit was the effect on Jennifer's business. In each of the three months after she filed her delinquent tax returns, Jennifer's sales *doubled.* Restored to financial integrity, she did business with renewed confidence, attracting and recruiting new team members.

> *Jennifer, a leader in her company with an active and growing team, carried a secret burden that was draining her energy and her enthusiasm.*

Restore Your Integrity Today

Are you among the direct sellers who ignore taxes? Have you missed filing with the IRS? Perhaps you simply haven't watched your finances as you should. That's okay! Here are the three steps you can take to make it right:

1. **Give it up.** Guilt or shame drain you and your business. Let go of the guilt and take action.

2. **Get help.** Find an accountant who specializes in home-based business accounting to maximize legitimate deductions and offset any fines you may owe. Visit the DSWA Accountant Referral Network at http://www.mydswa.org for referrals.

3. **Start fresh.** Once you have remedied the situation, develop the habit of taking care of your finances on a weekly, monthly, and annual basis. ■

■ Attend to the Business Side of Business

By Vicky Collins, CPA
Member of the DSWA Prosperity Center Panel

FINDING BALANCE AND CONFIDENCE

When you're so busy doing business that your financial picture becomes hazy, it's time to *develop a sound, streamlined financial routine.* While training thousands of women in home-based business finances and taxes, I've seen that following a routine gives them the confidence they need to take control of their money.

Knowing that you're in control of your business finances has a powerfully positive impact on your financial destiny and your attitude. In fact, 100 percent of top leaders interviewed agree that paying attention to business finances has been critical to their success. These leaders don't spend hours poring over financial statements and frittering away valuable selling time. Instead, they have developed sound financial habits that keep them in control of their financial affairs.

DEVELOPING SENSIBLE HABITS

Are you ready to take control of your business finances once and for all? If you answered Yes, here are the eight crucial steps:

1. **Get organized.** Business doesn't thrive in a cluttered environment. Being organized is a *process,* not a point. So plan days in your month to keep everything together.

2. **Prepare a simple business plan.** A plan helps you stay on track and serves as documentation to the IRS of your intention to make a profit in your business.

3. **Get a filing system that is easy for you to understand.** It doesn't have to be pretty, and it doesn't have to be complicated. It just needs to work for you.

4. **Keep up with automobile expenses.** Keep a log in your car so that you can easily record all the business miles you're driving. Keep an expense pouch handy as well. Put all your gas receipts and other receipts in the pouch, so you don't forget any more expenses.

5. **Commit to learning about taxes and how to reduce your tax bill.** Find a tax preparer with knowledge of home-business tax law. This could save you thousands of dollars every year. Visit the DSWA Accountant Referral Network at http://www.mydswa.org for referrals.

6. **Reconcile your bank accounts.** Banks do occasionally make mistakes and so do you. Protect yourself from unwanted bank charges and even possible identity theft by reconciling your accounts every month.

7. **Invest in your future.** Contribute monthly to your retirement accounts. Direct sellers have great retirement-funding options. With the help of a financial advisor or accountant, you'll find that certain accounts allow you to contribute up to 25 percent of your earnings to tax-deductible retirement accounts.

8. **Prepare monthly financial statements.** Even though this step can be intimidating, the results are worth it. Industry-specific financial software like *MLM Easy Money* can simplify the process and at the same time give you access to a wealth of additional tools to help run your business more efficiently.

   - The Income (Profit and Loss) Statement tells you how much you're earning (income) and where you're spending money (expenses), so you can take advantage of tax-planning opportunities, make better financial decisions, and run a more profitable business.

   - The Balance Sheet shows you what you own and what you owe with regard to your business. For example, if what you owe on your credit cards exceeds the value of inventory or samples you own, you'll know you are funding your business through debt and can then develop a plan to get those balances paid down.

Take Control Today

Paying attention to the business side of business doesn't have to be time consuming or boring. Commit to doing these things for 90 days—you'll see great changes! Nothing feels better than being in control of your financial destiny. ■

■ The Seven Money Skills of Extremely Prosperous People

By Mark Victor Hansen and Robert G. Allen
Creating a million millionaires in a decade

MAKING THEM YOURS

Why do some people earn ten times more money in their lifetime than do the rest of us? Do they work ten times harder? Are they ten times smarter? Of course not. The bottom line is that wealthy people are good at the seven following money skills that anyone can learn:

Money Skill #1—Value

Wealthy people value each dollar bill as a money seed. Just as a tiny acorn contains the power to grow into a mighty oak tree, each dollar has the power to grow into a mighty money tree. If you destroy an acorn, the oak tree inside also dies. So, too, with a money seed. Wealthy people know that a dollar a day can grow into a million dollars. So they are very respectful of every dollar they spend.

Money Skill #2—Control

They control their money down to the penny. Prosperous people take a few extra steps every time they spend money: (1) They shop for the best value; (2) they ask for and expect a discount; (3) they examine their receipt for mistakes; (4) they attempt to turn each expenditure into a legitimate tax-deductible business expense; (5) they balance their checkbook to the penny; and (6) they file their receipts on returning to their home or office. These activities take only an extra minute of time but build long-term financial peace of mind.

Money Skill #3—Save

Wealthy people love to save money by spending wisely. But they don't stop there. They save at least 10 percent of what they earn.

> **W**ealthy people know that a dollar a day can grow into a million dollars. So they are very respectful of every dollar they spend.

Money Skill #4—Invest

Wealthy people have a system for investing their money. Imagine a series of buckets into which money is siphoned from your main bank account. The first bucket is your emergency bucket. Let your 10 percent savings flow there first until you have at least three months of living expenses saved in an insured bank account. Once this first bucket is filled up, the stream of 10 percent overflows into one of three additional buckets: conservative investments, moderately aggressive investments, and very aggressive investments. Contact a reputable investment advisor to help you put your savings into these three types of mutual funds. The money should be automatically deducted from your bank account so you never forget.

Money Skill #5—Earn

Wealthy people are developing Multiple Streams of Income (MSI) outside their job. Your direct-selling business is one example of a stream of income that provides immediate as well as long-term, residual income. But don't stop there! Seek out information on diversifying your income portfolio by developing additional streams of income outside your primary income source, such as real estate investments, stocks, Internet income, or infopreneuring. The possibilities are endless. (Two recommended resources for learning about this money skill are *Multiple Streams of Income* by Robert Allen and

The One Minute Millionaire–The Enlightened Way to Wealth by Mark Victor Hansen and Robert G. Allen.)

Money Skill #6—Shield

The wealthy protect themselves with trusts, corporations, limited partnerships, LLCs, and other legal entities. In truth, you don't want to be a millionaire. You want to live like a millionaire but have very few assets in your own name.

Money Skill #7—Share

The wealthy are generous, donating at least 10 percent of their income. The secret is that money multiplies faster when it's divided. When you share freely, you prime the pump of the universe. We encourage you to establish a legacy that will outlive you. Plant money trees from which others will harvest the fruit. This is true prosperity.

Action Steps to Prosperity

- Take a look at the way you spend money by reviewing your check register and credit card statements. What two new spending behaviors are you committed to putting into practice immediately?

- If you have not established your emergency fund of three months income, arrange to have a specific amount deducted from your checking account each month and automatically deposited into a secure investment account.

- Get out your checkbook and write a check to a charitable cause that is near to your heart. If the money is not there today, date it for one week from today. The act of writing this check will begin to attract new opportunities that will enable you to honor your promise. ■

■ Seize the World

By Mary Lou Wilson
Building beyond our borders

LOOKING OUT TO THE HORIZON

The world is your oyster. Have you ever dreamed of going international? Maybe your company has opened up a new country and you would like to be involved in the next expansion. *Are you cut out for that kind of commitment—going international—both in time and money?*

Taking your business overseas will stretch you beyond your limits, scare you to death, work you harder than you have ever worked before, and cost you financially and physically. Did I mention it can be very difficult? As a result of following my passion, I assisted my company in opening up Japan and built an organization there of 400,000 distributors.

EYES WIDE OPEN

Opening distribution in a foreign country is definitely exciting and occasionally even glamorous! But along the way, I encountered many unexpected and hidden challenges. I want to expose them here so you can make an informed decision whether to pursue the opportunity. I suggest you consider these guidelines:

- Before you begin, build a strong base in the United States—a base so strong that it generates all the income you will need to expand.

- Don't assume that your company has done its due diligence to take care of the legal aspects regarding product registration, licensing, and so on. Get verification that these matters have been taken care of before you begin.

- As a leader, you must educate yourself about the laws pertaining to import, duty, and taxes. You can't rely on your company to educate you. Building an organization is *your* job, not the company's. Research the demographics and cultural perceptions.

- Discover if anyone else in your company is doing what you are attempting to do. Share resources.

If you are ready to proceed, ensure your success by expanding your vision. Take your passion for helping others and apply it to the individuals you will be serving in this new country. You must be passionate about your product, the opportunity, and people!

REALITY BITES

Expanding into a new area requires money. By the time your company is ready to launch into a new country, it has already invested millions of dollars. Consider what you, personally, are able and willing to invest in building your new organization. Here are some reality checks:

- Expect to visit frequently. Your expenses include airfares, hotels, meals, and dry cleaning.

- Expect it to take time. You will build a business by building relationships. It took me two years to develop a solid product following in Japan.

- Expect to learn a little of the language. It shows respect for the people.

- You will work with interpreters, so expect to compensate them. You may be able to offer them a position with your new organization in exchange for their time.

- Expect to work with international tax consultants, attorneys, and your company's policies for expansion.

- Expect to pay shipping and duty charges. Consider how they will affect your bottom line.

If you are still thinking of expanding your horizons, look for someone in your company familiar with the heritage and culture of the country into which you are expanding. Keep in mind your initial efforts should be focused on creating product loyalty rather than on immediately building a team. Be prepared to be honest with your new customers. Most cultures won't tolerate stretching the truth.

As they start using your products and find they work, your customers will want more. Find a local citizen who can assist you with such details as import laws. You may set them up as a U.S. distributor. Investigate the "not for resale" plan in the country so your new customers can call, fax, or e-mail the United States for their product orders. Let your customers and team members see you working right alongside them as they spread the word. Be available to support their new business.

Today's Actions for Spreading Your Wings

If this type of expansion intrigues you, within 48 hours:

- Investigate your company's expansion policy and plans.

- Evaluate your budget. Are you able to invest both physically and financially in consistent travel to a new area to build clientele, reputation, and exposure? ■

8

Integrating Home and Business

*T*ruly one of the greatest gifts of being a home-based entrepreneur is that, with everything under one roof, we can juggle our business and home life with a little more ease. No hectic commute, no office politics, no rigid schedule, and, if we are lucky, no day care for our precious children. As a home-based entrepreneur, you can process an order, coach a team member, and do a load of laundry all within an hour from the comfort of your home office. It's something millions of working women yearn for every day.

Working from home, however, is not without its challenges. It requires that you set boundaries, establish a schedule, and take time for the things that are important to you. To provide you with some solutions, we turned to some experts who have extensive experience in this area. Not only have these individuals achieved an impressive degree of success, they've all done it right from their home, and they impart to you some of their secrets to success.

■ Work from Home for Your Kids' Sake

C. J. Eisler
Son of direct-selling leader Shan Eisler

WHAT I LEARNED FROM MY DIRECT-SELLING MOM

I'll be the first person to admit that I had a privileged childhood. No, I wasn't born with a silver spoon in my mouth, nor was everything handed to me on a golden platter. Quite the contrary, there were times early on when my parents were unemployed and struggling to make ends meet. The privileges I am speaking of are far more intangible than any type of common luxury. I was privileged to grow up in a home with a mom who was in direct selling. Why was this such a privilege? First and foremost, it allowed my mom to stay at home to raise both my sister and me. There was comfort in knowing that I didn't have to come home from school to an empty house, and that there was always someone at home to take care of me if I were ever sick. Beyond that, the benefit of having a parent at home to supervise me certainly kept me out of some of the trouble that I watched a few of my friends get into and helped keep me a "good kid."

There were other benefits too, although I didn't realize them until I grew older. I learned how to work. Although I have never had what some would call a "real job," I have certainly developed a work ethic from watching and participating in my mom's business. I've hauled crates, stuffed envelopes, and stamped catalogs—and I've learned the value of hard work. I never had an allowance when I was a kid. I was an employee for my parents, and I was paid according to the work I did.

I learned how to set goals. My mom always had a definitive set of long-term and short-term goals, and I learned the value of knowing where you're going and what you want to do. Now that I'm older and starting life on my own, I know how to plan for my future. I was privileged to learn this skill at a young age, because now I don't have to learn it when I need it the most.

The privileges that I've had may not seem like much to the everyday person, but trust me when I say that there is no greater privilege than having parents who care. My mom cared enough about me and my sister to develop a business that could be run out of the house and, in doing so, helped make me into the person I am today.

You might ask, with all the benefits that come with a situation like this, why more women don't become involved with direct selling. I've asked myself the same question for the 12 years that my mom has been involved in her business. The number one excuse that I hear for not starting a business involves children and the lack of the time that can be spent with them when you're working. To everyone who thinks that becoming involved in direct selling will hurt their relationship with their kids, I would ask that they reconsider. My mom's business created more opportunities for our family, and those opportunities have helped shape me into a high-achieving, highly motivated person.

> **T**o everyone who thinks that becoming involved in direct selling will hurt their relationship with their kids, I would ask that they reconsider.

I won't say that life was always easy, but I will say that it was always worth the effort. There were weeks when my mom was out of the house almost every night, and there were times that she was on the phone for hours on end. There were times when it seemed she was always working. But in the end, she was always there for us. She was always there when we came home from school. She always had the time to come to all the events that my sister and I were in. She always was able to take time away from work to be there for us, and she was able to do it without fear of losing her job. The greatest privilege I've had in my life is having a mother who was able to provide for her family both financially and emotionally.

Today, Reflect on How Your Family Is Blessed by Your Business

- What are the three biggest benefits your business offers your family?

- Describe *how you feel* about the impact of your business on your family. ■

■ Make Your Children the Reason

By Kristin Rogers
The 23-year-old daughter of a direct-selling woman

SEIZE THE DAY

Over the years of watching my mom build a thriving direct-selling business, I saw it all—triumph to failure and everything in between. But I was always puzzled when I saw a mom use her kids as an excuse *not* to build her business. Having grown up with a direct-selling mom, I propose that you consider the very opposite: use your children as the reason *to* build your business. *Your direct-selling business gives you the opportunity to teach your children business skills, people skills, money skills, and, yes, even life skills!*

As a child of a direct seller, I was given this unique and extraordinary way of learning. My mom made me feel a part of her business and allowed me to work side by side with her. My mom's direct-selling business became *our family business.*

When I was in grade school, my mom's first office was in our laundry room. She had a card table as a desk and a metal folding chair. My mom would shut the door to the laundry room, while I was in charge of watching my brother. She was committed to not coming out until she sold $100 in product. Some days she would be in the laundry room for only a couple of minutes, but other days she was in there much longer. If it was one of those long days, I would slide a note under the door and she would slide one back with the amount she still needed to sell. Even at a young age, I learned to encourage her to meet her sales goal, because I knew when she reached her goal, we were off to the park or to Dairy Queen for an ice-cream cone.

Later on, I had a desk at the end of my mom's desk. I listened to her talk with people on the phone. I helped her make gift baskets, wrap gifts and prizes, and set up product displays. At first I was simply curling the ribbon, but as time went on I did all the gift baskets, wrapping, and product displays. When an order came in, I would check it off and help her label and put the product away. Soon after, I was able to do the entire task myself. I would also help my mom copy, collate, staple, highlight, and stamp her newsletters. As I got older, I was able to create the entire newsletter myself.

> **I** *learned a great work ethic and self-discipline from my direct-selling mom.*

I learned a great work ethic and self-discipline from my direct-selling mom. In fact, that work ethic shows in my education—in my study habits, in the quality of my schoolwork, and on my report card.

Yes, it may seem difficult or might take extra time to include your children in your business, but I'm living proof that the payoff is worth the effort. You might say that they are too young or can't stay focused long enough to help you. It could take you *twice* the time to do a task because they are doing it with you. But take a look at the big picture and see that by including your children in your business today, you are equipping them for *their* future.

If my mom hadn't taken the time to allow me to curl ribbon, put labels on products, or have a little desk next to hers, I would not have the life skills I have today. Every day I draw on the skills I gained as I helped build my mom's direct-selling business. Don't you want the same for your kids?

Ways to Involve Your Kids

- Share what's in it for them. Create a "Dream Board" and ask each of your children to select a picture of something they want to work toward individually and that everyone can focus on as a family. Display the board in a place that the entire family can see daily. Soon you'll notice your children have a more positive attitude about your business, because they feel they are a part of it.

- Ask each child to be responsible for a task that is age-appropriate. Understand that the children might not complete their tasks perfectly, but in addition to learning, they share quality time with you!

- Let go of the guilt! You are leading by example and affecting their life in a positive way. Someday, they'll say thanks! ■

■ Get Fired Up without Burning Out!®

By Carol Grace Anderson, MA
The "Fire Up" Expert

LIVING ON THE EDGE

As with many things in life, direct selling is a two-edged sword that can cut both ways. On one hand, we can work from home and conveniently meld our business into handling our family, community, and church responsibilities. On the other hand, we can work from home and be pulled in so many directions that we can't effectively deal with any part of our lives. The difference between these two scenarios is not how we choose to work but how we choose to *live*. ***The key to avoiding burnout and keeping fired up in our business is balance.***

It's so easy to get out of balance. When we believe strongly in what we're doing, we could easily work nonstop. The problem is that if we focus only on business, everything else in our life is negatively affected: our health, family life, work life, spiritual life, and social life are all challenged. If we work *without balance, we're less productive.*

Let's face it: as women, we want to have it all and do it all! In fact, our to-do lists are often longer than several people can do. But the truth is we can't do it all! We can do lots, but when we try the impossible, stress and burnout result and we feel overwhelmed, time challenged, or even exhausted, sick, and depressed.

BALANCING THE TWO-EDGED SWORD

Here are three simple but important steps to keep you in balance and fired up:

1. *Decide* to keep fired up by making balance a priority in your life. Whether you're married or single, working in sales full-time or part-time, young or old, balance makes life better. It's not easy to live a more balanced life, but without the decision to do it, you'll never achieve it.

2. *Discover* all the possible ways to keep *you* fired up. Everyone is different, so try different options to discover what brings *you* the best results. You might spend more time with positive, supportive people; read inspiring books; listen to motivating music; take a long bath; meditate; take walks; or just lighten up! Laughter is good for everyone.

3. *Devote* yourself to being fired up without burning out. Schedule variety and relaxation into your life and make sure you stick to it. This is where the big stuff really happens.

Yep. To get different results, we have to do something different. Now is the time. Just do a little at a time, but do it consistently. Your persistence is the secret!

Balancing Today

Today, look at your calendar and block out time for each facet of your life: physical, spiritual, intellectual, social, family, and business.

Today, commit to working within *your* balance. That's how you keep fired up. You're worth it! ■

■ Engage Your Kids in Your Business

By Connie Kittson
A successful single mom who raised amazing children

FINDING THE REWARDS

When I started my direct-selling business, my children were two and five years old. They had never had a babysitter, so I definitely was "Motherhood-Smotherhood." It was pretty traumatic for everyone when I began my business and started leaving the children with a babysitter. I realized right away that *I had to get them to see the benefits of my working and what was in it for them.*

In the beginning, my two-year-old's job was to stay with the babysitter without crying. My five-year-old was very mature and a great help with many small jobs.

What your children do in your business depends on their age. When mine were very small, sometimes their job was entertaining each other and playing nicely so I could talk on the phone. I would set a timer for 30 minutes and work like crazy. When the timer went off, I would play with them for 15 minutes and then set the timer again.

All kinds of tasks were recognized as helping the business. They picked up their toys, emptied the trash, labeled products, stamped brochures, and put stamps on envelopes. I started them with small jobs, realizing that they would not be perfect. As they mastered these skills, they could do more, and soon they were collating, stapling, folding, and stamping newsletters.

They helped me set up displays, made signs for open houses, and even made cookies for customers. My children learned to check off an inventory order, label it, and put it on the shelf. They could pull a customer order, write up the receipt, figure the sales tax, and record a customer's purchase on a profile card. They helped me make gift baskets, spray baskets, and cut shrink-wrap. Eventually, they could set up a meeting room and tear it down without my help.

As their computer skills grew in school, they were able to help me in the office by creating flyers and newsletters.

They both learned to drive while making deliveries to customers. It helped them understand where the products were going. While driving, we would listen to one of my motivational tapes, and then we would play one of their tapes. They were learning the business and not even realizing it. After each got a driver's license, they made the deliveries for me. They knew exactly where the customers lived.

The thing that I am the most proud of is not the business accomplishments and recognition that I have achieved but of who my children have become while working with me to create a successful business together.

As the children grew, so did the rewards: hockey skates, volleyball camps, trips to Disneyland, and cars when they turned 16. They have always looked at my direct-selling business as a family business and rightfully so. They learned goal setting by watching me set goals and move toward them. So when the kids got older, they created their own goal posters to help keep them on track for their goals—it just became ingrained into their thought processes.

I have always had an extra chair in my office. If one child came home from school and needed to talk, that child sat in the chair and waited for me to get off the phone. I would then hold all calls and give that child 100 percent of my attention for just listening. Also, we made mealtime family-talking time—we simply didn't answer the phone during meals.

Having your children work in your business will help them develop skills for their future. My daughter worked in my office during college break and in the summer. After graduating from college, she completely ran my office for nine months before getting the job of her dreams.

My children learned a work ethic, discipline, commitment, communication skills, and more from working with me in *our* direct-selling business. The thing that I am the most proud of is not the business accomplishments and recognition that I have achieved but of *who my children have become* while working with me to create a successful business together.

■ Partner with Your Partner

By Carol Ranoa
Partnering for prosperity

ALIGNING PURPOSES

Being a woman in the direct-selling profession for over 16 years has brought many joys and many challenges. One of the most difficult things for me and many other women has been to be taken seriously as a businesswoman—to be seriously supported by the men in our personal lives. Unlike a career or job, which is solitary and often not a threat, a direct-selling business is almost always run from home and anywhere else we happen to be. It pervades our lives more than does a typical nine-to-fiver situation and so is greatly helped by spousal support.

Whereas women like to feel empowered, men want to feel needed and in control. And the truth is, we truly *do* need their help and support. Gaining support starts from the beginning by initially enlisting your spouse's help in evaluating the business opportunity. Trying to convince an unwilling husband that your judgment is better than his when it comes to deciding to go into business is sheer suicide in many cases; it is a frontal assault and can be seen as a threat to his role as the family caretaker and provider. Asking for advice and help will crumble the walls of resentment and allow him to view your new venture with an open mind, enabling him to see the wisdom of your choice—although he will probably decide that it was his idea in the first place!

When a spousal partnership is forged, it can exert a strong force for success in a direct-selling business. Because it's not competitive by nature, such a business offers the opportunity to bring different strengths to the table in complementary synergy. It is important, however, to be very clear about the role each of you fills in the business. My husband and I both love the people contact aspect of our business. So our roles often overlap because our goals and interests are so alike. Sometimes he will pick up the slack at home while I'm out, and sometimes he'll make the follow-up calls. For us, it works to have blurred roles because we both like all aspects of the business. But for other successful couples, it works better to have a clear distinction of responsibilities. Very often the husband manages the business mechanics (computer, ordering, paperwork), while the wife does the personal contact tasks, such as phone calls and product presentations. But I've often seen that when given the opportunity, many men love the relationships and connections that we generally think of as part of a female role.

MAKING THE CONNECTION

So how do we do this? The first challenge is to achieve open-minded acceptance, followed by wholehearted support, and finally a blossoming into full partnership. But if you achieve only open-minded acceptance, you are way ahead in your road to success. You must never falter from the clarity of your goal: to build a profitable and lasting business. Doing what it takes to garner your partner's support is worth all the effort. Very simply, remember to defer to him, not demand of him; to empower, not assault.

Sure, this sounds great, but what does it look like in reality? I have found that it entails learning a whole new language (which, by the way, should also be used in your sales approach as well). It's saying things like:

- "I need your help."

- "I truly value your opinion."

- "Your experience and success can really help me."

- "I've never done this and you're so capable."

- "Would you do me a favor?"

- "I know I can count on you to be honest."

- "Would you check out the marketing plan and give me some ideas on how to maximize it?"

- *My favorite:* "I don't know if you can help me or not, but would you be open to taking a look and give me your honest thoughts and feedback?"

Then don't be afraid to ask him to "check it out for me and give me ideas on *how to make it successful.*" Always start with an empowering compliment such as, "I know you'll check this out with an open mind."

Getting Started

Within the next 48 hours, learn some of the openers presented here and give them a try. Nothing succeeds like success, and when you see how disarming and empowering phrases like these can be, they will change the face of your business forever—and possibly your role with all the men in your life. ■

■ Choose to Be Balanced

By Grace Keohohou Lee
Vice President and Cofounder of the DSWA

WHAT'S IMPORTANT TO YOU?

Balancing a direct-selling career and a family is a challenge faced by millions of women each year. Although many guess that a home-based business would, by its nature, bring more balance to our life, it also challenges us to separate our business and our personal life as we juggle taking a customer call, caring for a scraped knee, and coaching a new team member—all in the course of 15 minutes. *The truth is, balance is not a matter of fitting everything into your life; it is a matter of deciding what is important to you and fitting all the important things into your life.*

A direct-selling woman can have balance amidst the madness, but you must consciously choose what you do with your time and with whom you spend your time. Here are some conscious choices you can make to bring balance to a hectic life.

Have a Plan That Includes All Facets of Life

Give yourself one day a week. Select a day when you don't schedule *any* business, better known as a *freedom* day. Sure, you'll meet people that you want to follow up with later, but having one day off will rejuvenate your spirit.

Schedule in playtime, just as you do work time. Whether it is a date with your spouse or an outing with the kids—don't leave *having fun* to chance. It is much too important. When it's time to play, turn off the phone, close the office door, put the papers away, and *play!*

Work hard, play hard. When it's time to work, stay focused and productive by giving the task at hand your full attention and working your specific plan for that time. This is a day of laser-light *focus* when you are working specifically on income-producing activities.

Take time to learn. It is important to continually refuel your mind with positive information. Even if you simply take 10 to 15 minutes a day to recharge your brain and learn something new from a book, tape, article, conference call, or mentor, you've achieved a great accomplishment!

Strengthen your spiritual connection. Take time to grow spiritually as well as personally. Know that you are not alone on your journey and that faith and love will bring forth your ability to do more than you ever thought possible. Believe in God, yourself, and others; and doors will open for you.

Establish Variety in Your Life to Stimulate Your Soul

Rev up your social life. Seek out friendships with people who are fun, positive, uplifting, and excited about life. Then, make time to socialize—have a good laugh, share a good meal, learn to let go.

Create a calming personal environment. Life seems more out of balance when there are clothes on the floor, the kitchen is a mess, and every surface is covered with *stuff.* I'm not suggesting that you become obsessive, just adopt the philosophy that when it comes to your personal environment, less is more.

Control Your Inner World

Let go of guilt! Do you ever feel guilty about not being with your kids when you are working, and then feel guilty about not working when you are with your kids? Let go of guilt by being present in the moment. Tell yourself, "I am doing exactly what I should be doing *right now;* there is time for everything important in my life."

Give up time wasters. What are your time wasters? It may be watching TV, chatting on the phone, e-mail, surfing the Internet doing "research," shopping, or reading romance novels. Imagine substituting 30 minutes of that time for something that nurtures your soul: reading an inspirational book, taking a walk, or indulging in a bath. Take good care of yourself so you can take better care of others.

Actions for Today and Tomorrow

1. Select items from the list above and decide which actions you will take in the next 48 hours to bring more balance to your life.

2. Make a date to complete them in your calendar and be sure to keep the appointment.

A balanced, joy-filled life can be yours—but it doesn't just happen overnight. You have to make the right choices and then design your life around the things that matter most. ∎

∎ Nurture Your Professional Image

By Marion Gellatly, AICI, CIP
The DSWA Image Center Director

DETAILS COUNT

Whether your office consists of hanging files and a cardboard table, whether you build your direct-selling business on a part-time basis, or whether you plan to rise to the highest level of management within your company, *paying attention to the details of your professional image is vital to your success.* Consider these facts:

- Opinions are formed and people are sized up in as soon as seven seconds in today's fast-paced world, studies now show.

■ Ninety-three percent of a person's conclusion about you is influenced by your appearance, body language, tone of voice, and attitude. Only 7 percent is influenced by what you say.

■ The moment you meet a person, she begins to subconsciously assess whether she wants to get to know you better.

With this in mind, can you see why it is vital that you give your professional image *top priority*?

Your professional image is all about how you project to the world and how you conduct yourself. It's the energy you bring into a room and the way you make others feel when they meet you. It's something I refer to as your *personal power*, and it has a huge impact on your success.

DETAILING A PROFESSIONAL IMAGE

So how do you increase your personal power to gain the attention and respect of others?

Project Your Best You

The way you look conveys your commitment to building your business. This means always looking your best and being well groomed, whether you leave your home or not. Dressed for business, you'll feel more professional and be treated more seriously. Looking your best doesn't have to cost you a fortune. Invest in an up-to-date hairstyle, flattering makeup, and a few well-chosen professional outfits that make you look and feel your best.

Communicate Professionally

Customer service and first impressions begin with the way you communicate by phone. Teach children to answer the phone properly, or ask them not to answer. Your outgoing calls are equally important. Keep your tone friendly and upbeat, yet professional. One way to improve your phone skills is to record your incoming and outgoing calls and listen for how you can improve.

Invest in Your Business

A professional is ready to do business, whereas a hobbyist can't find her business cards, date book, or order forms. Invest in the tools that show you mean business. From an effective voice mail system to a personal e-mail account just for your business, the right tools can have a considerable impact on the way others view you and your business.

Network with Style

Become involved in your community and develop a reputation for being *professional* and *reliable.* Whether at a local chamber mixer, a Little League game, or at the grocery store checkout, you never know where you will make a great connection. Be the person others want to meet and watch your business soar!

Prepare in Advance

A hobbyist is always running late and when she finally gets where she is going, she has forgotten something. A professional follows the Girl Scout rule to *be prepared.* Prepare the products and supplies for your next product presentation a day in advance. Make mornings stress-free by making sure your clothes are cleaned, pressed, and ready to slip on.

Be a Student

Enhance your *personal power* by constantly learning and growing. By attending workshops, participating in teleclasses, reading books, and listening to tapes, you can hone the business and personal skills that will build your self-confidence and your business.

Developing your *personal power* does not happen by accident, nor will it come about overnight. It is something that is consciously developed over time by paying attention to the details and making small, daily improvements to your professional image.

Getting Down to Business

- Review the six areas that make up your professional image and choose one to focus on this week.

- Write down three action items that will improve your professional performance. For example:
  1. Rerecord a more professional voice mail message.
  2. Get a full-length mirror for checking your appearance.
  3. Buy blank cassettes, record five calls, and listen until you find three ways you can improve. ■

■ Make Your Life Partner Your Business Partner

By Deby Sorensen
Building with strength and conviction

GAINING HIS COOPERATION AND SUPPORT

When I began my direct-selling career, my husband had two things to say to me:

"If you have to pay money to get started, it isn't a real job."
"I'll never see that 20 bucks again!"

Ouch! But despite his "wise counsel" and "optimism," I started to work. Now, seven years, two all-expense-paid cruises, and a couple of hundred thousand dollars later, he has changed what he says to me. Now he says: "Hey, Honey, wanna go for a ride on the Harley?" The Harley was purchased with money from my direct-selling business!

So how do you go about making your life partner your business partner as well? Do you have to turn a profit before you can turn his head? No! *When you involve your spouse in your thought processes and decisions, he can share in even the tiniest early successes and see that you are on the right track.* Here are three principles that helped me involve my husband during the early years.

1. Communicate

Make sure the two of you share your *common goals.* Think back to *why* you chose this route in the first place. Was it to stay at home with the kids; you didn't like your boss; you wanted to finally get paid what you are worth? Whatever the reason, you need to be clear about *why* you are creating your business and share that with your spouse.

What does your partner see happening? Often we have an idea of what we are doing and why, but our partner is left in the dark. Make sure you have communicated with your partner to decide together your common goals, and then write them down so you can measure your progress. (My husband prefers a multicolored pie chart or graphs.) After all these years, I have just recently discussed with my husband his personal goals and was rather surprised by them. Even though they are not my goals, they are goals that are important to our family. Therefore, his goals *are* my goals, and I work just as hard to make his dreams come true as I do my own.

2. Cooperate

Realize that phenomenal success isn't going to happen overnight, and make the necessary adjustments. In other words, you may think that you have to give 150 percent to the business to get it off the ground, but if you neglect your family–*often the very reason you started your own business*–you have missed the mark! Cooperation is important because it lets you share the load and stay on the same side of business issues, so you can solve them together.

At this point, you are hoping I'll give you pointers on how to get your partner to cooperate or at least give passive support. The truth is that sometimes you have to give (and give and give) to get! Most guys are "programmed" to get a job and simply don't believe that you can start a successful business on only $20.

Arm yourself with facts and statistics. How long does it take the average independent representative in your business to break even or make a profit; what are common income levels; who is making that (preferably someone you know); what level of activity is required to make decent money; why would the company be willing to pay you this much money to do what you do for them? Compare your opportunity with one in a start-up retail business, making sure to include things like start-up costs, ROI (return on investment), inventory (or lack of it), long-term and short-term schedules, activity requirements, time commitments, and overhead (or your lack of it). And for goodness' sake, don't forget all the tax advantages of a home-based business.

3. Celebrate

Make sure to *congratulate* each other on a job well done and take time to *celebrate* even the smallest of milestones. As you are discussing your goals, identify little milestones that you will celebrate when you achieve them. This is what makes it all worthwhile! After all, how sweet is our success if we don't enjoy the journey?

Today's Actions for Involving Your Spouse

Think back to the last time you discussed goals with your spouse. Is it time for an update (or to do it for the first time)? Make a date to identify your goals, his goals, and mutual goals. Write them down, begin tracking your progress, and get ready to celebrate! ∎

■ Win the Dinner Dash

By Annick M. Gunn

Making a difference with joy in her heart

MAKING HOME *THE PLACE TO EAT*

You can bring your busy family back to the dinner table by presenting **high-quality, affordable, and easy-to-prepare meals that take the stress out of your dinnertime!** Interested? It doesn't even matter whether you like to cook! If you are looking to connect and *build stronger relationships* with your family, while providing fresh, flavorful, and nutritional meal options, family meals are the place to do it. As with most things in our lives, a little planning goes a long way toward relieving stress and improving performance—even in the kitchen.

We are a grab-and-go nation! This country seems to have forgotten the importance of sitting down and eating together at mealtime. How many times a week do you find yourself driving through for takeout, picking up the phone to speed dial for pizza delivery, or getting out a bowl of cereal for dinner? In fact, the average family household spends 47 percent of its food dollars in restaurants, vending machines, and takeout. In addition to building communication, shared mealtimes foster a healthier lifestyle.

According to several studies, when children are asked what defines "happy family," 90 percent of them answered "time spent together." Think about that—time spent together *defines* love and happiness to a child! Mealtimes teach values and social skills, so set aside time to communicate with those who are most important to you. Providing a simple, nutritious meal every night or several nights a week is worth the effort and develops long-lasting rewards for your family.

WORKING YOUR MEAL PLAN

If you don't plan meals, they don't happen! Planning is the only way to ensure that you have regular mealtimes together. Careful planning saves time, money, family relationships, and your sanity!

There are four simple steps to meal planning:

1. **Check your calendar.** What nights have interfering activities that require a quick meal or short preparation time? What nights are you gone? What nights can you plan to spend more time preparing a family meal?

2. **See what you already have in inventory.** What is sitting on your pantry shelves, in your freezer? Use your current food resources before investing money in more.

3. **Plan menus by finding recipes that fit your calendar challenges and ingredient resources.** Write down these menus and the needed ingredients on recipe cards for future reference.

4. **Make a grocery list.** Check the store ads to find what is on special and worth stocking up on. With proper meal planning, you save money and time by making fewer trips to the grocery store, freeing more time to enjoy your family and friends or to work your business!

Food preparation takes time, and there is no way around it. You can maximize your effectiveness if you plan to prepare several days' worth of food at the same time. Many foods can be prepared in bulk, bagged, and frozen for later use. This provides yet another opportunity for a family project, teaches kids and spouse how to navigate in the kitchen, and ensures your teenagers have not snacked you out of ingredients. Bagged and frozen meals are now fast food that even a child can prepare.

Now you can put your family first and take back your dinner hour!

Meal Planning for Today and Tomorrow

- Schedule time to plan the meals for the next week. Check your family's calendar and schedule time to plan your future meals *as a family.*

- Check the food you already have on hand and plan to use it. Then make a shopping list.

- Check grocery ads and go shopping. Remember that your children and spouse can assist and contribute, and you can help make it an outing they enjoy.

- Use one evening or a weekend for preparation, remembering that your spouse and even small children can help. Make preparation a fun family time together. ■

■ Choose Success Systems to Stay Motivated

By Dr. Zonnya
The First Lady of Motivation

CHOOSING MOTIVATION

Having been part of the Direct Selling industry for many years and a trainer in the field, I have often been asked this question: "I can get myself or my people motivated, but how do we stay motivated in times of challenges and crisis?" You can go to a meeting and get all pumped up. But what happens when you get back home and the pump loses its zip? *In my experience, motivation is a matter of choice.*

Part of the challenge lies in the definition of *motivation*. For too long we have had a misguided impression of what motivation is and is not. So, let's define the terms for this discussion.

First, a *system* is an *accurate, established procedure* that works every time, for everyone, each time it is used. That is precisely why direct selling works. Once a company has developed its system, positive results can be duplicated every time that system is worked.

Second, *motivation* is defined as four parts of a single sentence. It is

1. making a choice

2. to take action

3. for a result

4. *whether you feel like it or not.*

Motivation is not about how you *feel;* it is about what you *choose.*

WORKING SUCCESS SYSTEMS

My first basic motivation system is this:

- Everything is a matter of choice.

- Choice equals results.

- Good choices = good results; bad choices = bad results.

With the terms being clearly defined, we can now move forward with a clarity that I believe has been lacking. Because too many have confused what motivation is and is not, it has lost its value as a tool to help achieve results.

Motivation is simply about *making a choice to take whatever action to achieve the clarified results.* Can every day be a motivated day? Yes, if you choose to take action for results *whether you feel like it or not.* There will be those days when you do not choose to take action for results, and that is necessary in our busy lives. As women, very few of us have ever been given permission to take time for ourselves. Even when we do, we play the "oughta, coulda, woulda, shoulda" game with ourselves and do the guilt trip. When you know what motivation is, that old programming can be replaced, you become more productive and effective, and you can even take time off without guilt.

Consistent motivation (choice making) is a key factor in the success of a direct seller. What does that mean? Primarily, that you have a game plan in place to keep you on the path to your selected result. To stay result-driven is the objective, all the time remembering that we are *making choices.*

Why do we in direct selling choose to stay motivated? I believe the reasons are many and very individual. Some possibilities include these:

- To book more appointments

- To increase sales

- To make more money

- To plan a family vacation

- To put a child through college

- To provide braces for a child

- To remodel your home

- To do whatever your heart desires

I had the honor and privilege of tutoring under Dr. Norman Vincent Peale until his death. His wisdom still lives in me, and I will share it with you. He said to stay motivated (making choices); first, you must *love yourself,* because if you don't, you will be at war with yourself. Second, *love where you live,* because if you don't, you will be at war with your geography. Third, *love what you do* or you will be at war with the clock.

Identify Choices for Today and Tomorrow

Within the next 48 hours, take a personal inventory of who you are and what results you have clearly defined and clarified for your business as well as for other areas of your life. Get up every morning and follow your game plan of the day for the choices you will make to achieve your desired results. Then you will have mastered the art of staying motivated. ■

■ Get a Running Start

By Susan W. Miller
Creating systems for success

BEGINNING A DYNAMIC DAY

Do you feel as though time is slipping through your fingers? Professional organizers estimate that workers waste about one hour a day (totaling more than six weeks annually) searching for misplaced items as a result of disorganization, and 43 percent of working people struggle with managing time. No matter where you are in your personal or professional life, *you must be organized so you can be as productive as possible and waste the least amount of time.*

Achieving a running start begins the night before. Start your day at night—*the night before.* When you start the morning already organized, your entire day runs more smoothly and successfully. So after dinner, set aside 15 to 20 minutes to complete the following tasks:

- ■ Before leaving the kitchen, prepare snacks and lunches. Refrigerate the perishables and put the remaining items in sacks or lunch boxes ready for quick assembly.

- ■ Check your calendar and planner for tomorrow's activities. Identify conflicts and time crunches.

- ■ Discuss any changes in schedules or activities with your family.

- ■ Write down "Five Things I Want to Accomplish Today."

Now you are ready for tomorrow—ready to succeed. You can go to bed with a clear conscience and get the rest you need to deliver peak performance.

FUNDAMENTALS OF ORGANIZATION

Getting organized is the first step to success. Persistence and follow-through are the keys to staying that way. And that's exactly why you should commit to only a few things at first. Do them consistently, do them well, and you will have developed new life-planning skills. Later, when these new activities become habits, you can add more ideas that will further streamline your business and leave you time to enjoy life.

Counting on Your Calendar

- Carry your calendar with you everywhere, every day. It is your new best friend!

- Write down every event.

- Review activities at least one week in advance.

- Color-code business, social, and family events.

Desk for Success

- Clear all clutter off the top of your desk and file or refile documents immediately. If more than 15 percent of your work surfaces are covered with "stuff," then clutter is *hampering* your productivity!

- Use daily, weekly, and monthly files to simplify managing your recurring activities.

- Set aside daily time for paperwork, and clean your desk every night.

What's in the Mail?

1. Establish a specific time and place to sort mail daily, preferably near a large wastebasket or recycling container.

2. Sort by family member and put mail in a designated area. Store in a large envelope when someone is out of town.

3. Sort your own mail by the four Ds: Do, Dump, Delegate, and Delay.

Tips for Efficiency and Productivity

■ Limit personal early morning visits and telephone chitchat. Instead, plunge right in to your work, following your daily plan.

■ Do your most important job first. Completing the difficult jobs first and getting them out of the way gives you an immediate sense of success and boosts your energy. Besides, you never know what's going to happen this afternoon!

■ Work in blocks of time. Do all routine jobs at one time. But don't hesitate to take breaks. You need a rest or your productivity level will fall.

■ Don't jump from one job to another. Focus on and finish one job, and then move on to the next one.

■ Review your progress throughout the day and adjust your schedule if necessary.

Smile, breathe, and have fun creating the success you know you can achieve. As you assimilate these habits into your life, you not only find that you are more productive but that you are also more able to relax when it's time to relax, because you know you have used your time wisely and your business is under control!

Today's Actions to Improve Organization

Review the tips above and choose two or three to implement this week. Give yourself a few weeks to make the methods habitual, and then choose a few more. Be on the lookout for other organization tips to implement once you have mastered these. ■

9

Building through Technology

Technology can be a direct seller's dream. You can connect with customers and team members at the speed of light, improve your efficiency, and expand your market to reach beyond the borders of your state and even your country. From teleconference meetings to personal Web sites, the business-building options available to you because of technology are mind-boggling. But where do you start? What tools are essential? And how can you strike the right balance between high tech and high touch?

These answers and more unfold in the pages ahead. For the insights on technology, we turned to direct-selling leaders who are plugged in and turned on to technology. Their guidance helps you navigate the many options available to you and gives you food for thought as you incorporate the technology that fits with your goals and your personal style. But before you head out to buy the latest gadgets with all the bells and whistles, heed this warning: never ever allow technology to replace the human touch. You are in a relationship business, and no amount of bandwidth or roaming airtime can make up for the person-to-person connection that has made this profession what it is today.

■ Conduct Engaging and Effective Teleclasses

By Carly Anderson, MCC
The Virtual Learning Guru

REACHING OUT TO TOUCH SOMEONE

If you are an aspiring leader not yet using teleclasses to inspire and motivate your team members, you are missing out on a safe, fun, and convenient way to inspire greater results and build a supportive community committed to each other's success. *Teleclasses cut to the heart of a training meeting, stripping away travel time and expense, refreshment cost, and the inconvenience of going to a meeting, while preserving idea exchange and promoting accountability.*

What is a teleclass? It is a structured, group telephone call that links people together to inform, educate, and promote the sharing of ideas. Participants call a special phone number at a designated time and enter a numeric code to join the call. If you have experienced a teleclass, you know they can be lively, interactive, and very effective, making them ideal for teams with members located across the country or around the world.

I've led thousands of hours of teleclasses over the past seven years on a wide range of topics. Here's what I've noticed are the vital components required to create an inspirational and effective teleclass.

LEADING THE CALL

Be specific about the purpose of the teleclass. Include how participants should prepare for it and what they will be able to do as a result of participating.

For example, if the purpose is to convey leadership skills, you might ask participants to prepare by observing leadership techniques, and tell them that as a result of their participation, they'll become more authentic leaders who inspire by example.

Designate a facilitator who can continue bringing the group back to the agreed-on purpose. At the same time, she must be in tune and flexible enough to see what the group needs at any given moment. The facilitator can be the team leader, one of the participants, or a professional who is skilled at group learning and can use coaching skills to draw out the best in everyone.

Limit the number of participants. The more intimate the group, the more individual attention people will get. An ideal number is 6 people for a one-hour call, although you can be effective with 20 or more people once you master the skills of leading a teleclass.

Set a regular call time on a weekly or biweekly basis. I recommend having the group meet three to four times per month for the first three months. Then review the progress gained by each participant and decide whether to change the call frequency.

Cocreate team agreements that provide a safe environment. Do this on the inaugural call. It's best to have no more than five agreements, so participants can remember and adhere to them easily. Typical agreements include the following:

- Arrive in the first two minutes and stay until the very end—start and finish on time. Be in a quiet place where you won't be interrupted, and switch off cell phones.

- What's said in the group *stays* in the group.

- Get to the essence of what you want to say, or what you need, as quickly as possible. Avoid getting into a long story.

- Listen with an open mind to differing points of view.

- Avoid interrupting when someone is speaking. Be respectful by being fully present and listening to the speaker.

Have an agreed-on format for each call. Create a structure that uses the time most effectively. Here's a sample format with six segments:

1. Welcome everyone *by name* in the first three minutes.

2. Ask who has had a win this week, especially in regard to the fieldwork everyone agreed to take from the last call. Avoid chit-chat about the kids or the weather!

3. Acknowledge each participant for her win by *recognizing the qualities or strengths* she used to achieve that win.

4. Find out what stopped people from following through with their agreed-on action from the last call. Hear them out, ask open-ended questions, be nonjudgmental, and discover what they need to follow the action through this week.

5. Discuss a topic you've previously agreed on, or one that arises from what's been shared.

6. Finish up by having everyone state what she got from the call and what she's committed to doing this week.

In the Next 48 Hours

- Decide whether you will hold regular teleclasses with your team.

- Check out various providers such as Black & White Communication, Flashtalk, and COA Network. For information, search "technology" on the DSWA Vendor page: http://www.mydswa.org/search_vendor_profile.asp. ■

■ Build Strong Teams by Phone and Web

By Judy Marshall
Tuned in and turned on to technology

THE POWER OF YOUR VOICE

To strengthen your ability to stay involved with your team through thick and thin, ***steadfastly connect your team members to yourself and to each other.*** For decades, local weekly meetings were the backbone of building relationships and connections with your team. In today's global economy, many organizations have distributors all over the world. So how do you maintain that sense of relationship and connectivity in a global organization?

One of the most effective tools for keeping a global team connected is *conference calling.* Today, conference calls can be done by phone or on the Internet, providing those essential feelings of connection while minimizing costs. With phone rates available for pennies a minute and Internet services available for free, this technology is available to everyone.

LET'S GET CONNECTED!

Have you ever attended a local meeting that was fun and informative and left everyone feeling inspired? An effective conference call can be structured in exactly the same way. Bringing guests is as easy as making the "pick-up" by three-way call technology.

The teleconference call is an excellent way to deliver product updates, training, the business opportunity, or even a weekly sales meeting. As the leader, you can either deliver the content yourself or brief the participants and elect a speaker to deliver the training component, stepping back to simply facilitate—and train others in the process.

PREPARING YOURSELF

If you were inviting a small group over for coffee or preparing for an event, you would orchestrate your resources to create an appropriate environment. A conference call is no different. The call might comprise five parts:

1. Picking up your guests via a three-way call

2. Introductions, networking, or mixing

3. Formal presentation and testimonials

4. Announcements and reminders

5. Inviting guests to get together with the person who invited them to the meeting

After the call, the people who brought guests have the option of calling their guests and discussing the call with them, usually asking something like, "What was your favorite part of the call?" and moving the relationship to the next level. When the guest has specific questions, there's a great opportunity to include you in a three-way call to answer them.

THE FINE ART OF THE TELECONFERENCE

Long distance is no longer an obstacle to building relationships. Phone rates are inexpensive, and technology lets people in any time zone participate in teleconference training or meetings.

Services range from "for free" to "for fee," and each service provider has unique strengths and weaknesses. The downside to some of the free teleconferencing services is that your conference call is not exclusive to your group. Outside callers can potentially interrupt your meeting.

You might find a paid conference call worthwhile because it lets you mute other callers when you're talking for a clearer presentation. This gives you more control of the conversation, maintains your listeners' attention by reducing noise on the line, and makes a cleaner recording if you tape or digitally capture the call. Most paid conference services include the option of recording your call, or you can record it yourself with an instrument from Radio Shack. You can then upload the recording into a voice mail or Web site, where team members in any time zone can listen at their convenience.

Another option to investigate is conference calling via the Internet. Some team members might have a better experience with this kind of call than with others because the quality depends on the speed of your computer and Internet connection. Nevertheless, everyone in your group can participate because most conference providers offer a regular phone number to callers with no Internet connection. As you explore the advantages of Web conferencing, you'll see other benefits. At a Web conference, you can display reports and data sheets, presentations, and slides—almost any kind of document—and get feedback immediately from all participants.

Get Ready to Connect!

Today and tomorrow, research the following:

- What is your budget for training or meetings? If you have no budget, use free services while starting out or share the expense with another leader from your company.

- Investigate service providers by visiting the Vendor area at http://www.mydswa.org.

- Schedule a sample conference call and ask your team members how they like it! ■

■ Build Relationships on the Internet

By Jude Hodge
Connecting hearts and minds through technology

NETWORKING MADE CONVENIENT

Picture yourself sitting in your living room and connecting with your team and with prospects from across the nation using your laptop computer. Imagine growing your business with people in other cities, other states, and even other lands. Does this sound like someone else's life? It can be yours when you ***meet new people and build relationships online.***

When you're online, you build rapport, trust, and value the same way you do in person. Here are some great ways to create powerful connections and successful partnerships:

- Meet new people in an *online chat room.*

- Reduce meeting costs by connecting with your team via *online conferencing.*

- Let others get to know you through a *personal Web site.*

- Leverage the power of your voice with *online audio training.*

- Qualify prospects with a *lead-capture page.*

Are you interested yet? The technology is here to support your business development efforts, but to be effective you must do your homework. Researching these technologies costs no more than ordinary Web surfing. And many of these services are free. However, before you sign up for any paid service, consult with other leaders who are already using that technology. Don't make any investments until you are confident they will pay off.

CONNECTING ONLINE

One of the easiest ways to get familiar with these resources is a free *online chat room.* If you have never participated in a discussion forum or chat room, check one out. You can find a group or even create your own through http://groups.yahoo.com or a variety of other service providers. Invite your team or friends to discuss a topic. When you join a forum that interests you, you'll find plenty of opportunity to meet and help others. These forums can be a wonderful information resource! You will make great friends and find strategic partners for growing and expanding your business.

If you want more personal contact, schedule a *conference call.* The teleconference environment is ideal for connecting a group individually separated by long distances. Imagine offering a weekly get-acquainted call or, better yet, an opportunity meeting. Don't let the cost of long distance deter you. Many call programs cost only pennies per minute. While you are investigating the value of conference calling, check out Web conferencing too. If viewing Web pages online with audio and feedback options would support your training efforts, join a direct-selling discussion group to get tips from those who are using this resource.

Leverage your time with a *personal Web site* if your company allows you to have one. As you develop interest both locally and on the Web, you can direct prospects to a Web site that lets them get to know you. When you set up your site, keep in mind that cultural perceptions may be different from your own. Tailor your message to your audience. Be real. Be genuine. You may add a photo of yourself, a personal mission statement, testimonials about yourself and your product, and a link to your company site. Some Web site providers offer a page where your visitors can sign up to join your mailing list, and others offer a feedback form to collect information on prospects.

Let others get to know you online with the power of your voice. *Online audio* lets your site visitors hear you, your voice, and your message. This tool is fantastic for training too. For more information, visit http://www.instantaudio.com.

Now that you are connecting out in your local market and on the Web, *a lead-capture page* will help you screen interest so you can follow up more effectively. Many direct-selling professionals have built a successful online business by optimizing their Web site for search engines using key words to improve their search ranking. Many also place ads on popular search engines such as Yahoo and Google to drive traffic to their Web site and lead-capture page.

When you are responding to leads from another country, make sure you check the time before you call! One easy way to verify that your prospect is awake is to visit http://www.TimeandDate.com. The best time to return calls is after 6:00 PM or on weekends. When you receive a lead online, follow up on it promptly. A customer who takes the time to complete your information page is *very* much interested and expects a speedy response!

The Internet is changing the face of our business at the speed of light. I realize the World Wide Web, search engines, and Web pages can be daunting to less experienced surfers. But if you are serious about making money, you'll recognize the high-payoff potential for learning to use the Web. Stay informed. Don't hide behind your computer! Step out. Learn from others. You can be warm, friendly, and fun! Even electronically! Connect in every way possible to build your reputation and offer your service to others.

Today's Actions for Networking on the Web

- Chat with others in your organization who use the Internet to build their business.

- Decide which resources on the Web would best support and complement your business.

- Join a discussion group about those resources at the DSWA, Yahoo, or Google. Start planning how you will add these new technologies to your networking methods. ■

■ Train with Technology

By Maria Little

Harnessing the power of technology

ANSWERING THE MAIL

With ever-increasing communication technology and company growth spanning the globe, it's possible that many members of your direct-selling organization will be far distant from you. This is the case with my organization of over a thousand people. Despite the fact that I may never meet some of these people face-to-face, developing and training them is very important. I have found that *training via the Internet by using e-mail communication is an excellent way to get and stay connected, provide training tools, give valuable information to your team on a regular basis, and help ensure success in their business.*

FINDING AND GIVING YOUR MESSAGE

Successful training over the Internet is best done on a regular weekly training and communication schedule that your team will recognize and come to rely on for information, tips, and motivation to achieve *their* goals. People seem to better understand training that comes to them like a gentle rain rather than like a deluge. This gives them a chance to incorporate training principles in their business and see gradual improvement rather than simply being given a large amount of information in a short time, creating a lot of information "runoff." Here are some of the principles that have worked for me.

Foundations of Successful Training through Technology

■ Use training memos to communicate several times a week with your team.

- Develop two to three different types of memos that you will send the same day each week. Each type of memo should have a consistent style in the subject line. Your team members will begin to regularly identify a specific memo type with a specific day.

- Focus your training memos and information on the basics of the business, motivational tips, and company initiatives.

Examples of Creative Style Memos

- Best business practices—A brief, one-paragraph memo that highlights a simple yet successful business practice with three or four bullet points that support that particular business practice. Visit the DSWA Learning Center for a ready supply of success tips and articles.

- Recognitions and results—A memo designed to highlight both the efforts and achievements of your individual team members who are actively pursuing their business.

- Focus corner—A creative memo that highlights, reviews, and reinforces any new policies, company initiatives, upcoming events, and other news. You may also include a small, one-sentence training tip in this type of memo.

- Weekly focus—A more detailed type of training memo. You can develop one training topic for the month and then break it down into four main subtopics, highlighting each subtopic in a weekly focus for that particular month.

What Makes a Creative and Successful Training Memo?

- Make your training e-mails eye-catching and fun to read!

- Generate excitement and motivation in the tone of your e-mails with the words and punctuation you use.

- Use different fonts and font colors.

- Insert graphics and clip art when applicable to your training themes.

- Make your content easy to read, simplistic in presentation, and no more than one page in length.

TRAINING TIP—ABOVE AND BEYOND REGULAR TRAINING

- Develop a team Web site as a resource tool for your team. It is a great way to highlight the current week's training memos for easy team reference as well as to archive past memos.

- Setting up message boards, online chat sessions, and regular teleconferencing are also great ways to communicate and train your team.

Answering Today's Mail

Develop a weekly training schedule by selecting the specific days of each week that will be dedicated to sending out training communication.

List the types of memos that you would like to use to communicate training information. Feel free to adapt from the examples presented here, or you can create your own.

Evaluate the needs of your team and the areas of the business for which you would like to develop additional training. Begin making a list of topics on which you can expand and incorporate into your weekly training schedule. ■

■ Boost Your Online Image

By Marion Gellatly, AICI, CIP
The DSWA Image Center Director

EXPEDIENT COMMUNICATION WITH A HITCH

E-mail is a home-based entrepreneur's dream. It's convenient, fast, and saves time and money. The pace at which we send these messages and the expectation of how quickly we expect a response is getting faster and faster.

However, if you think it is easier to send an e-mail than it is to send a business letter or typewritten memo, think again. There's a thorn on the e-mail rose! *Written communication is perhaps the most difficult form of communication.* This is because we have a tendency to write in shorthand, expecting our reader to know what's in our mind at the time we are writing. Consequently, written communication is often confusing and can hurt your professional image.

Because people can't see or talk to you through your e-mail, *it* becomes your professional image to them. Your preparation of e-mail responses is just as important as the business letters you once churned out on the typewriter.

Here are 15 tips guaranteed to boost your professional image when using e-mail:

1. E-mail is written communication, and that means complete sentences are a must. Spelling and grammar count, so always use the spelling and grammar checking features on your computer before you hit the Send button.

2. Short, concise e-mails are best. Organize your thoughts and write short sentences and short paragraphs. Whenever possible, limit your message to two screens or fewer.

3. Create a subject line that summarizes your message. This facilitates the initial review or later retrieval of messages.

4. Don't send messages to people who don't need them. Carefully select the intended audience for your message.

5. Don't participate in Internet junk mail and chain letters. If you receive these kinds of messages, simply hit the Delete key and move on.

6. Healthy debate on e-mail is okay, but know when it's time to pick up the phone or have a dialogue in person.

7. It's appropriate to sign your e-mails. Often, when a number of messages have been forwarded or replied to, it becomes difficult to sort through and determine who sent which message.

8. Courtesy and a presumption of innocence work miracles in e-mail messages. When you are writing a message, imagine that you are looking directly at the person and talking with him or her. *And if you write an e-mail while angry, don't send it until you can review it away from the heat of the moment.*

9. Using boldface type or all capital letters is considered impolite—it looks as if you are SHOUTING in e-mail language.

10. Carefully consider the use, and possible misuse, of blind carbon copies (BCCs), whereby each person who receives a message doesn't know the identity of the other recipients. Using BCCs can create an atmosphere of distrust, thereby undermining your communication efforts.

11. Check your e-mail a minimum of once a day. Whenever possible, respond immediately. If you know your response will take longer than normal, send a message to say you have received the message and will follow up.

> **W**e *have a tendency to write in shorthand, expecting our reader to know what's in our mind at the time we are writing.*

12. Use the Reply to All feature very sparingly when responding to messages. If a reply is required, respond only to the person who sent the original message, or at least limit your message to a smaller audience.

13. If you need a response, be very specific about when you expect a response and what you expect that response to contain.

14. Ask permission before forwarding others' e-mails or portions of them even if it's good news. Mary may not want the world to know her news.

15. E-mail should never replace personal interaction, ongoing dialogue, and spirited debate.

Finally, the most basic rule of correspondence still applies: be careful not to put anything in writing that you wouldn't say in person. Once it's on paper—or once you've hit the Send button—it's impossible to take it back. Still and all, e-mail is a wonderful way to communicate conveniently, and it can help your business if you follow these guidelines.

Today's Actions for Improving Your E-Mail Messages

■ Identify three tips from the list above that you want to incorporate in your e-mails this week.

■ Next week, pick three more.

■ Enjoy clearer communication and fewer misunderstandings! ■

■ Become a Master Networker on the Internet

By Sue Seward

Powerfully promoting online

THE ART OF THE VIRTUAL CHAT

Building your direct-selling business without building relationships, whether on or off the Internet, is like building a house without a *foundation!* As soon as the first big storm hits, it all washes away and you have to rebuild, don't you? ***Approach relationships online the same as you would in person.***

Virtual (online) chat rooms and discussion forums are a fabulous venue for getting to know others and expanding your knowledge at the same time. The World Wide Web has given millions a way to connect and share varied interests. Your initial interest may be in expanding your direct-selling business, but consider your other interests as well. There are discussion groups for every interest under the sun!

GET CONNECTED

Finding a discussion forum is fairly simple when you have Internet access. If you are new to discussion groups, type in http://www.goo gle.com or http://www.yahoo.com and enter "MLM Discussion Forum." The search brings up links to thousands of Web sites and chat groups. Join one that looks interesting by following the instructions to sign in, and read the conversation postings. You will quickly get a feel for the ideas that are being shared. Once you've found a forum to discuss business-building ideas, check into other areas that interest you. For example, book discussion forums, moms' groups, and so on. This arena lets you connect, just as if you were there in person. What happens when you connect with others? They want to know more!

What if you were told never to reveal who you are online?
This is business. If you were meeting someone at a networking event, you would introduce yourself, your company, and your seven-second personal tag line. Be professional and genuine. The same commitment you bring to networking locally—offering service, value, and opportunity—builds true lasting relationships.

You have heard that people are the same everywhere. They are. Just like you and me, they want the same things. The virtual environment simply lets you bring your desire to help others get what they want to a larger world. Cultivating relationships on the Web is like gardening. It takes patience, planting seeds, watering, pruning, and weeding.

When you begin participating in forums and chat rooms, you make friends and contacts, and you learn from others who are building strong successful businesses.

Planting Tips

- Imagine yourself entering a room filled with people. When you join a chat room, watch for the conversation streams.

- Join conversations you are interested in. Contribute and ask questions. When others ask about you, be honest.

- Be prepared to follow up when someone shows interest. A personal Web site, a newsletter, and a link to your corporate site will help your new online friends get to know you.

When you're engaged in "Internet farming," I suggest the *drip* approach. Drip little bits of information to your friends on a consistent basis. Sooner or later something clicks with them, and when the timing is right, they ask about your products and services. Most of my business partners have come from this approach!

It's always about serving people! Keep a nonpressured, low-key attitude to help people feel comfortable. This servant's approach also helps you guide and advise a new friend without pressuring her into something that may not be right for her. Not only must you decide if it's right for her, but is *she* right for us?

After some practice, you'll start to pick up on little clues, and you'll know in what direction to point your new friends. Remember it's *always* about them!

Ready to Start Farming

Take these two steps within the next 48 hours to begin reaping your harvest:

1. Join a forum in an area of your interest. Watch your balance of time; it's easy to become so involved in the online environment that you lose track of your schedule.

2. Develop a presence online. Become a promoter of the Direct Selling industry. ■

■ Make Friends with Technology

By Jeanette S. Cates, PhD
The Technology Tamer™

THE CHARM OF YOUR RECEPTIVE VIEWPOINT

When the avalanche of technology seems overwhelming, ***take a genial approach to what you have to learn.*** While teaching and coaching thousands of students and clients, I've learned that their mind-set makes the biggest difference in how quickly and comfortably they adapt.

Whether you're just getting started in direct selling or are an experienced direct seller who's been putting off using technology, you know you should use the available tools to leverage yourself. Technology can multiply your effectiveness, just like a lever can magnify your strength—saving time and making duplication and delegation easier.

So how do you approach technology? How do you start using it, or move to the next level in using it? None of us were born with a chip in our heads, even though it seems like some people were. Everyone has to go through the same steps to learn a new technology. What seems to make the difference is *attitude*.

DEVELOPING AN ATTITUDE OF ENJOYMENT

Here are pleasurable approaches to adopt as you learn to take advantage of technology.

Make technology fun! Decide that learning a new piece of software or how to use a new piece of equipment is an adventure. Approach each new task with a sense of excitement and the wide-eyed wonder of a child. Don't try to be perfect—just enjoy it! It's impossible to "break" software and very difficult to harm most hardware. Kids on a playground don't worry about breaking the swing or the slide. Just have fun and explore!

Make your computer as unique as you are! If you like pale blue flowers, set your screen to a desktop pattern or wallpaper that reflects your taste or feeds your dream. Put the programs you use all the time into your start-up folder so they'll automatically open when you start the computer.

Create computer directories that match your paper files. If you have a folder for marketing in your file cabinet, have a folder for marketing in your "My Documents" file and another for marketing in your e-mail file.

Combine your personal and professional appointments and contacts into your electronic calendar and contact program so you have only one place to look with fewer things falling through the cracks.

Customize your Internet browser's home page so you can see your favorite page each time you start your browser.

Invest in tools you *like*. You'll probably find you like the tools that give your productivity the biggest boost for the shortest setup and learning time. You don't have to buy the latest and greatest, but don't be afraid to look at new tools. Try them out if you can. Borrow them from a friend for a few hours. Go to your local office supply store and test different models and ask questions. Make a list of features you want.

Recognize that new isn't always better. For example, I'm using a copier that has been obsolete for the past 12 years. I've looked at the newer models, but I don't need their capabilities; instead, I need exactly what I have. It's not fancy, but it copies documents, important papers, permission slips, newsletters, and homework very well.

Give yourself permission to say "uncle." "Uncle," as you recall, was what we said when we were kids and we'd had enough. That same phenomenon occurs with technology. Sometimes, you just don't want to check your voice mail or answer the phone. Sometimes you want to draw on paper instead of on the computer. Sometimes you want to go somewhere where beepers and cell phones don't work. That's okay. The long-term survivors in the technology world do that. They withdraw, regroup, and come back for more—with more enthusiasm.

Have Fun with Technology Today

We've known for more than 40 years that the desire for lifelong learning contributes to a longer life. In today's society it's a necessity, both personally and professionally. In the next 48 hours, make technology an ongoing part of *your* learning. Buy a DVD to learn a new program. Check your local evening classes or computer store to see what training is offered. Get together with friends to explore your new software. Just keep learning. And remember to have fun while you're doing it! ■

10 *Strategies for Success*

*C*ongratulations! You've made it to the last chapter. If you've read this book all the way through and allowed the ideas and suggestions to take root in your business and your life, you are very likely a different person from the one when you began. Consider this last chapter icing on the cake, the extra something that makes something good even better. The insights shared in the following pages ask you to go a little deeper—to think carefully about your fears, your faith, your dreams and desires. Let it all in and carefully consider how you might use these strategies to raise the bar—to squeeze even more nectar out of life so that your cup runs over with joy. Because beyond the compensation plans, the award conventions, and the bonus checks, isn't that why you are really building your business? To experience the freedom that allows you to live your life on your own terms? The choice is yours to make every day, when you decide to take one more step toward your goals.

If you are new to the world of direct selling and are looking for a place you can call home, we offer you four important insights that will help you find a company that is right for you. Don't take lightly the decision you are about to make, for it is what dreams are made of. To your success!

■ Voice Your Power . . . in Public!

By Dawn M. Holman
Helping you and your business rise and shine

WHY BECOME RECOGNIZED AS AN EXPERT?

Using the media to voice your message is the most powerful positioning strategy you can employ for yourself and your business. It establishes you as a player. Doors will open that otherwise would remain closed. Why? Because ***creating that "celebrity edge" by becoming known as the expert in your field plays right into your business model.*** Yet it remains the most underutilized strategy for business growth.

Nonetheless, the more media exposure you receive, the more the customers call—ready to buy because they are *presold* on you and your offering. Your peers will notice too. This results in opportunities that only "experts" get, and the spin-offs lead to even greater things. In short, the more you raise the bar on your efforts to establish yourself with the media, the more both you and your business will grow. It's just a matter of courage . . . for you have everything you need to start now!

Many direct-selling professionals are searching for a way to express what they do . . . in a way that helps them feel good about themselves. Yet I have also witnessed a sense of shame about "tooting your own horn." Such feelings are usually rooted in some childhood incident or remark. Why would you allow the perceptions of a five-year-old manage your business today?

The real issue: are you competent in what you do? If so, then you have every good reason to believe that someone else's life is better because you take pride in your work. You serve well. Then why would you hide this fact so fewer people benefit?

THE IMPORTANCE OF PERCEIVED COMPETENCE

Competence is much more than applying what you know. You must also develop *perceived* competence. You can be very good at what you do, but if you don't tell enough people how you can help them, you aren't perceived to be as competent as you really are.

Have you ever felt the frustration of lagging behind a competitor who knows how to promote herself well yet is less competent than you are? The fact of competence *and* the perception of competence are equally important to creating the success you deserve.

Create Newsworthy Angles

- **Research past coverage of your area of expertise.** How topical can you be in relation to the top stories by taking a fresh approach? Can you offer a new, valuable insight?

- **Position yourself online.** Become a regular contributor to relevant e-zines with high readership. This increases the likelihood of being discovered as an expert because the media scour the Internet daily.

- **Think from the fringes.** Do or say something that is counterintuitive. What techniques and strategies are individuals and companies outside your industry using that are producing big results? How could you cross-apply them? Identify the biggest problem in your industry; then *solve it!* This will set you apart as the "go to" expert.

- **Create a buzz.** Organize your knowledge into a doable system of action with a definite end result. Give it a catchy name.

- **Create a high-impact "bio."** Take an inventory of your professional history and how you have made an impact within your industry and on others.

- **Create third-party endorsement.** Donate your product or service to an appropriate and appreciative organization. Involve it in a media event and let *it* extol the benefits of what you offer.

- **Create a "high-pull" event.** Bring in well-known speakers to create third-party validation by association and increased media coverage. Create great visual opportunities for television and print photographers. Add human interest whenever possible.

- **Note your initial responses to news reports.** If you blurt out, "I could have commented on that," then act! Formulate your thoughts and angle your fresh point of view for the media to consider.

- **Keep up-to-date on mainstream coverage relevant to your area of expertise.** Scan industry-specific media for ways to bridge the gap.

Remember, it only takes one brilliant twist of an idea with your local media to land major coverage. The topic on which you've just been interviewed could suddenly turn into a regional or national news item.

Turning On the Spotlight

- Decide for yourself if your business would benefit from your being recognized as an expert.

- Start looking at news reports from the angle of promoting your business. ■

■ Be the Change

By Garvin DeShazer
Facilitating positive change in others

KNOW YOUR PURPOSE

Have you ever thought about why you do the things you do? The prevailing belief in our society is that you must *do* certain things to *have* success so you can *be* happy in your life. Do, have, be. However, there is a wisdom tradition that suggests a different order—be, do, have. *Be* a happy, fulfilled, purpose-driven person, *do* the things that kind of person would do, and you will *have* the benefits of success. This wisdom was best summarized by Gandhi, when he said, **"You must be the change you wish to see in the world."**

Given this paradigm, how would you describe who you "be"? Are you a person of integrity? Are your actions consistent with the values you claim to hold? Have you ever taken time to consider your values and decide what's truly important to you? Do you know your purpose—in life, in business, in every choice you make? Are your choices fundamentally in alignment with your purpose in business and in life? If not, it is highly unlikely that you will attain the success you seek.

CHOOSE WISELY

You were born with an amazing gift: the power of choice. You have the ability to manifest whatever reality you choose in your life. Now, I'm not suggesting things won't happen in your life or that you won't have hardships and hurts along the way. These are part of the fabric of life. The important thing is how you choose to respond to the circumstances and events that befall you.

Will you be a victim of what happens to you, investing all your energy in complaining about things outside your control? Or will you take *whatever* comes your way and use it to shape building blocks for the temple of your life? Ultimately, this choice determines the person you will become and the results you will create.

BECOME ACCOUNTABLE TO YOU

People often mix up the principle of accountability with the idea of blame and shame. Nothing could be further from the truth. Simply stated, accountability is the *ability* to *account* for the choices you make and the outcomes of those choices. This is the key to personal empowerment. It boils down to a commitment to be ruthlessly honest with yourself.

If you're still trapped in a victim mentality, you might find yourself arguing with the notion that you can be 100 percent accountable for all the outcomes of your life. You might say, "What about the things that happened to me as a child?" or "How can I change all the things other people have done to me?" You might even ask, "What if something happens to me in the future that is clearly beyond my control?"

If you want to be powerless, it's easy to justify your powerlessness. By all means, focus on your past or on the unknown future. Attempt to control them. Of course, they are impossible to control, just as the actions of other people are impossible for you to control, so your success at proving you are a victim is assured. If this is where you go with these ideas, ask yourself what subconscious benefits you are receiving from holding on to your slavery.

There is only one person you can control, and that's you. Whatever happens in your life, you have the power to choose what you will make it mean and what you will do with it. Viktor Frankl spoke of this in *Man's Search for Meaning*. He described his experience of being a prisoner in Auschwitz, knowing each day might be his last. In that terrible situation, he chose to find purpose in holding on to the hope of telling his story, so the world might learn from that experience.

Be Powerful

If you acknowledge that you can influence the world around you and you're willing to live each moment as if now is all you ever have, you already *are* more powerful than you could have previously imagined possible. All that remains is for you to *be* that powerful person, *do* what a powerful person would do, and *have* the rewards of that power in your life. ■

■ Take My 101 Goal Rush Challenge

By Mark Victor Hansen
The Ambassador of Possibilities

THE GREATEST EXERCISE OF YOUR LIFE

Today, you are going to start on a wonderful path of making your dreams reality by writing down 101 goals that you want to accomplish in your lifetime. Before we set off on this path together, let me acknowledge that the word *goals* can be intimidating. In fact, it can feel so overbearing that it keeps people from beginning the process. So while you are thinking about your 101 goals, pretend you are a kid again. What kid do you know who didn't have a bazillion things she wanted or wanted to do?

Why 101 goals? First, because when we reach a goal, it loses power and importance for us. We need plenty more to keep our conscious and subconscious mind at work! Second, goals have different gestation periods. Some are accomplished quickly, some take many years. And, finally, the rule of the universe is abundance. Because you can have almost everything you really want, why settle for less?

Do your goals have to be accomplished tomorrow? Next week? This year? Of course not! Your goals can be added to, subtracted from, and achieved as you move through life.

Here is a checklist to ensure you're using a successful framework to set your 101 goals:

- Your goals must be *yours*. Not your spouse's. Not your child's. Not your employer's. When you let other people determine your definition of success, you're sabotaging your own future.

- Your goals must *mean* something to you. Your reason for charting a new course of action gives you the drive and energy to get up every morning.

- Your goals must be *specific* and *measurable*. Vague generalizations and wishy-washy statements aren't good enough. Be very specific!

- Your goals must be *flexible*. A flexible plan keeps you from feeling suffocated and allows you to take advantage of genuine opportunities that walk in your future door.

- Your goals must be *challenging* and *exciting*. Force yourself to jump out of your comfort zone to acquire that much-needed energy and edge.

- Your goals must be in *alignment* with your values. Pay attention to your intuition, your gut. When you set a goal that contradicts your values, something inside will twinge.

- Your goals must be *well balanced*. Make sure you include areas that allow time to relax, have fun, and enjoy.

- Your goals must be *realistic*. Be expansive but don't be ridiculous. If you're four-feet tall, you'll probably never play in the NBA.

- Your goals must include *contribution*. Don't get so wrapped up in pursuing your goals that you don't have time in your life to give back to others.

- Your goals must be *supported*. Share your dreams selectively with people who will support and encourage you. This is your web of support and accountability.

> **W***hat kid do you know who didn't have a bazillion things she wanted or wanted to do?*

You're now ready to embark on the greatest exercise of your life by making your list of 101 goals. In your journal or on a sheet of paper, number the lines 1 through 101. Turn on some relaxing music. Close your eyes. Take a deep breath. Now, open your mind to *all* the possibilities. Limitations and restrictions have *no* place in your life anymore. They don't exist.

As you begin to visualize *everything* you want, write your goals down. Start each goal with "I am" or "I will." Ask yourself questions like these:

- "What do I want to do?"

- "What do I want to have?"

- "Where do I want to go?"

- "Where do I want to live? How many homes do I want to have?"

- "What contributions do I want to make?"

- "What do I want to learn? From whom? Where?"

- "Who do I want to spend my time with?"

- "How much do I want to earn, save, and invest?"

- "What will I do for fun and optimum health?"

As you write your goals, don't go back and read them. If you do, you'll probably find that you begin judging every goal—and yourself—for wanting them. Just write . . . then say to yourself: "This is so. I'm predicting and announcing it to myself." Do it *now* and change your *life!*

Life-Changing Actions

- Set aside a few uninterrupted hours for completing this exercise.

- Find a beautiful journal if you don't already have one.

- Stay committed to keeping your date with destiny. ■

■ Say No to the Good, So You Can Say Yes to the Great

By Janet Switzer
Empire Builder and Success Strategist

ARE YOU MAJORING IN MINOR THINGS?

What a simple concept this is, yet you'd be surprised how frequently even the world's top saleswomen, entrepreneurs, educators, and civic leaders get caught up in projects, situations, and opportunities that are merely good, while the great is left out in the cold—waiting for us to make room in our lives. In fact, *concentrating on merely the "good" often prevents the "great" from showing up,* simply because there's no time left in our schedules to take advantage of any additional opportunity.

Is this your situation—constantly chasing after mediocre prospects or pursuing misguided schemes for success when you could be holding at bay opportunities for astounding direct-selling achievement?

SELECTING GREAT OPPORTUNITIES

How can you determine what's truly great, so you can say no to what's merely good? Here are six important steps you can take:

1. Start by listing your opportunities. It sounds simple, but often writing down your opportunities is enough to steer you away from ordinary activities and even potentially damaging ones. Seeing them in writing somehow tends to help us crystallize our thinking about an opportunity. It also helps us determine what questions to ask, what information to gather, what our plan of attack might be, and so on.

2. Decide if an opportunity fits with your overall life purpose and passion. Most of the opportunity that comes our way is really life's way of taking us down side roads—paths that deviate from

our overall purpose and passion. This is particularly common for successful direct-selling women. It seems that once you've created a successful enterprise in one area, people want you to "jump in" and replicate the same kind of success in an area *they* are passionate about. But is the opportunity in sync with *your* passion and purpose?

3. Talk to advisors about this potential new pursuit. Women who have traveled the road before us have vast experience to share and hardheaded questions to ask about any new life opportunity we might be contemplating. Investigate other women who have done this successfully, find out how they succeeded, and learn how you can too.

4. Gather information and make educated decisions. It's easy to get excited about something new, but what can truly help you determine whether an opportunity is good or great is to educate yourself about the actual activities you'll be undertaking—before making a decision. Interview people. Visit with experts. Ask for advice. Survey customers. Talk with your family.

5. Consider the *hassle factor.* One way to look at any opportunity is to measure the possible outcome against how much time, money, effort, stress, and commitment it will require. In short, determine the hassle factor. Is it easy to outsource much of the work or at least the less appealing or more time-consuming aspects of the opportunity? Is there a specific amount of time or a certain level of expenditure you'll be locked into? Is it possible to pursue this opportunity while maintaining your current lifestyle? How will it affect your spouse and children?

6. Test the waters. Rather than take a leap of faith that the new pursuit will proceed as you expect, conduct a small test, spending a limited amount of time and money. If it's a new direct-selling career you're interested in, see if you can do it part-time for a while.

Discovering Greatness Today and Tomorrow

- Identify and write down what is important to you—identify your values.

- Make a list of opportunities presented to you and determine which one most closely matches your value system.

- Do an intuitive cost-benefit analysis and decide if the opportunities you select are worth your time. Remember that money is not necessarily the deciding factor.

    Once you find the opportunity for you, it deserves your heart and best effort—greatness awaits! ■

■ Get the Monkey off Your Back

By Peggy Long
Peggy "Like a Rock"

PERMISSION TO COACH

We all know how a problem, a complaint, or some other kind of negativity can race through an organization, poisoning everyone it touches. *Here is a simple, fast, and effective way to diffuse any negative situation.*

First, make a practice of securing two clear agreements with each new person before she joins your team:

1. She will never go to her team with any problem. Instead, she will come upline to you.

2. She will grant you advance permission to coach her through any situation, whatever it may be, because that is your role.

These agreements allow you to contain the negativity and turn it into an opportunity for leadership training.

WHEN THE CALL COMES

Quickly assess how much energy she has on this issue and whether she is willing to see her own accountability in the situation. If she is highly agitated, tell her you acknowledge the reality of her feelings and are willing to allow her to vent for a certain amount of time—usually between 30 seconds and 2 minutes, depending on how deep the agitation seems to go. Encourage her to rant and rave as loudly as she wants during that time, but then be prepared to set her feelings aside and focus on solutions.

This is an important point: it's not your responsibility to take on her garbage. Give her the two minutes, if that's what it takes for her to feel heard. But then remind her that *feelings do not solve problems.* If you allow her to stay in her upset state, her negativity will gain momentum and soon she'll be like a hamster in a wheel—unable to stop because of all the energy she's put into it. Tell her that if she goes back into her upset state after the venting time is over, you will hang up, not to be harsh, but to make the point that continuing the trauma and drama doesn't serve either of you.

Ask the Basic Questions

Ask her if she remembers giving you advance permission to coach her in situations like this. Ask her also if she is committed to reaching a solution. If the answers are yes, you're ready to begin asking the basic questions. Tell her you're only interested in the bottom-line facts, not her emotional reaction to them:

- "When did this situation arise?"

- "Where exactly have you looked for possible solutions?"

- "Who is directly involved in the situation and could possibly resolve it?"

■ "What could be two possible solutions to this situation?"

■ "What do you think is the best way for you to put the solution into action?"

■ "Why do you feel these are the best avenues for you to take at this time?"

This is a gentle, leading process of solving the problem rather than saying, "Send me everything and I'll solve the problem." In that case, you would not be developing a leader but rather fostering codependency in your organization. By asking these questions, you are empowering your team member to discover her own solution and develop leadership skills in the process.

When she has come up with some answers, you might say something like, "It sounds like you're on the right track. Why don't you go ahead with these solutions and either call me or e-mail me to let me know how everything works out. And if this situation ever comes up again, you now know exactly how to handle it, right?"

Your leader will feel great about solving the problem, and you will have replicated your leadership skills within your organization. The word will soon get around your organization that you don't solve other people's problems but that you do support them in finding their own solutions.

Acknowledge Her Progress

The final step in this proven process is acknowledgment. Once she's taken ownership of the problem and formulated a plan of action, be sure to acknowledge what she's achieved. She has taken big steps that will make a big difference in your organization. Celebrate her accomplishment, and then teach her how to pass it on to the members of her team. In this way, you will be passing along the baton of leadership.

Today's Steps to Prepare for Crisis

Work with current team members to secure their agreement to be coached in a crisis. Then study and practice the coaching steps and questions, even in the smallest conflict that arises. ■

■ Paint a Picture of Your Faith in Your Business

By Doug Firebaugh
Fun, faith-filled, and on fire

IN BUSINESS WITH GOD

In direct selling, we can easily live our faith through our business. It is important to show Whom we believe in, Whom we work for, and Who is running our life and business. Many folks shy away from that because they don't want to offend others. I understand. I was that way myself until I came to the question: *"Who should I worry about offending . . . other people or God?"* Even though it is unimportant whether others believe as we do, it *is* important that we are not afraid to show that *we believe.*

I believe that God is interwoven throughout the tapestry of our lives and business, and we can be unashamed to let people know that *we* walk in faith. If we operate our lives by tapping into a Higher Power, we simply cannot be afraid to show it. Operating a business outside of a partnership with God would be like an alcoholic getting dry without God. Sure, it can be done, but why do things the hard way? And if God is your partner, you need not make Him a silent one.

JOINING THE SOCIETY OF THE UNASHAMED

When I want to signal that I believe in God and am a Christian, I quite often use certain simple words and phrases. I encourage any believer to use these daily, as they *identify* you as a believer. These words won't convert others or make them uncomfortable, but they will strengthen *your* sense of integrity as you put your public image in harmony with your deepest feelings and show gratitude to God. Here are some of my favorite words and phrases:

"**Blessings.**" I use this word frequently to acknowledge the many blessings in my life. "It is such a blessing to be here tonight" or "What a blessing it has been to meet you." This paints a picture of gratitude to God.

"**Blessed.**" Like *blessings,* this word carries a wallop. I use it when talking about what has happened in my life and business. "I have been so blessed!" or "We all are blessed, aren't we?" This lets people know that you acknowledge events in your life to be from God.

"**Thankful.**" This word lets people know that you are grateful to God for your blessings, success, and income, as well as for the life you are living. This word paints a powerful picture that you recognize where your blessings come from and illustrates how you feel about them.

"**Divine Intervention.**" These are great words to describe God's work in your life. You can use this in many ways, such as "It was Divine Intervention that I met you!" or "You have to admit, this is a great case of Divine Intervention!" This phrase is a powerful way to acknowledge an unexpected blessing.

"**This is an answer to prayer.**" I love this one! When you truly trust God and surrender the success of your business to Him, you can honestly say this whenever you experience success. It expresses humility—your right relation with God—by acknowledging the Divine Support who made your success possible.

Operating your business with total integrity, honesty, and ethics is the best way to paint a picture of your faith for others. There are times that we can compromise, and no earthly person would know. *God knows.* Let people know by your consistent actions that God owns and runs your business and uses it to reveal Himself in the marketplace.

Painting a Picture of Your Faith

If God is your partner:

- During your next presentation, use the words *blessings* and *thankful.* Let your prospects know that you believe in God with all your heart and are grateful for your business!

- Use the phrase *Divine Intervention* when sharing your business and products.

Paint a picture of God in your business and watch Him paint a picture of success in your life! ▪

■ Professionalism and Direct Selling

By Charles W. King, PhD
Professor and Evangelist for Direct Selling

THE OPPORTUNITY FOR THE DSWA

For over a decade, I, as a Professor of Marketing at the University of Illinois at Chicago, have been evangelizing to the Direct Selling industry as follows:

- *Direct selling should be viewed as a* **profession!**

- *Individuals building distributor organizations should* **professionalize** *their business practices.*

Operationally, what does this challenge really mean?

THE CONCEPTS OF "PROFESSION" AND "PROFESSIONALISM"

A survey of 15 major dictionaries revealed many definitions of these concepts. Synthesizing these definitions produced some contemporary themes:

Profession generally referred to an occupation requiring special education and mastery of a body of knowledge and continuing development of technical skills—for example, "the learned professions . . . medicine, the law, theology . . ." Physicians *"practice"* medicine.

> *Professionalism* refers to the *process of the "practice" of the profession.* It relates to particular standards involved in performance of the "practice," that is, the *character and integrity* of the practitioner, the *purpose and "seriousness of manner"* of the practice, the *"high-level training, operational effectiveness and competency, expertness, commitment and organization . . ."*

As distinguished from an *amateur . . .* not expert or professional . . . one who does something without professional skill . . .

DIRECT SELLING AS A PROFESSION

Direct selling, while admittedly not one of the "learned professions," does have similar dimensions of a profession as currently defined. To be successful in building an organization, the distributor should have *special education and mastery of a body of knowledge* about the Direct Selling industry. The body of knowledge focuses on the following:

- A comprehensive knowledge of the Direct Selling profession, including the evolution of the industry; the current size measured by sales volume; number of distributors in the United States and internationally; competitive forces across the industry; the dynamics of the current direct-selling business model; the legal status of the industry; major growth trends; and so on.

- A strong belief system regarding the credibility of direct selling as a channel of distribution and as a career path for entrepreneurs in generating full-time or part-time income.

- In-depth understanding of the generic direct-selling process of relationship marketing.

- A passion for, and knowledge about, the company's products and services.

- Thorough understanding of the company's unique market positioning strategy—market strengths—and the company's internal operating policies and procedures.

DIRECT SELLING AND PROFESSIONALISM

To be successful in building a distributor organization, the individuals should continually *develop technical procedures and skills necessary in the performance of the "practice" of direct selling.* More specifically, professional researchers, educators, and industry trainers have identified at least nine different techniques and skill sets that direct-selling business builders should master and continue to develop. Those involve:

- Prospecting

- Inviting

- Presenting

- Handling objections

- Closing and signing

- Training

- Coaching

- Supporting

- Tracking performance

The DSWA's Role in Promoting Professionalism in Direct Selling

There are over 146 million women in the United States based on census statistics, circa 2004. Many of these women are interested in entrepreneurial, home-based business opportunities.

- In its most recent research in 2002, the DSA reports that of the 13.0 million direct sellers in the United States, *women accounted for 74.2 percent, or 9.6 million direct sellers.*

- Those 9.6 million women accounted for over *$21 billion in sales in 2002.*

In summary, *women represent the largest single demographic market segment in the Direct Selling profession.*

The DSWA has a powerful opportunity for promoting professionalism to its contingency of female entrepreneurs involved in or potentially interested in direct selling. The DSWA, through its multifaceted array of member services and educational programs directed at the female direct-selling salesforce, can make an enormous contribution toward building professionalism in this dominant market segment. ■

■ Water Your Own Lawn

By Peggy McColl
The Diva of Destiny

LONGING FOR THE OTHER SIDE

Have you ever felt that someone else's life or business was *so* much better than your own? I think we've all felt that way at one time, and perhaps even considered uprooting and making a big change. But is that other person's situation really more appealing, or are you forgetting that you have the power to change how you *feel* about circumstances, and how positive feelings can lead to real improvements in your own situation?

When the grass looks greener elsewhere, use these tried-and-true techniques to extend your appreciation for your own blessings, shift to a positive attitude, and experience a new bloom of renewal and growth right where you're planted.

WATERING YOUR GRASS AND PULLING THE WEEDS

Evaluate your life from an *observer's* point of view rather than a place of judgment. An observer views each situation as a *learning experience,* appreciating the opportunity to discover how to choose more wisely in the future. An observer never judges an action or reaction; instead, she recognizes the opportunity to express her true self in her response. Self-confidence is diminished with judgment; judgment serves no purpose whatsoever! This does not mean you should ignore destructive behavior. Instead, evaluate the behavior with your observer eyes and simply choose to no longer partake in destruction going forward.

Recognize the benefits, gifts, blessings, and treasures in your own life and business. Turn your attention to yourself and focus on the wonders! These questions can help you get started:

- "What is great about my direct-selling business?"

- "What do I enjoy most in my life?"

- "What are my strengths?"

- "What are my unique talents?"

- "What have I accomplished that I'm particularly proud of?"

- "Who do I love?"

- "Who loves me?"

- "What am I most grateful for in my life?"

- "What are my greatest memories?"

- "What do I look forward to in my business?"

As you read those questions, do you start feeling better? Write some of your favorite questions on an index card and hang it on your bathroom mirror. While you're brushing your teeth, ask and answer the questions to discover more of your joys and shift to an attitude of gratitude.

Create a self-improvement program and get to work on it.

> *If you think the grass is greener on the other side, try watering your lawn.*

Just as a coach does for her players, evaluate the areas where you need to improve your performance, create a plan for improvement, and then get to work. It's easier than you think to create subtle improvement and growth every day. And those little changes soon add up!

Know that another person's life isn't always as rosy as it seems.

Everyone has challenges. Most people do a great job of concealing their problems. So when you think someone has an easier life, a more supportive company, or greater success in business than you, think again. Maybe the grass isn't as green as you think it is!

Don't compare your life or business to anyone else's.

When you feel someone has "more" of something than you do, perhaps your longing is a clue that it's time to bring that something into your own life. And maybe that person can help you! Find out what she has done and is doing to get that something into her life, and learn from her how you can do the same.

Make consistent efforts.

When I was a child, our lawn and gardens were the envy of the neighborhood. My father was an avid gardener, working every single evening and on the weekends to create the beauty that we all enjoyed. He knew that if he neglected the landscaping chores, the lawn and the gardens would suffer, and he chose not to let that happen. Just like a successful businessperson, a gold-medal winning athlete, or a straight-A student, he knew he had to put in the effort to enjoy the rewards.

So water your lawn, pull the weeds, plant the seeds, fertilize, and keep an eye on the results, so that you can determine what needs to be done to keep that lawn beautiful, healthy, and green. Enjoy the beauty!

Use Your Watering Can Today

- Decide to step up and give more value today than yesterday.

- Do one thing today that benefits you and others, and makes you more today than you were yesterday. ■

■ Ask! Ask! Ask!

By Jack Canfield
America's Peak Performance Expert

THE WORLD'S MOST POWERFUL AND NEGLECTED SECRET TO SUCCESS AND HAPPINESS

Why are people so afraid to ask? They are afraid of several things: looking needy, looking foolish, and looking stupid. But mostly they're afraid of experiencing rejection. They are afraid of hearing the word *No.*

The sad thing is, though, they're actually rejecting themselves in advance—they're saying No to themselves before anyone else even has a chance to.

But the truth is, *there's nothing to really lose by asking.* For example, if you ask an energetic friend to join your team and build a business with you—and she says No—you didn't have that leg of your team before you asked her and you don't have that leg of your team now. Your life didn't get worse. It stayed the same.

Think about it. You've spent your whole life not having her on your team. And you already know how to handle that.

HOW TO ASK FOR WHAT YOU WANT

There's a specific science to asking for and getting what you want or need in life, which is why Mark Victor Hansen and I wrote a book about it called *The Aladdin Factor.* Here are some quick tips to get you started:

- **Ask as if you expect to get it.** Ask with a positive expectation. Ask with the attitude that you have already been given it. Ask as if you expect to get a Yes.

- **Assume you can.** Don't start with the assumption that you can't get it. If you are going to assume, assume you *can* get a registration, that your prospect *will* say Yes to you, and so on. Never assume against yourself.

- **Ask someone who can give it to you.** Qualify the person. "Who would I have to speak to, to get . . . ?" "Who is authorized to make a decision about . . . ?" "What would have to happen for me to get . . . ?"

- **Be clear and specific.** Vague requests produce vague results. Your requests need to be specific. When it comes to money, ask for a specific amount. When it comes to when you want something, don't say "soon" or "whenever you get around to it." Give a specific date and time. When it comes to a behavior, be specific about what you want from others.

- **Ask repeatedly.** One of the most important principles of success is persistence—not giving up. Whenever you ask others to participate in the fulfillment of your goals, some people are going to say *No.* They may have other priorities, commitments, and reasons not to participate right now. It's not a reflection on you.

But keep asking. Because even the same person might say Yes . . .

- on a different day;

- when she is in a better mood;

- when you have new data to present;

- after you've proven your commitment to her;

- when circumstances have changed;

- when you've learned how to close better;

- when she trusts you more;

- when the economy is better;

- and so on.

Herbert True, a marketing specialist at Notre Dame University, found that 44 percent of all salespeople quit trying after the first call, 24 percent quit after the second call, 14 percent quit after the third call, and 12 percent quit trying to sell their prospect after the fourth call.

This means that 94 percent of all salespeople quit after the fourth call. But 60 percent of all sales are made after the fourth call. This revealing statistic shows that 94 percent of all salespeople don't give themselves a chance at 60 percent of the prospective buyers.

JUST SAY "NEXT!"

The next time you ask anyone for anything, remember, *some will, some won't, so what, someone's waiting.* Some people will say Yes to you, and some are going to say No. You have to keep asking until you get a Yes.

Get used to the idea that there's going to be a lot of rejection along the way to your goal. But the secret to success is to not give up. When someone says No, you say *"Next!"* If one person tells you No, ask someone else. Don't get stuck in your fear or resentment. Move on to the next person.

You may have the capacity, but you also have to have the tenacity! To be successful, you have to ask, ask, ask, ask, ask!

Today's Actions to Build Your Asking Power

Think about the last time you asked someone for something important and didn't get it.

- Did you ask as if you expected to get it?

- Did you assume you would?

- Did you ask the right person, a person who could give it to you?

- Did you make your request crystal clear?

- Were you graciously persistent?

Identify three ways to improve your asking power and *ask again!* ■

■ Select the Right Opportunity

By Donna Marie Serritella
Industry consultant, speaker, and author

IT'S YOUR *CHOICE;* CHOOSE WISELY!

Congratulations on making the *choice* to become involved in direct selling! Direct-selling opportunities can be powerful, profitable, and fulfilling. Initially, you might get introduced to a program because of a product you try or introduced perhaps by a friend, neighbor, relative, or even a business associate. It is a rare occasion when anyone wakes up and proclaims, "Today is the day that I am going to select a direct-selling opportunity!" Because of this, more often than not, people find themselves in a direct-selling opportunity before they realize it has happened. Sound familiar? Truly, however, *joining a direct-selling company is a choice you make, not a circumstance you fall into.* Making the selection of which opportunity is right for you deserves your best efforts.

Here's the problem. People rarely make a conscious *choice* when selecting an opportunity. Most often they don't even give any consideration to *which* opportunity would be best for them. What typically happens is that people allow an opportunity to select them, and before they know it, they are in deep—or they can't get going and give up in disgust.

If you are reading this book, I assume that you have decided to learn more about becoming successful in direct selling. If you are an opportunity seeker, than you may be searching for tips on how to select the best opportunity. Or possibly you have found yourself in a situation related to direct selling and are looking for some answers. Perhaps you want to figure out what went right, or even *what went wrong*, with the last direct-selling opportunity you undertook.

Maybe you are just wondering how *they* did it—those friends of yours who you may think are, let's say, as dumb as a box of rocks, yet *they* are making *obscene incomes* from selling vitamins or from getting their friends to switch long-distance services. You may be sitting there scratching your head and asking yourself, "What do they know that I don't?"

Well, you don't need to worry any longer. If you are ready to discover the secrets that many don't know, then keep reading. Open your mind to the world of direct selling and the potentially unlimited opportunities that await you. The truth of the matter is that *you can do it too!*

USING THE RIGHT TOOLS

Look carefully at all the details of the opportunity. Take time to consider all your options, based on the advantages and disadvantages that each opportunity offers, and then compare the choices. You will be making a calculated decision instead of just being selected. In the long run, you'll feel really good about your final decision and be in an environment where you can succeed.

When you attend an opportunity meeting, you must protect yourself from the emotion of the meeting and from the representative soliciting you. Opportunity meetings are *designed* to give off lots of energy and be exciting. Whoever invited you to the meeting wants to be *your sponsor* and has a vested interest in your selecting *her* program on *her* team. Just be careful of making an emotional decision you may later regret.

Use these tips to evaluate a direct-selling opportunity:

- Protect yourself from the excitement of others.

- Take your time and do your research.

- Ask quality, fact-finding questions from multiple resources.

- Evaluate, evaluate, evaluate, and then compare.
    - Evaluate the company, compensation plan, and product; then compare.
    - Evaluate the marketing tools and upline; then compare.
    - Evaluate your value system and mentally project yourself into the opportunity. Does the result pass the "snicker test?"

- Calculate the cost of your involvement in both time and money. Be clear about what is required before you decide.

- Make your final decision, and then commit to a one- to two-year action plan.

Sorting Information

Any direct-selling opportunity must be examined from a minimum of three points of view: the company's, the upline's, and your personal values. Misalignment of the company's or upline's viewpoint with your personal values makes *any* opportunity a bad deal. Your quest is to find the *match* that will *support your success*.

Today, visit the DSWA Web site where you can download an opportunity evaluation form to guide your opportunity quest. Happy hunting! ■

■ Watch Out for Red Flags in Network Marketing

By Kevin D. Grimes
Leading attorney with a passion for the profession

PYRAMIDS BELONG IN EGYPT—NOT IN NETWORK MARKETING

There are only two possible business models for direct-selling companies: (1) a sales-based model with its primary emphasis on product sales and customer acquisition, and (2) a recruitment-based model with its primary emphasis on recruiting participants into the program. ***Recruitment-based programs are illegal pyramids and must be avoided.***

Check out the following red flags and warning signs for pyramids and other problematic programs.

Poor Product Value

The first indication of a possible pyramid is poor product value. If, in your opinion, the company cannot sell its products or services to nondistributor customers, it is likely recruitment based. A primarily recruitment-based program *is* a pyramid. Avoid any company that offers poor value or overpriced products.

Recruiting

The following characteristics signal trouble:

■ Inventory loading—a practice requiring a new distributor to buy, for a large sum of money, a large amount of (usually nonreturnable) inventory. Similarly, be careful with large product packs. There *are* legitimate reasons for companies to offer them, and cost will vary from company to company. If, however, packs exceed $1,000 and a significant percentage of distributors purchase them, you *may* be looking at a pyramid.

■ Be wary of any program in which recruiting *intertwines* with a product "sale."

■ Watch out for any compensation plan based on the number of "sales" rather than on an accumulation of *sales value* (like dollars, sales volume, or purchase volume).

■ Does compensation come primarily from enrollment or participation fees, or does it come from the sales of the goods or services to end consumers? Compensation flowing from fees constitutes a pyramid unless the following question can be answered affirmatively: *If compensation comes from membership fees, does the company have a customer program that ties distributor compensation to sales of the memberships to customers (nondistributors)?* A negative answer signals a fatal weakness.

■ Be wary of an opportunity to "buy in" at a certain rank. Remember that advancement in a legitimate compensation plan comes *only* by earning it—not by buying it.

■ Watch out for an automatic debit from bonus checks to pay for new products or continued "qualification." It is most likely a "pay-to-play" situation, or it could be a one-time purchase compensation plan, either of which is problematic.

■ Ask this question: "Can I still make money if distributor recruiting comes to a dead stop?" If not—run away!

Costs

■ Starter or distributor kits should cost less than $200 (less than $100 is better) and sell at the company's cost.

■ Distributors who only come in with the basic starter kit must be able to potentially participate in *every* aspect of the plan.

■ Watch out for any type of *personal purchase requirement* (PPR) for distributors. A PPR requires a distributor to purchase a certain amount of products *to be eligible to receive compensation.* A PPR is illegal. Legitimate compensation plans often have a personal sales requirement (PSR), which requires distributors to generate or produce a certain level of personal sales *to achieve levels of compensation.*

■ Watch out for compensation plans with any part that requires participation in an auto-ship or backup order program. Doing so violates antipyramid laws.

Training Programs

Training programs have frequently violated antipyramid laws. The bottom line: it is legal to

■ charge attendees for training;

■ make a profit from *nonrequired* training; and

■ pay the person(s) actually training the attendees.

It is not legal to pay multilevel compensation on training program revenues. The only exception is when the majority of attendees are nondistributors, that is to say, customers.

Compensation Plans

■ Watch out for unreasonably high personal sales volume requirements. Although there is no established amount, if a company requires over $300 a month in personal sales, you should be concerned, unless it is a party plan program.

■ Look at the total possible compensation from a sale. A company cannot pay out more than 50 percent of its gross revenues and still provide value to the market. If it cannot provide value to the market, it will be recruit-based and thus a pyramid.

Miscellaneous

- Avoid programs offering certificates rather than products or services.

- *Layaway* = *stayaway*. Avoid any program that offers to lay away products.

- Any program saying that "no sales" are involved is a flaming pyramid and is operated and promoted by idiots. Stay away!

Today's Actions

Visit the DSWA Web site where you can review listings of many opportunities and download an opportunity evaluation form to guide your opportunity quest. ■

■ Assess the Compensation Plan

By Gerald P. Nehra
Direct-Selling Legal Eagle

BUILDING ON A SURE FOUNDATION

Even though we all expect to do great things with the products we sell, compensation plans provide the money that makes all the effort worthwhile. *Nobody wants to spend effort promoting a company that is either operating illegally or that is not designed to pay you for your efforts.* I suggest you look at these two factors when evaluating a new compensation plan: legality and how it pays.

MAKING SURE IT'S LEGAL

Make absolutely sure that the act of sponsoring alone can never trigger a commission payment or qualification. All *compensation must be based on business volume,* and no compensation can ever flow solely from the act of sponsoring. Even plans that are technically correct in design but use *inappropriate language* to suggest you are paid for sponsoring should be looked on with suspicion. This error is a red flag to regulators investigating pyramid schemes.

MAKING SURE IT PAYS

Typically, you're paid based on business volume, which comes in two types: (1) sales *you* make and (2) sales your *team* makes.

Personal Volume

Business volume directly created by the representative is the first type, commonly called "personal volume." The three most common forms of personal volume are these:

- Purchases for resale to customers

- Purchases for personal and family use

- Commission credit for any customers you send directly to the company

Note that some plans are designed to treat the third type of business volume as personal volume even if the customer also signs a representative application, but such a treatment doesn't change the tenor of this tip. The issue is simply that you have found and brought to the company users of the products or services, and the compensation plan rewards you for that effort.

Here is what to look for: Is the compensation for selling product worth the effort? Ask this question now, before looking at the rest of the compensation plan. If a compensation plan doesn't make sense for personal sales, it doesn't make sense. Even if you focus on building a team, personal sales must make sense to *team members* if the compensation plan is to work. You cannot skip by this evaluation and expect to find a good compensation plan. In a legally designed plan, no one—not the company or any representative—makes any money unless products or services are sold to consumers.

Business Volume

The second type of business volume is that volume generated by other representatives you sponsor and the business volume of those they sponsor and so on. "Group volume" is the most common name. *But unless the last person recruited believes the compensation being offered for generating personal volume is worth the effort, we have a house of cards about to fall. No amount of "goodies" offered for generating group volume can overcome the flaw of an inadequate reward for generating personal volume.*

The Final Analysis

Here are three important steps you should take before choosing your company and signing on the dotted line:

1. Get an authorized, written copy of the compensation plan (drawings supplement a plan but are not useful in making analyses).

2. Determine if the plan even hints at making money from sponsoring others into the business. If it does, the plan is not valid and will not work for you.

3. Determine if you are adequately compensated for your personal sales volume. If not, the plan doesn't have the financial teeth to serve you or your potential team.

Above all, remember that a compensation plan is the company's method of rewarding and shaping representative behavior that most profoundly affects *its* bottom line. Look at the activities the company is willing to pay the most for and decide for yourself if you are willing to do the things required to earn that money. If the compensation plan meets the criteria mentioned above, if you are willing to do what the compensation plan rewards you for doing, and if you think you can build a team of people who will reach the same conclusions, then you have found a compensation plan that can work for you. ■

■ Zen and the Art of Selecting a Company

By Mike Russell
Enlightened Innovator of the Direct Selling Profession

THE ANSWERS ARE WITHIN

Let's assume you've found a company and everything looks right on the money. You *love* the product, management team, and the compensation plan. The timing is good, and the investment of money and effort seems sure to give you a *positive return.* The company has a rich history, and there are plenty of independent reps who think highly of the firm's *positive culture.* From the outside, all the t's are crossed and the i's dotted. Now what?

Go within, little grasshopper, because **the most important part of choosing a direct-selling company is about to begin.**

Get Clear

First, pay careful attention to whatever you're *feeling,* remembering that even if all indications are that the prospective company is the perfect choice, nothing happens if you can't or won't *resonate* with your final decision. Listen to those important little whispers! If you've never been in direct selling before, are you *willing* to ride out this new stretch in your comfort zone? Even if you're a veteran of the industry, you're just as vulnerable to the forces that could distract you from a laser focus on success in your new direct-selling home. Give yourself every chance to succeed by acknowledging that who you *are*—that inner choices you make based on your understandings, your behavior, and therefore your outcomes—is the *other half* (the most important?) of the company selection equation.

Get Receptive

You've already done the homework on your new company, and there's ample evidence that you have as much opportunity as anyone else to grow into a rewarding career (*be objective* about this) with your prospective company. So take a walk or do whatever you do to get out of your own skin for a moment. Get relaxed. Make a list (mentally or in writing) of your thoughts, mindful that you have the ability to choose them. Are you focused on the positives?

Get Perceptive

Ask yourself: Can you (are you willing to) learn from your sponsor and your company? Are you personally okay with the company's style of duplication? Will you feel supported? Are you self-directed? Will you need nurturing to get going? Is there evidence that your potential sponsor has provided support to other recruits? Do your personal strengths and weaknesses "connect" with the framework of your future company's public persona?

Get Strong

Most of us have our fair share of negative people in our lives. In choosing a new company or by joining the direct-selling marketing force, you will likely be setting yourself up for waves of opinion that run counter to yours. Negative vibes can be motivated by everything from love to jealousy and range in form from concerned doubts to outright attack. Brace yourself and do whatever is necessary to not get sucked into others' negativity. Your success depends on it.

Get Going!

Give yourself a huge pat on the back! It's not easy to look in the mirror and ask these questions—and to pay attention to the answers (even if you don't like them). But in the direct-selling world, there's a gigantic reward for going through this exercise, and *that's a tighter company fit from a more informed self-assessment.* When you can *accept* what drives you, what makes you happy, what excites you, what *challenges* you, then you can plan and respond more proactively for the circumstances you're now far more likely to experience.

Choosing a company doesn't have to be a roll of the dice. It can be a comfortable decision based on recognition of both external and *internal* conditions. And with a good corporate fit, it makes sense that you'll earn far higher commissions and enjoy your direct-selling life infinitely more. ■

■ Additional Resources

The DSWA: Support and Encouragement for Direct Sellers

The Direct Selling Women's Alliance is a community of individuals who share a love for direct selling and are committed to making an authentic difference in the lives of direct-selling professionals around the world. The DSWA Executive Team is comprised of the three DSWA Founders—Jane Deuber, Nicki Keohohou, and Grace Lee—as well as industry consul-

Jane Deuber,
Nicki Keohohou,
and Grace Lee

tants, top trainers, quality vendors, and respected experts who have served the direct-selling industry for much of their careers and now want to share their expertise for the betterment of the members and the direct-selling profession.

Since its inception in 2002, the DSWA has gained a reputation for providing exceptional industry-specific training, cutting-edge resources, and heartfelt inspiration. Our members share that, as a result of participating in our programs, they stay committed to their businesses, remain loyal to their companies, and are able to advance more rapidly to higher levels of leadership.

The membership is comprised of thousands of women (and men) who own home-based businesses with one of over 250 party plan or network marketing companies. These individuals understand that their success depends on the skills, habits, and character they develop. They look to the DSWA for information and resources that complement that which they already receive from their companies.

We are teachers, cheerleaders, coaches, confidantes, and mentors who respect your choice to own a direct-selling business and understand the challenges you face every day. In every way possible, tangible or otherwise, the Direct Selling Women's Alliance is devoted to the development of your personal power and ultimate prosperity.

DSWA Members: Learning, Connecting, and Growing

Members of the DSWA enjoy an extensive array of benefits. Our 250-page member-only community features six *Educational Centers* filled with success-enhancing content relevant to building a direct-selling business. Members also work with top industry trainers through *live teleclasses* held every week. The *Learning Library* contains hundreds of articles and success tips on every aspect of growing a direct-selling business and can be easily accessed through a state-of-the-art search tool. In addition, members can also establish a *Success Circle* or *Area Chapter* in their community, providing a safe and welcoming place for direct sellers to learn, grow, and support one another.

In addition to these resources, the DSWA has put together a tremendous *Member Bonus Package* that includes free subscriptions, admission to live events, and complimentary e-books and CDs—and that's just a sample of the built-in bonuses! For as little as a few dollars a week, you can gain the support of this community of direct-selling professionals. Visit http://www.dswa.org to join today.

- Member benefits: http://mydswa.org/list_of_benefits.asp

- Why join the DSWA: http://mydswa.org/member_area_tour.asp

- Who is the DSWA: http://mydswa.org/who_we_are.asp

- The Leader's Task Force: http://mydswa.org/leaders_link_promo.asp

- Find a company: http://mydswa.org/leaders_link_promo.asp

Discover Solutions: Products and Services from the DSWA

The Direct Selling Women's Alliance is your first stop for educational products and services designed exclusively to help you grow and manage your person-to-person, party plan, or network marketing business. Here's just a sample of what you will find in the DSWA Store:

- ■ *Managing Your Business Finances.* A comprehensive, easy-to-understand audio program and workbook that show how to manage your business finances, reap tax benefits, and keep more of what you earn.

- ■ *The Accountant Referral Network.* A select group of Certified Public Accountants who specialize in home-based business taxation, and understand and respect your decision to build a direct-selling business.

- ■ *MLM Easy Money.* Without a doubt, the best direct-selling business management software that enables you to manage your contacts and appointments, track genealogy and sales, and produce monthly and annual financial records.

- ■ *Coaching Your Team to Success.* A unique and effective audio program and workbook that teach you how to support your team for improved results, increased accountability, and more fun.

- ■ *The Coach Referral Network.* A team of Certified Professional Coaches who are ready to provide one-on-one and team coaching that will accelerate your success.

- ■ *Enhancing Your Personal Power.* A fun and comprehensive audio program and workbook that guide you to create a professional image that will accelerate your rise to the top.

- ■ *Group Medical Benefits Program.* Health insurance backed by the collective buying power of the DSWA that offers affordable, comprehensive coverage for you and your family.

To learn more visit the DSWA Store at http://www.mydswa.org/dswa_store.asp.

■ Distributors

Debi Agee
National Representative, Country Bunny Bath and Body

Working with Country Bunny since its inception, Debi has built her success by focusing first on the needs of those in her organization. Her achievements include "Queen of Sponsoring" in 2001, "Queen of Sales" in 2002, and "Queen of the Bath" for "Top in Sales and Sponsoring" in 2003 and 2004.

Gale Bates
Senior Executive Sales Manager, Weekenders, USA

The #1 manager in Weekenders in 2003, Gale gives presentations that bubble with her love to educate women about fashion, but her true passion is teaching women on her team to have a successful home fashion business.

Delores Douglass
Independent National Sales Leader, The Longaberger Company

Delores started with The Longaberger Company in 1983. Her organization grew to include over 1,300 consultants in 33 states. Frequently recognized on the national level, she consistently maintains her personal sales and sponsoring.

Maria Dowd
Manager at Warm Spirit, Inc.

In just two years at Warm Spirit, Maria has grown her team to 400 and is still expanding. She's proud of her involvement, because "Warm Spirit is a culturally rich company. Staunchly committed to community development, Warm Spirit quantifiably 'walks the walk.'"

C.J. Eisler

The son of Shan Eisler, CJ is a 20-year-old sophomore attending the Carlson School of Management at the University of Minnesota, where he is pursuing a double major in finance and marketing.

Shan Eisler

Senior Executive Director, The Pampered Chef

An experienced direct seller, trainer, and coach, Shan leads one of the top-selling and recruiting teams for Pampered Chef, where she has served for over 13 years.

Carol Garvey

National Vice President, AmeriPlanUSA®

In addition to Carol and her husband Joe, only four others in AmeriPlanUSA have risen to the position of national vice president. Carol has been with AmeriPlan for seven years and works the business with her husband and two sons. Their team includes over 4,500 individual brokers and sales directors serving more than 10,000 customers.

Annick M. Gunn

Senior Director and Meal Planner, Homemade Gourmet®

Annick has been with Homemade Gourmet for four years. Her team includes two Directors and other leaders guiding almost 350 distributors. Annick enjoys knowing that Homemade Gourmet will influence lives in such a positive way for years and generations to come.

Jude Hodge

Jade Distributor, Tahitian Noni International

Jude has been in direct selling for over 15 years. She is proud of working full-time in the industry for the last six years, and for earning a full-time income.

Rachel Kerr Schneider

Senior Regional Vice President, Fire Spirit Region of PartyLite

With 12 years of experience in direct selling, Rachel is proud of her ability to have her own business, work it around her lifestyle, and influence and coach others to have and do the same.

Connie Kittson

National Sales Director, Mary Kay Cosmetics

With Mary Kay for over 17 years, Connie leads a team of 26 sales directors and over 1,000 consultants. She received the Go-Give award at the Diamond Seminar in November 2002.

Marcy Koltun-Crilley

Diamond Distributor, LifeForce International

During her seven years in direct selling, "Marcy from Maui" has reached the very highest pin levels in three companies, including a Triple President in Traffic Oasis/Madison Dynamics. She is proud of duplicating success through coaching within her team. She is co-founder and Chief Financial Abundance Officer of PowerfulIntentions.com.

Terra Larsen

Executive Sales Director, Epicure Selections

In direct selling for only six years, Terra has achieved the following at Epicure every year since 1998: winning the Top Sponsoring Award, being in the Top 3 in Sales, and earning the incentive trip. She is happy to have helped so many people find success and freedom with Epicure.

Delbra and Tim Lewis

Diamond Director, USANA

After joining USANA in 2002, Delbra and Tim built a team of about 2,000 associates in a little over 14 months. Tim is also a popular speaker and travels throughout the United States and abroad, bringing inspiration, motivation, and hope to thousands around the world.

Maria Little
Regional Director, Affordable Luxuries, Inc.

The very first consultant for Affordable Luxuries, Maria is proud of her key role in its development over the last two years, as well as to be at the top of the field today. Her team currently includes over 1,200 consultants.

Peggy Long
Corporate Trainer and Marketer, Nouveau Riche

After being downsized from a six-figure income in 1992, Peggy vowed she would never allow anyone to own her calendar and paycheck again. In the past 15 years, she has become a well-respected icon in our industry and has developed a network of over 120,000 sales colleagues.

Linda Lucas
Diamond Infinity, Home and Garden Party

To crown her 40-year career in direct selling, Linda recently received the State of Minnesota's "Working Woman of the Year" award, primarily for building her Home and Garden Party group's volume from $0 to $3 million in 18 months. She also received the company's Spirit Award.

Judy Marshall
Cofounder, KingsWay

A wife, mother, and grandmother, Judy has been CEO of her own home-based business for 12 years. She loves having the freedom to establish her own priorities in how her time is spent.

Joan Nilsen-Robison

Director, Sensaria Natural Bodycare

Joan joined Sensaria in 2001 and has risen to the prestigious position of director. She is one of the top performers in her company and continues to build a thriving business.

Barb Pitcock

Presidential Level at VitaCorp International

Barb and her husband Dave live in a small town of about 3,000 people, yet in their first six months as direct sellers, they built a team of 5,000 people. In less than eight years, they have built an organization that spans the globe.

Grace Putt

Sales Director, Viviane Woodard

Grace executes the basics consistently and works her business with a focus on excellence. She has achieved the prestigious level of Queen many times, and has won many incentive trips to places such as Hawaii, Paris, and Puerto Rico based on her achievements.

Carol Ranoa

National Marketing Director with National Safety Associates, makers of Juice Plus

Carol began her career 16 years ago and has become one of the most successful women in NSA, with business on three continents and in every state. A highly sought-after speaker and trainer, Carol is thrilled with the difference she's made in the lives of other women.

Lorna Rasmussen

Platinum Executive Director, Pre-Paid Legal Services

As one of Pre-Paid Legal Services' top associates, Lorna has received many recognitions and awards. She's been honored as a trainer and speaker at a number of the company's national conventions. Through her work with the DSWA, Lorna has demonstrated an unwavering commitment to elevating women in the Direct Selling profession.

Sue Seward
Diamond Director, Scent-Sations

Sue has been creating residual income online from home since 1996. She's a published writer, an Internet marketing trainer, a distributor building salesforces with Xango, a Diamond Team leader of ScentStations MiaBella Soy Candles, and the publisher of two online marketing newsletters.

Deby Sorensen
Senior Executive Unit Leader, Avon

After years of corporate sales management, Deby learned that time is money, and "waiting to be served" didn't suit her well. On a whim, she became an independent representative for a company she loved but couldn't find a reliable source. Today, she is in the top 50 income earners for Avon, out of four million worldwide.

Carla Spurgeon
District Manager, Jafra Cosmetics

During her 20 years with Jafra, Carla has spoken to and influenced thousands of direct sellers. She loves direct selling because it gives her the freedom to be herself, the stable income and benefits she needs to feel secure, and the excitement of a flexible schedule and travel opportunities.

Joellen Sutterfield
Senior Executive Sales Manager, Weekenders

During her 15 years in direct selling, Joellen has promoted eight offspring units, created a combined team of more than 600, and by God's grace has repeatedly achieved the million-dollar circle. She has also received the Weekenders President's Award.

Jeri Taylor

Queen Emeritus, SeneGence International

After just five years as a direct seller, Jeri is an award-winning field leader, recruiter, and trainer; has built a team whose sales exceed $25 million; and achieved the highest level of recognition at SeneGence. A respected author and speaker, Jeri is also president of the Las Vegas chapter of the DSWA.

Shirley Tyson

Executive Coordinator, Shaklee

Recognized in the top 100 of executive managers in the nation while with Tupperware, Shirley is now very successful at Shaklee, where she has been #1 in overall growth in the United States. Outside of direct sales, she was in banking for 15 years and owned and operated a retail store.

Janet Wakeland

Senior Director, Stampin' UP!

Janet is passionate about sharing the direct-sales opportunity and helping others discover greatness and hidden gifts through training, recognition, and networking. She's proud that her personally sponsored recruits achieved #1 status in just seven years, and for having served three terms on her company's advisory board.

Karen Walter

Silver Chef, Demarle At Home

Karen has been one of the top recruiters and salespeople for Demarle At Home this year, and earned the incentive trip. She has also been appointed to the Roundtable Team, a group of ten representatives who give input on programs and products to the company's executives.

Sarah Janell White
National Sales Director, Discovery Toys

The youngest person ever to be promoted to national sales director, Sarah has been a speaker at Discovery Toys convention 2003. She also has been featured in *Network Marketing Lifestyles Magazine.*

Mary Lou Wilson
Presidential Diamond, Unicity International

In her 30-year direct-selling career, Mary Lou has risen to the top ranks of every company she has joined. For Unicity, she has built an organization of over 400,000 across the globe; she opened Japan and has her largest team there. Mary Lou has received every top award afforded by our industry.

Linda Wiseman-Jones
Independent Senior Sales Director, Mary Kay

A former high school Spanish teacher, Linda is on a mission to empower and support women to be "all they can be." She has been a director with Mary Kay for almost eight years; earned six free cars, including three pink Cadillacs; and has entered the $300,000 Circle of Achievement twice and the $400,000 Circle three times.

■ Speakers, Trainers, and Experts

Robert G. Allen

The author of two of the largest-selling financial books in history, Bob has trained thousands of people in his cutting-edge investment seminars over the past 20 years. His current bestselling books are *Multiple Streams of Income* and *The One Minute Millionaire.* To contact Bob, write to robertallen@multiplestreamsofincome.com, or visit http://www.multiplestreamsofincome.com.

Carly Anderson, MCC

Carly is a masterful leadership coach and expert on virtual learning. Her course, "How to Use Teleconference Calls to Build Your Team and Profit," teaches business builders and managers how to lead effective virtual team meetings and develop programs to create more success. To contact Carly, call 949-716-9265, write to carly@carlyanderson.com, or visit http://www.carlyanderson.com.

Carol Grace Anderson, MA

Carol is a popular speaker and author of the book, *Get Fired Up . . . Without Burning Out.* She fires up audiences across the country. To contact Anderson Programs, Inc., call 800-758-2964, write to carol motivates@aol.com, or visit http://www.getfiredup.com.

Gary Ryan Blair
President of The GoalsGuy

A visionary and gifted conceptual thinker, Gary is highly regarded as a speaker, consultant, strategic planner, and coach to leading companies across the globe. More than 80,000 organizations and four million employees use the GoalsGuy handbooks, training programs, and coaching services. To contact Gary, call 877-462-5748, write to gary@goalsguy.com, or visit http://www.goalsguy.com.

Jim Britt

During his 33 years in direct sales, Jim has built large distributor organizations, consulted and trained with more than 300 companies, and written numerous books. Today, he's considered one of the industry's leading experts and educators: he has trained over a million people. To contact Jim, call 530-268-2724, write to jimbritt@jim britt.com, or visit http://www.jimbritt.com.

Les Brown

Les is an authority on maximizing human potential, teaching and inspiring millions of people through empowerment speeches, motivational materials, and personal development programs. He has written books, such as *Live Your Dreams,* and earned numerous honors, including the Golden Gavel Award. To contact Les, call 800-733-4226, write to speak@lesbrown.com, or visit http://www.lesbrown .com.

Jenny Bywater

After starting several successful home businesses, Jenny founded The Booster to help those in the Party Plan industry achieve greater success. Over the past 23 years, Jenny has developed more than 3,000 products and helped over 300,000 customers to build their businesses. To contact Jenny, call 800-553-6692, write to jennybb@ thebooster.com, or visit http://www.thebooster.com.

Jack Canfield

Cocreator of Chicken Soup for the Soul

Jack has been a leading authority in the area of self-esteem and personal development for the past 30 years. He leads three organizations—The Foundation for Self-Esteem, Self-Esteem Seminars, and Souperspeakers.com—to bring self-esteem resources and training to people in any walk of life. To contact Jack, write to info4jack@jack canfield.com, or visit http://www.jackcanfield.com.

Jeanette S. Cates, PhD
Founder of TechTamers

Jeanette works with experts who are ready to turn their knowledge and their Web sites into gold. She is the creator of the Online Success System and offers products and courses to help you build your online success. To contact Jeanette, call 512-219-5653, write to cates@tech tamers.com, or visit http://www.techtamers.com.

Nick "Keeper" Catran-Whitney
CEO of NWM Entertainment Group

Keeper leads direct selling's only urban entertainment, marketing, and promotions company, which specializes in helping direct-selling companies get their products and services to the Urban Youth markets. To contact Keeper, call 818-598-0092, write to keeper@mpower ment.com, or visit http://www.mpowerment.com.

Vicky Collins, CPA
DSWA Prosperity Center Panel Member

Vicky teaches others how to keep more of what they make, so they can enjoy more freedom and greater peace of mind. A respected author and trainer, she is one of today's most sought-after experts in home-based business taxation. To contact Vicky, call 214-824-6890, write to prosperitycenter@mydswa.org, or visit http://www.mydswa .org.

David Cooper

David has given over 7,300 speeches; well over a million paid attendees have experienced David's winning sales training. His exciting style is highly acclaimed by direct sellers from around the world who have implemented his techniques for increased sales and sponsoring. To contact David, call 901-386-6191, write to ispeakt00@aol .com, or visit http://www.davidcooper.com.

Camilo Cruz, PhD
CEO of Taller del Exito, Inc.

Dr. Cruz is an entrepreneur, coach, and author of 20 books on personal development and business excellence. He founded a unique Spanish-language Web site providing information and tools that teach and inspire people to reach their most ambitious goals. To contact Dr. Cruz, call 954-321-5560, write to ccruzs@elexito.com, or visit http://www.camilocruz.com.

Garvin DeShazer

Garvin is a freelance writer who graciously contributed his talents to capture the stories of many contributors to *Build It Big*. To contact Garvin, write to garvind@sbcglobal.net.

Jane Deuber, MBA
President and Cofounder of the DSWA

Jane has worn all the hats: a distributor, a company founder responsible for a nationwide salesforce, and a consultant creating significant change in the industry. Also an author and a highly rated trainer, Jane is bringing professional coaching skills to direct sellers through the DSWA Principle-Centered Coaching Program. To contact Jane, call 888-417-0743, write to Jane@mydswa.org, or visit http://www.mydswa.org.

Jennie England, PCC, CPCC
Director of the DSWA Coaching Center

The founder of Wisdom in Action, a coaching and training company dedicated to bringing wholeness and harmony to a challenging world, as well as a respected trainer, Jennie has 25 years' experience working with individuals, businesses, and organizations in the areas of communication, leadership, and teamwork. To contact Jennie, call 831-624-2525, write to coachingcenter@mydswa.org, or visit http://www.mydswa.org.

Doug Firebaugh

Chairman and CEO of PassionFire International

Doug has been in direct selling for over 19 years. He loves this industry because it is the bastion of free enterprise: the greatest way to embrace financial, time, and personal freedom. To contact Doug, call 972-998-3473, write to dfirebaugh@yahoo.com, or visit http://www.passionfire.com.

Richard Flint

Richard's career has included university teaching, private counseling, professional speaking, and working as a private coach to many of North America's leading sales and business leaders. He has written ten books, recorded 45 audio albums and 27 videos, and for two years hosted his own television show. To contact Richard, call 877-875-8255, write to richard@richardflint.com, or visit http://www.richardflint.com.

Stephanie Frank

For over 15 years, Stephanie has been helping people grow their businesses without losing their minds. The founder of the Rich Living Worldwide Community for Empowering Entrepreneurs, she helps business builders have more focus, sales, freedom, and fun. To contact Stephanie, call 480-963-3590, write to sfrank@stephaniefrank.com, or visit http://www.StephanieFrank.com.

Marion Gellatly, AICI, CIP

Director of the DSWA Image Center

A successful motivator and founder of Powerful Presence, an image management training and consulting firm, Marion has been in direct selling for 13 years. To contact Marion, call 831-625-2000, write to imagecenter@mydswa.org, or visit http://www.mydswa.org.

Kevin D. Grimes

Kevin is one of a handful of attorneys in the country who specializes in law for direct selling. His clients include Herbalife, Shaklee, and USANA. Before serving as an attorney, Kevin was a distributor and built his last organization up to a volume of over $40,000 per month. To contact Kevin, call 208-524-0699, write to kgrimes@mlm law.com, or visit http://www.mlmlaw.com.

Mark Victor Hansen
Cocreator of Chicken Soup for the Soul

For more than 25 years, Mark has helped people and organizations reshape their vision of what's possible. With Chicken Soup partner Jack Canfield, Mark created what *Time* magazine calls "the publishing phenomenon of the decade." With partner Robert Allen, Mark's current bestseller is *The One Minute Millionaire*. To contact Mark, write to service@markvictorhansen.com or visit http://www .markvictorhansen.com.

Dawn M. Holman
Dawn has transformed the lives of millions as an author of internationally acclaimed, award-winning audio programs and books, and as the presenter of life-changing keynotes and experiential events. She is also a media relations and direct-marketing strategist. To contact Dawn, call 619-709-1637, write to dawn@dawnholman .com, or visit http://www.dawnholman.com.

Augusta Horsey Nash, MCC, CPCC
Managing Director, CPS (Coactive Process Systems) LLC

Augusta has 20 years of international professional experience in academia, industry, and government. She is a Master Certified Coach (ICF), a Certified Professional Coactive Coach (CTI), a Certified Birkman Method® Consultant, and a graduate of the Newfield Network Graduate Coaching Program. To contact Augusta, call 404-352-8048, write to augusta@cpscoach.com, or visit http://www.cps coach.com.

Beth Jones-Schall
Founder and President, Spirit of Success, Inc.

Beth started as a sales consultant and grew to the positions of director of training and sales director, where she was responsible for leading more than 1,000 consultants. Now she is a powerful, proven speaker and trainer who equips others for success. To contact Beth, call 813-654-1540, write to beth@spiritofsuccess.com, or visit http://www.spiritofsuccess.com.

Nicki Keohohou
CEO and Cofounder of the DSWA

Active in the direct-selling profession for more than 30 years, Nicki has personally worked with thousands of direct sellers from around the world and is on a mission to empower more people to achieve their dreams through a career in direct selling. To contact Nicki, call 808-230-2427, write to nicki@mydswa.org, or visit http://www.mydswa.org.

Charles W. King, PhD
Professor of Marketing, University of Illinois at Chicago

A graduate of Harvard University, Dr. King develops the professional image of direct-selling careers through university-level education and practical training. Dr. King is cofounder of the UIC Certificate Seminar in Network Marketing, which sets the standard for direct-selling education worldwide. To contact Dr. King, call 630-668-1251, write to thekings1976@yahoo.com, or visit http://www.netwkmarketing.com.

Lisa Kitter
President, Empower You Now Publishing

A respected speaker, trainer, and author who's been active in direct selling and personal coaching for over 18 years, Lisa loves this industry, because it allows average people with above-average dreams and desires to accomplish greatness at all levels of their being. To contact Lisa, call 888-212-0759, write to riskit0823@aol.com, or visit http://www.empoweryounowpublishing.com.

Grace Keohohou Lee
Vice President and Cofounder of the DSWA

Growing up among direct sellers and eventually becoming one, Grace appreciates the dedication it takes to achieve success. She wants more women to be able to leave the "job" that keeps them away from their family and home. To contact Grace, call 888-417-0743, write to grace@mydswa.org, or visit http://ww.mydswa.org.

Mike Lemire
Founder of Millionaires' Lifestyle Marketing and Development

"Motivated Mike" has trained over 80,000 people in more than 70 countries on all aspects of direct selling and personal development. He offers free, expanded trainings about working leads, developing ratios, long-distance sponsoring, and many other topics to help you experience success in your business. To contact Mike, write to mike@mlmdevelopment.com, or visit http://www.motivatedmike.com.

Carol McCall, MA, MCC
Founder of The Institute for Global Listening and Communication

Carol has more than 40 years of experience as an educator, therapist, and award-winning entrepreneur. She has influenced the lives of more than five million people through her public workshops, books, tapes, and personal appearances. To contact Carol, call 480-513-6244, write to wigc4u@aol.com, or visit http://www.listening profitsu.com.

Peggy McColl
Founder and President of Dynamic Destinies Inc.

To help people define their goals and reach their maximum potential, Peggy has written three bestselling books: *On Being the Creator of Your Destiny, The 8 Proven Secrets to SMART Success,* and *On Being a Dog with a Bone.* To contact Peggy, call 613-299-5722, write to peggy@destinies.com, or visit http://destinies.com.

Ron McMillan

Coauthor of Crucial Conversations: Tools for Talking When Stakes Are High

Ron received degrees in sociology and organizational behavior and cofounded the Covey Leadership Center, where he also was vice president of research. Ron is coauthor of two *New York Times* bestselling books and is cofounder and vice president of VitalSmarts. To contact Ron, call Dave Taylor at 208-542-5284, write to dtaylor@servicequest.com, or visit http://www.crucialconversations.com/direct sales.

Susan W. Miller

Founder of Financial Network Specialists

An award-winning businesswoman and public speaker, Susan is the author of *The Pro Notebook,* a life-planning tool to help you eliminate clutter and gain control over your personal and financial records, and *113 Great Tips for Your Family's Health & Education.* To contact Susan, call 303-221-2224 or write to susan@fnspecialist.com.

Gerald P. Nehra

An MLM specialist, private-practice attorney, Geri is one of only a few nationwide whose practice is devoted exclusively to direct selling and multilevel marketing issues. His 32 years of legal experience includes 9 years at Amway Corporation, where he was director of the Legal Division. To contact Geri, call 231-755-3800, write to gnehra@mlmatty.com, or visit http://www.mlmatty.com.

Richard Neihart

Author, educator, and speaker, Richard has honed his craft over 20 years, and joyfully inspires and motivates people in the Direct Selling profession. One of the world's most powerful voices on personal potential, he has delivered over 5,000 presentations to more than a million people. To contact Richard, call 614-475-1692 or write to richardneihart@aol.com.

Kathie Nelson

Kathie was in the top 2 percent of her direct-selling company for seven years, thanks to the tools she teaches today. Author, speaker, and success systems creator, Kathie trains and connects her clients to the tools they need to grow flourishing businesses. To contact Kathie, call 503-641-4354, write to kathie@kathienelson.com, or visit http://www.kathienelson.com.

Christie Northrup

Christie teaches business owners, team leaders, and independent salespeople how to TWIST Sour Situations—like not having enough business—into Sweet Successes and Juicy Profits. She is an expert in the Direct Selling industry, where she has been active for over 20 years. To contact Christie, call 940-498-0995, write to lemonaidlady @yahoo.com, or visit http://www.lemonaidlady.com.

Michael Oliver
Founder of Natural Selling Sales Training

Using his 24 years of sales experience, Michael teaches how anyone can achieve far greater and long-lasting results when they understand and use principles that allow people to persuade themselves to make positive changes in their life . . . naturally. To contact Michael, call 775-886-0777, write to info@naturalselling.com, or visit http:// www.naturalselling.com.

Pat Pearson, MSSW

An internationally known author and speaker with a passion for inspiring individuals to claim their own personal excellence, Pat has spoken to over 250,000 direct-selling professionals in the United States alone. To contact Pat, call 949-718-0313, write to pat@patpear son.com, or visit http://www.patpearson.com.

Karen Phelps

An author, trainer, and international speaker, Karen brings 22 years of experience in direct selling to her students. While pursuing her career goals, she managed to be there for all her family's important life events. She believes you can, too, and get what you want! To contact Karen, call 248-673-3465, write to karen@karenphelps.com, or visit http://www.karenphelps.com.

Caterina Rando, MA

As a master certified coach and author of the national bestselling book *Learn to Power Think,* Caterina passionately helps women succeed in direct selling. She is also a dynamic keynote speaker and is the entrepreneurship expert for Staples.com. To contact Caterina, call 415-668-4535, write to cpr@caterinar.com, or visit http://www.caterinar.com.

Kristin Rogers

Kristin was a National Teen Spokeswoman for Mary Kay Cosmetics while she worked with her mother, Connie Kittson, in her direct-selling business. Kristin is currently working for Dr. John C. Maxwell, bringing leadership resources to people in direct selling. To contact Kristin, call 404-808-8986 or write to kristin228@hotmail.com.

Teresa Romain

President and Founder of Access Abundance!™ Services International

Teresa founded Access Abundance! to educate, inspire, and support people to access and experience greater levels of abundance, freedom, and fulfillment in their daily lives. To contact Teresa, call 608-356-0929, write to tromain@accessabundance.com, or visit her Web site at http://www.accessabundance.com.

Bonnie Ross-Parker

Drawing on her background as an entrepreneur, speaker, trainer, author, and direct seller, Bonnie has created her own publishing company, as well as seminars, workshops, and keynotes on "The Joy of Connecting." Women around the globe have experienced her programs. To contact Bonnie, call 770-333-9028, write to bootgirl@bonnierossparker.com, or visit http://www.bonnierossparker.com.

Sue Rusch

President and Founder of Direct Sales Resources, Inc.

Over the past two decades, Sue has spoken to thousands of direct sellers in the United States and Canada. What Sue values most about the industry is the opportunity it provides for women to realize their personal potential, while working in a home-based atmosphere. To contact Sue, call 952-893-0025, write to sue@suerusch.com, or visit http://www.suerusch.com.

Mike Russell

Founder of Russell Communications

An Emmy-winning television producer, Mike spent two decades in local and network TV, in both journalism and marketing roles. Now Mike uses his skills to develop branding, marketing, and communication strategies for direct-sales companies and their reps. To contact Mike, call 303-771-5971, write to mikerussell@tde.com, or visit http://www.russellcommunications.com.

Donna Marie Serritella

Founder of Downline Solutions, Inc.

An accomplished writer, speaker, and trainer, Donna Marie has touched thousands of direct sellers worldwide. She and her team consult with start-up direct-selling companies and to date have served over 150 clients. To contact her, call 407-833-8170, write to tyg dms@aol.com, or visit http://www.downlinesolutions.com.

Jeff Shafe

President, MLM Software Solutions, Inc.

After a career in engineering, marketing, and product management, Jeff founded MLM Software to develop and market MLM Easy Money, which is widely regarded as the most comprehensive and user-friendly software available for managing a direct-selling business. To contact Jeff, call 877-632-9988, write to jeff@kynetics.com, or visit http://www.mlmeasymoney.com.

Marilyn Snyder

During her 18-year sales career, Marilyn was consistently honored for reaching sales and new business development goals. As a speaker and author, Marilyn enlivens audiences and encourages them to seek their passions in life. She also leads a Mastermind Power Coaching program. To contact Marilyn, call 218-631-7191, write to snyder@di recway.com, or visit http://www.marilynsynder.com.

Janet Switzer

Coauthor of The Success Principles: How to Get from Where You Are to Where You Want to Be

Over the past 13 years, Janet has not only built highly visible empires for some of the industry's most recognized business experts (such as Jack Canfield and Mark Victor Hansen), she's engineered countless marketing campaigns and generated millions of dollars in the process. To contact Janet, call 805-499-9400, write to janet-swit er@leadingexperts.net, or visit http://www.janetswitzer.com.

Terrel F. Transtrum

Cofounder of TeamRetention.com

Terrel is the leading retention advisor to direct-selling companies. He has worked with thousands of corporate executives and hundreds of thousands of direct-selling professionals, implementing best practices for the retention of customers and team members. To contact Terrel, call 208-529-9698, write to terrel@servicequest.com, or visit http://www.servicequest.com.

Cheryl Walker, PCC

Certified by the International Coach Federation and successful as a small business owner for over 20 years, Cheryl helps her clients develop leadership and communications skills and create action plans. To contact Cheryl, call 410-531-1267 or write cherylwalker @comcast.net.

Marcia Wieder

America's Dream Coach, Marcia is a top-rated presenter on visionary thinking, goal achievement, and team building to companies such as Avon, The Pampered Chef, and Creative Memories, and reaches tens of thousands more through appearances on shows like *Oprah* and *Today*. To contact Marcia, call 415-435-5564, write to mw @mydreamcoach.com, or visit http://www.my dreamcoach.com.

Lisa Wilber

Owner, The Winner in You

Avon's number four money earner in the United States, Lisa has a team of more than 1,600 representatives who sold over $8 million in 2002. Lisa is an accomplished speaker and reaches thousands more through the media. To contact Lisa, call 800-258-1815, write to lwilber@aol.com, or visit http://www.winnerinyou.com.

Dr. Zonnya

On a mission to "touch lives with inspiration, information, encouragement, and motivation," Dr. Zonnya delivers over 200 presentations each year to reach over 250,000 people, and through her media appearances, several million more. To contact Dr. Zonnya, call 888-725-9103, write to drzonnya@drzonnya.org, or visit http:// www.drzonnya.org.

■ Index